COLUMBIA COLLEGE

3 2711 00056 7705

C0-DKM-499

DATE DUE

MAR 3 0 2009			
GAYLORD			PRINTED IN U.S.A.

2 7 2005

MEDIA POLITICS
AND DEMOCRACY
IN PALESTINE

For my parents
Hannah and Ahmad

COLUMBIA COLLEGE LIBRARY
600 S. MICHIGAN AVENUE
CHICAGO, IL 60605

MEDIA POLITICS AND DEMOCRACY IN PALESTINE

Political Culture, Pluralism, and the Palestinian Authority

Amal Jamal

sussex
ACADEMIC
PRESS

BRIGHTON • PORTLAND

Copyright © Amal Jamal, 2005

The right of Amal Jamal to be identified as Author of this work has been asserted in accordance with the Copyright, Designs and Patents Act 1988.

2 4 6 8 10 9 7 5 3 1

First published 2005 in Great Britain by
SUSSEX ACADEMIC PRESS
PO Box 2950
Brighton BN2 5SP

and in the United States of America by
SUSSEX ACADEMIC PRESS
920 NE 58th Ave   Suite 300
Portland, Oregon 97213–3786

All rights reserved. Except for the quotation of short passages for the purposes of criticism and review, no part of this publication may be reproduced, stored in a retrieval system, or transmitted, in any form or by any means, electronic, mechanical, photocopying, recording or otherwise, without the prior permission of the publisher.

British Library Cataloguing in Publication Data
A CIP catalogue record for this book is available from the British Library.

Library of Congress Cataloging-in-Publication Data
Jamal, Amal.
    Media politics and democracy in Palestine : political culture, pluralism, and the Palestinian Authority / Amal Jamal.
        p.   cm.
    Includes bibliographical references and index.
    ISBN 1-84519-039-4 (hardcover : alk. paper)
        1. Mass media—Political aspects—West Bank. 2. Mass media—Political aspects—Gaza Strip. 3. Democracy—West Bank.
    4. Democracy—Gaza Strip. 5. Political culture—West Bank.
    6. Political culture—Gaza Strip. I. Title.

P95.82.W47J36 2005
302.23′095695′3—dc2   2004022659
                                                              CIP

Typeset and designed by G&G Editorial, Brighton
Printed by MPG Books, Ltd, Bodmin, Cornwall
This book is printed on acid-free paper.

Contents

Preface

Yasser Arafat has been the main figure in Palestinian politics over the last forty years. His death, understandably, has had a severe impact on the dynamics of Palestinian politics. This was more than just the passing away of the man who symbolized Palestinian nationalism and aspirations for statehood; in the immediate political sense it constitutes the end of an era of the central leader in Palestinian politics, of one leader holding all the strings of Palestinian politics together. Arafat, as this book demonstrates, managed to manipulate all official Palestinian institutions, controlling their external and internal policies. He intervened at all levels of decision-making, and managed to place his loyalists in the central political junctures. This pattern of political control figured predominantly in the Palestinian Authority (PA) in the last ten years, right up to the time of Arafat's death. Since 1994, Arafat had orchestrated the institutionalization of a quasi-state authority in the areas evacuated by the Israeli army. He established national institutions, creating an impression that the Palestinian Authority functioned as a state-in-the-making, and ensured that all the rituals of the modern state were made apparent in his regime.

This policy of 'rituals' was borne at a heavy price, demanded from him by Israel, which insisted that he act as head of a state, curtailing any opposition to Israeli occupation, despite the fact that the PA was not sovereign over its own territory and inhabitants. The rituals of the state were thus a double-edged sword: on the one hand, enabling the Palestinians, for the first time, to operate a political space, running some aspects of their public life for themselves; but asking them, on the other hand, to behave as if in a sovereign state, in terms of exerting control over their society, during a period when most Palestinian territories were still under Israeli control, exploited for settlement policies. This contradiction put Arafat, as well as the PA, in a position where it had to rely on the behavior of two opposing forces to maintain the illusion of sovereignty: Israel on the one hand and the Islamist opposition on the other. Israel failed to show much understanding for the intricate situation of the PA and its leader, especially concerning land confiscation and settlement building. The Islamist opposition, namely Hamas and Islamic Jihad, has been uncooperative with the PA leadership when formulating their resistance policies against Israeli occupation. The PA, and mainly its dominant elite, was squeezed between these two forces with a lack of maneuvering ability, other than seeking to deepen its control in Palestinian society, and continuing to act like a state.

Despite the external Israeli pressure and the internal authoritarian tendencies led by the dominant national elite in the PA, with Arafat at its head, Palestinians in the occupied territories managed to establish a very lively civil sector, composed of social movements and civic organizations. The active civil sector in the West Bank and Gaza Strip, whose roots preceded the establishment of the PA, became a central player in internal Palestinian affairs. The interplay between the PA, and the civil sector that sought democratization of PA institutions, and the setting of the rule of law in Palestinian politics, forms a central dimension of Palestinian politics. Although most civil organizations in the Palestinian territories were heavily damaged by Israeli occupation policies during the second Intifada, they still form the backbone of Palestinian society. Civil organizations managed to maintain some of their activities, especially service providers such as medical care, education, and welfare.

Arafat's death seems to have brought new waves of optimism into the Middle East. Arafat's formal powers were swiftly passed to political figures in the PA and in the PLO. The Fatah movement, the central movement in the PA, agreed on appointing Mahmoud Abbas (Abu Mazen) as head of the PLO and on endorsing him as its candidate for the PA presidency. Immediately after his election as PA president on January 9, 2005 Abbas began intensive talks with opposition groups in the West Bank and Gaza Strip, so as to bring an agreed end to the current circle of violence between Palestinians and Israelis. The negotiated cease-fire agreement (*Hudna*) aims at allowing him a chance to promote negotiations with Israel, especially concerning the proposed disengagement plan promoted by Israeli Prime Minister Ariel Sharon. Additionally, the PA leadership has initiated talks with the Syrian government, after a prolonged period of icy relations between the two. The main aim of the Palestinian delegation visit to Damascus was to coordinate positions regarding peace talks in the region, and to guarantee Syrian containment of the operation of Palestinian opposition groups located within its borders.

These political and diplomatic steps represent an attempt to stabilize the Palestinian transfer of power, and to facilitate Israeli withdrawal from Palestinian cities. Palestinian society, meanwhile, remains dynamic, with new forms of political organization and pressure emerging. Besides Abu Mazen, there were several other candidates for the PA presidency elections. These candidates came from different political and social backgrounds. They reflect the competition between social forces for power and influence in Palestinian politics. The social dynamics taking place since Arafat's death reflect the liveliness of Palestinian society and the vigor of civil institutions still active in it, despite the harsh policies of the Israeli army over the past four years. The current political dynamism in the West Bank and Gaza Strip cannot be separated from what has occurred since the establishment of the PA in 1994.

Understanding the conflicting dynamics between the PA and the civil sector during the Arafat period is essential in order to identify what processes may develop in the post-Arafat period. This book provides a thorough analysis of the main dynamics of political processes that will determine how Palestinian politics develops. The attempts made by the dominant political elite in the PA, principally Abu Mazen, to reach a broad coalition with all the active political forces in Palestinian society, demonstrates the importance of the politics of consensus in Palestinian political culture. The politics of negotiations and mutual agreements over common political formulas may become the main marker of Palestinian politics in the post-Arafat period. Such a tendency, in a situation where none of the active political figures enjoys the symbolic power that Arafat had, may reshuffle the relationship between the PA and the civil sector, and lead to the liberalization and democratization of Palestinian politics. To understand how this may become possible one has to understand the historical nature of the relationship between the PA elite, especially Arafat, and the civil organizations active on the political stage. The chapters that follow provide a through analysis of the role of NGOs, the media, the women's movement and the Islamic movement in shaping Palestinian politics. The attempts made by these forces to influence Palestinian politics, and the efforts made by some to democratize the PA by constituting an effective public sphere and an active civil society, are examined systematically throughout the period 1994 to the present (December 2005). It is difficult to anticipate how these efforts may develop in the post-Arafat period, but it is almost certain that Palestinian politics will be determined by efforts made by these social forces to exert influence in the political sphere, and to broaden the ability of civil society to make its voice heard in governmental institutions, such as parliament, government and the courts. The lack of a central symbolic figure available to replace Arafat, and the existence of extensive and lively civil institutions, is a major opportunity for the democratization of Palestinian society, providing Israel respects the Palestinian basic right for a sovereign state, and facilitates its establishment, based on peaceful negotiations, without stipulations that make such an option effectively impossible to achieve.

Acknowledgments

Many people were involved in seeing this book through to publication. Some were involved from the start with collecting the basic materials and others stepped in and out at different stages for particular tasks. I would like to begin by thanking Palestinian friends in the West Bank and Gaza, who provided some of the materials for this book and supported me along the way, providing good advice and sound ideas. I would like to express my gratitude to Dr. Bassem Ezbeidi from Bir Zeit University near Ramallah for discussing with me several topics discussed herein and for providing analytical and critical views that have certainly enriched the volume.

I would like to thank all the women and men at the Women Affairs Technical Committees, Palestinian Non-Governmental Organizations Network, Women Center for Legal Aid and Counseling, and the editors of the bi-weekly *Sawt Al-Nisa'*, for providing me with data and for discussing with me many issues that came up during the research. Many other Palestinian friends facilitated my meetings with political leaders and civil activists, all of which enriched the book enormously. I acknowledge with thanks their sincere help. I am grateful also to all the political leaders and civil activists who shared their experiences with me. I would like especially to thank Prof. Carolyn Landry for her professional and personal support and dedicated assistance. She read the manuscript with critical but supportive eyes and assisted in making it a better book. Anthony Grahame, Editorial Director at Sussex Academic Press, has been supportive and helpful throughout. Of my students, Umayma Diab helped in organizing the bibliography and Tomer

Zeigerman helped in the process of editing. I would like to thank them both very much for their dedication.

Several chapters of this book underwent substantive revisions during my stay at the Solomon Asch Center for the Study of Ethnopolitical Conflict at the University of Pennsylvania. I would like to thank the academic and the administrative staff for providing the good atmosphere that made this task possible.

To my family, thank you for providing me with support and encouragement.

This book is dedicated to my parents. They taught me the value of scholarship.

Abbreviations

CPRS	Center for Palestinian Research and Studies
DFLP	Democratic Front for the Liberation of Palestine
GUPW	General Union of Palestinian Women
JMCC	Jerusalem Media and Communication Center
NGOs	Non-Governmental Organizations
PA	Palestinian Authority
PFLP	Popular Front for the Liberation of Palestine
PGUCS	Palestinian General Union of Charitable Societies
PLC	Palestinian Legislation Council
PLO	Palestinian Liberation Organization
PNGO	Palestinian Non-Governmental Organization Network
WATC	Women's Affairs Technical Committees
WCLAC	Women's Center for Legal Aid and Counseling

MEDIA POLITICS
AND DEMOCRACY
IN PALESTINE

Introduction

STATE FORMATION, SYMBOLIC POWER AND POLITICAL HEGEMONY

The Palestinian socio-political experience after the Oslo Accords remains a major subject of study for scholars and produces fresh insights into that experience. Few attempts, however, have been made to explain the dynamics of Palestinian politics after the establishment of the Palestinian Authority (PA) in July 1994. Nevertheless, research by Palestinian sociologists and political scientists has laid the foundations for the understanding of vital aspects of Palestinian society and politics. The influence of social structures on the emerging political entity in the West Bank and Gaza Strip has been highlighted by various studies addressing different dimensions of Palestinian public life.[1]

Various theoretical approaches were utilized to explain sociological developments. The establishment of an autonomous Palestinian authority on a portion of Palestinian territory in the West Bank and Gaza Strip has greatly influenced the dynamics of Palestinian politics. The institutional structure and the bureaucratic apparatus of the PA established a state system that played a key role in every aspect of Palestinian society and politics. The prominent role of the executive authority in the PA and the lack of established constitutional rules have had a significant impact on the course of the Palestinian political process. The dominant position of the security forces, and the terms of the peace agreements with Israel (especially the latter's continuing grip over Palestinian lands for the purposes of settlements and roads), have also affected developments in the PA. These conditions have been a major cause of the second *Intifada* and are possibly be related to the constitutional changes and administrative reforms that have been taking place in the PA since early 2003.

This book will examine the interdependence between institutional and cultural developments in the Palestinian society of the West Bank and Gaza Strip. The institutional regime of the PA and the structure of power within it, the effect of the patterns of regime institutionalization on the emerging public sphere in its areas of jurisprudence, and the relationship between the political elite that dominates the PA and the social movements that seek to undermine the hegemony of the elite over society are all explored. The political process is the aggregate of interactions between different social players, each seeking to influence the outcome according to their individual interests and ideas. The processes of state building and centralization of power are therefore not detached from contentious movements that seek to undermine them or influence their nature. Palestinian politics is a fluid process conditioned by internal and external players.

Palestinian politics is not simply a linear process dominated by a homogenous group of people.[2] Indeed, Palestinian society has always been pluralistic, and internal splits have historically played major roles in determining its course of development. The differences within the dominant political elite, and the role played by opposition movements in civil society and their strategies of protest, are no less important than attempts made by dominant political institutions or elites to consolidate power and centralize authority. It is essential to take a close look at both realms of Palestinian politics – elite and grass roots – in order to comprehend the ways in which mechanisms of interaction between institutionalization from above and contention from below determine the character of the emerging Palestinian polity. Social movements' attempts to counter the communication order and media regime (the institutional and cultural structures of the media and their discourse) imposed by the dominant national elite of the PA represent a significant aspect of this contention. The communication order in Palestine serves not only as a means of control, but also as a field of contention between different political agents and a way of articulating different worldviews. Examination of the communication order provides a point of departure for evaluating the chances of democracy in a future Palestinian state.

The PA experience over the years 1994–2003 can be turned into a learning process for the Palestinian process of state building, if assessed correctly. In recent years, this process has been disrupted by the outbreak of the second *Intifada* in September 2000, and the subsequent reoccupation of all Palestinian areas by the Israeli army. Notwithstanding this development, and assuming that the peace process will be resumed some time in the future, it is important to learn from the experience of the PA, to try and determine what form the process of state building should take in the future. The seven years of partial PA rule were problematic for many reasons: corruption, mismanagement, and authoritarianism were apparent in every PA institution, which meant, that the expectations of many Palestinians were not met. To that, one should add Israeli policies of land confiscation, settlement expansion, and construction of the separation wall. These measures cause much disillusionment among most Palestinians regarding a possible peaceful settlement in the near future and add to the resentment felt towards the conduct of the PA.

Between 1994 and 2003, a central source of Palestinian jurisdiction attempted to establish its power in areas evacuated by the Israeli army in the West Bank and Gaza Strip and to realize Palestinian aspirations for national self-determination. The PA formed the nucleus of a future Palestinian state and assumed the right to monopolize power. Attempts by the PA to institutionalize Palestinian nationalism through the framework of the Oslo agreement, and the circumstances that surrounded this process, have had far-reaching repercussions on the dynamics of Palestinian politics. Contentious social forces that opposed the peace process, or were not satisfied with their position in the national reconstruction process, criticized the patterns of institutionalization engineered by the governing elite and sought to influence the public agenda in order to achieve a greater balance in decision-making. Among the PA's most vocal critics are the secular civil organizations, the women's movement, and the Islamic movement. These forces sought to influence PA policies by capturing the communicative "space" created by the establishment of the PA, or by constituting alternative counter-public spheres. Different civil organizations initiated public debates about the character of the Palestinian polity that might emerge as a result of the peace process with Israel. Other social movements, especially those that strongly identify with Islam, tried to compete with the PA's dominant elite for the hearts and minds of the Palestinian people. Different Palestinian voices protested against the PA's hegemonic attempts to dictate, without consultation, the future of the Palestinian people based on authoritarian political measures.[3]

Palestinian politics during the period of PA dominance therefore cannot be viewed only in dichotomous theoretical terms. Different political forces, especially social movements, sought to exploit the political opportunity opened with the establishment of the PA to assert their political interests and influence the nature of the emerging Palestinian state.[4] The "state in society" model, which contends that the distinctive patterns that characterize society are a result of struggles over conflicting demands between different group interests, is of especial relevance here.[5] Different groups – elites, parties, organizations – engage in struggles over the sets of rules and codes that they would like to see dominate society and organize its different formations. These conflicts lead to the formation of rules by which the state institutions function and the way in which they are subject to conflicting interests.

However, not all social groups have equal access to state power. The attempts of civil organizations and social movements to influence the process of state formation usually founder against the hegemonic social power and its attempts to assert its authority by different means. As a result, the struggle for power becomes a useful vehicle for the examination of the Palestinian state-building process, revealing a great deal about the operation of political regimes in general.

Public debates between different social forces concerning the character of the state determine many of its features; contentious Palestinian movements that were mobilized against the authoritarian tendencies of the PA authorities in the process of state formation have disputed the institutionalization of corruption and authoritarianism as permanent characteristics of Palestinian politics. At the same time, contentious politics that lacked coherence and consistency did not lead to the democratization of the regime in Palestine. The authority of the dominant elites and the narrow political opportunities open for protest under the circumstances of Israeli domination and control have given the latter the opportunity to assert its policies of colonization and dismantle the peace process. The outbreak of the second Palestinian *Intifada* and the reoccupation of all Palestinian areas by Israel rendered the efforts of opposition movements futile and, in some cases, even harmful to endeavors for independence. Nevertheless, civil contention has succeeded in establishing deliberation as a character trait of Palestinian politics and placed limitations on the desire of the dominant elite to expand its power over all realms of public life. Palestinian politics in the period between 1994 and 2003 became a competition between different social forces to determine the political–legal regime and the cultural–symbolic order that would dominate society.

Palestinian society still struggles for independence and remains under occupation. This situation conditions the mode of state building and the relationship between the state-in-the-making and society. Although Israel withdrew from several Palestinian cities, it remained the key player in the area and has continued imposing its terms on the ground. This has influenced the state-building process and the *modus operandi* of the various political actors, especially after the outbreak of the second *Intifada*.

Israel's reoccupation of the Palestinian territories and destruction of the infrastructure of the PA have obstructed the Palestinian state-building process. Despite the fact that this study is based mainly on the experience of 1994–2000, it also addresses developments that took place (and are still under way) after the breakdown of the peace process and the reoccupation. The constitutional changes and the administrative reform that has been taking place in the PA since January 2003 are discussed briefly. The study is placed in a comparative theoretical context that helps re-conceptualize the meaning of state formation, social movements, and public spheres. The examination of Palestinian politics will thus make a theoretical contribution to the general study of politics.

State Formation, Social Movements, and Symbolic Power

State formation has never been about institution building alone; it is a much broader social and cultural process, which includes setting procedural rules that determine the space, and patterns of behavior, of collective and private life. According to this understanding, the state cannot be characterized as an institution independent of the society in which it is forming.[6] Any attempt to understand the nature of a "state-in-the-making" and its particular characteristics must consider the social context in which this process is taking place. Furthermore, state formation is an open-ended process that never actually reaches its final destination for the duration of the state's existence. The structural features of the state involve the entire set of rules and institutions that contribute to forming and implementing policies. In Steinmetz's view, these may include "the arrangement of ministries or departments, the set of rules for the allocation of individual positions within these departments, systems for generating revenues, legal codes and constitutions, electoral rules, forms of control over lower bodies of government, the nature and location of boundaries between state and society, and so forth".[7]

Charles Tilly has emphasized coercion as a special characteristic of the state. Tilly defined the state as "coercion wielding organizations that are distinct from households and kinship groups and exercise clear priority in some respects over all other organizations within substantial territory".[8] This definition points to the importance of defining territorial boundaries and the concentration of the means of violence as central features of the state, despite the fact that Tilly does not insist on a complete monopoly of coercion. But Tilly's definition, like that of Max Weber,[9] assumes territory as a given, something that ought to be problematized. The territorial dimension is central to the Palestinian state-formation process because of Israel's continued occupation and the lack of Palestinian sovereignty. The symbolic–cultural dimension, however, is just as important in the process of state formation, as the Palestinian case demonstrates.[10]

The symbolic–cultural dimension is important for understanding the Palestinian experience because of the existing conflict about the meaning and character of the future Palestinian state. The importance of the symbolic–cultural dimension has been argued by Pierre Bourdieu, who views the state as an entity that "successfully claims the monopoly of the legitimate use of physical and *symbolic* violence over a defined territory and over the totality of the corresponding population".[11] According to this definition, the grip of the state is felt most powerfully in the symbolic–cultural realm, where the state manifests itself in the form of mental structures and categories of perception and thought, implanted in citizens by socialization processes run by ideological institutions of the state, such as schools, media, and universities.

Palestinian politics centers, among other things, on the character of the future state. The process of state formation is about the attempts of different social movements to determine the territorial, structural, and symbolic features of the Palestinian state. Debates over these characteristics take place in the public sphere, which is continually being constituted by the different discursive formations presented by social players. At the same time, political elites influence what is allowed to be said, where, and by whom in the public sphere. The symbolic capital each social movement acquires through the dissemination of its discourse influences the process of state formation and influences the institutionalization of the administrative and physical structures of the state. Ideological mechanisms, such as the media, represent the state in mental structures and categories of perception and thought among the targeted population.

As Laclau and Mouffe contend, the state apparatus does not, though, ever attain full control over the means of symbolic violence.[12] As political communication theory and media studies have demonstrated, the state is a major player in setting the public agenda, but not the only one.[13] The state is also shaped by social movements that seek to incorporate their worldview in its institutional structures and rules. Therefore, to understand the process of state formation, one must consider the overall complexity of society and the interactions between its different components: social movements, political parties, elites, and media institutions. These processes differ from one state to another and from period to period.

In Western Europe state formation has been a process of authority centralization in which the predominant feature is the surveillance and supervision of one group of human beings by another within clearly demarcated geographic boundaries.[14] The state wields administrative power, specifically with respect to the accumulation of information and the setting of accepted rules of action, with an established set of sanctions for situations that deviate from the rules.[15] An important aspect of the process of state formation has been differentiation: the separation between state and religion on the one hand, and between state and civil society on the other.[16] This separation, argues Gianfranco Poggi, "conveys the state's recognition that the individuals subject to its power also have capacities and interests of a non-political nature, that they may express and pursue autonomously, and its commitment to disciplining and ordaining the resulting private activities only in a general and abstract manner".[17] This process of differentiation distinguishes between the "logic of the political and economic systems, regulated respectively by administrative power and money, and the life-world of self-organized public spheres based on solidarity and communication".[18]

According to this understanding of state formation, continuous tension exists between the expansionist logic of the political economy and the authority welded by the elite that dominates the state, and the self-organized public spheres that constitute civil society. Regulation of this tension through constitutional law in Western European states ensures freedom and explains the stability of democracy. The European experience illustrates that a conditional relationship exists between the emergence and durability of democratic rule and the unification of public discourses that exist outside the state and seek, legitimately, to influence its policies. Public spheres are an integral part of democracy, both in theory and practice. This form and process of European state formation is not universal. It is particular to the Western European experience. But several aspects of this process – for example, the interdependence between the institutional and cultural influences and the functionality of public spheres for freedom and democracy – are relevant to the understanding of other, non-European, state-building experiences.

Some aspects of the processes of state formation in the Arab world are also relevant to the understanding of the Palestinian experience. In a recent study on the theory of the Arab state, Nazih Ayubi writes: "The Arab state is not a natural growth of its own socio-economic history or its own cultural and intellectual tradition."[19] That is, the structure of the modern state did not emerge from the social web of Arab society and culture, because the institution, the very concept of the state, was imposed from outside of Arab society. The European idea of the state does not take into account the social structure natural to Arab society, where personal connections play a major role in both private and public spheres. The formal rigidity of the modern state does not (and cannot) provide a place for the rich personal and social bonds familiar within Arab culture. Consequently, the Arab state is "fierce" and resorts to raw coercion in order to protect itself. Yet this fierce state is not a "strong" one. In Ayubi's view, the state has neither the infrastructural power that would enable it to penetrate society nor the ideological hegemony that would allow political elites to establish their legitimacy. This analysis of the Arab state draws upon the distinction that Jackson and Rosenberg made between the legal, juridical concept of the state and the sociological, empirical one.[20] In the West, states emerged as political, military, and social entities first, and only then endeavored to gain legal recognition of their existence through competition and war. Third World states, however, as part of their colonial legacy, emerged as juridical entities before socio-organizational factors had developed. This process has led to a crisis of legitimization in the Arab world, where state authority is disputed.[21]

In former colonial societies, states were not created by national elites but rather by a foreign colonial power that over-inflated the size of its bureaucratic–administrative machine to serve its own interests. As a result, postcolonial states are underdeveloped in certain respects but overdeveloped in others.[22] This is most apparent in the highly developed administrative governmental machinery, especially the armed forces, as opposed to the weak nature of civil society.[23] Postcolonial states have developed a considerable amount of "relative autonomy" *vis-à-vis* the native economic and social forces. This autonomy had taken the state beyond mediating different socio-economic forces – as states tend to present them-selves – to involvement in processes of economic accumulation and consequently the creation of its own classes.[24]

This type of postcolonial state-formation process partially explains the predicament in which democracy finds itself in these states. The alienation between society and the state is the product of a fluid class map, where classes are dependent on the state and usually supported by external forces. Within the class map, there are intermediate strata where several of the classes compete for social and economic preeminence. As a result, politics in Arab society is characterized by continuous conflict between forces competing to dominate the state or resist its control.[25] The social elite in power seeks to maintain its position, especially by excluding the general public from political participation by denying them free and trans-parent elections, or granting them responsibility over the civil areas of social life. The political process in most Arab countries is devoid of any real form of power sharing. The "state classes" control all aspects of life and limit other socio-economic forces' ability to freely maneuver.

The Palestinian experience of state formation shares many of the characteristics of other postcolonial states, with a few significant differences. The Palestinians still live under occupation for example; the occupying power still has claims over their territory. As a result of territorial differentiation imposed by Israel, the organization of coercion and the extension of the administrative apparatus of the Palestinian state system (especially the establishment of a system of revenue generation and the holding of normal elections) has been impossible. Despite these difficulties, the PA managed to establish the nucleus of a future state. The dominant Palestinian national elite has pursued what has been called by political theorists, a process of homogenization by restructuring society and creating an overarching political order – more than establishing a mere legal state framework. [26] As a result, a new moral order began to emerge. Until the reoccupation of all Palestinian areas by Israel in April 2001, national institutions were established and functioned in several areas, albeit under limited circumstances. The special circumstances that condition the process of state formation are not to be ignored when examining the emerging Palestinian polity and the state-in-the-making's relations with society.

Internal Palestinian dynamics exist which have influenced the process of state formation. The methods used by different social movements to influence state formation, and the extent to which they were utilized, determines the characteristics of the process and the nature of the state. The examination of how and by what means social movements seek to influence the territorial, institutional, and cultural character of the Palestinian state are crucial for understanding the PA and its emerging regime, and for comprehending the strategies of contention and the modes of resistance employed by the social movements, and the "state's" responses to them.

Public Spheres, Social Movement, and Symbolic Power

Despite its authoritarian characteristics, the PA has not succeeded in achieving complete hegemony over civic society. Public avenues exist through which social forces emerge to impose limits on state domination. [27] The rise of self-organized public spheres that challenge the central state authority and seek to make it accountable has been an important feature of Palestinian politics since 1994. Political theory suggests that democratization requires the constitution of a public space for action that mediates between the realm of the state and the private sphere.[28] This space, described by Habermas as a "placeless place", is where critical discussions of cultural and political matters take place, and where popular sovereignty is best manifested.[29] The existence of Palestinian social movements instituting self-governing public spheres is perhaps an expression of democratic developments.

Charles Taylor claims that the public sphere is a central feature of modern society. He contends that it exists "even where it is in fact suppressed or manipulated".[30] Public spheres are best viewed through the deliberative power of civil organizations and social movements. These social formations use the structural opportunities open in society to appropriate resources and mobilize them for their interests.[31] Palestinian social movements, especially civic and Islamist organizations, utilized different material and symbolic means to influence the political process. In the context of state formation, these social movements sought to become an integral part of the public sphere to achieve a maximum impact on the framing of public opinion and through it on state structure. Can the competition between national, civil, and Islamic social forces regarding the proper political and moral order in Palestine be considered a manifestation of democratic public spheres?

Jürgen Habermas defined the public sphere as "the sphere of private people come together as a public; they soon claimed the public sphere regulated from above against the public authorities themselves, to engage them in a debate over the general rules governing relations in the basically privatized but publicly relevant sphere of commodity exchange and social labor."[32] This concept of the public sphere has been criticized for corresponding with liberal democratic theory and for failing to consider the possibility of multiple public spheres.[33] Nevertheless, Habermas's definition emphasizes that public spheres are not physical locations but rather spaces where the flow of information created by different voices creates an impact on the state and influences its policies.[34] The public sphere means freedom of argumentation for all and has procedural as well as the normative dimensions. It emerges as such whenever and wherever those "affected by general social and political norms of action engage in a practical discourse, evaluating their validity".[35]

As a result, depending on the number of controversial general debates in society, there may be more than one public sphere.[36] Cohen and Arato claim that the public sphere in a society "aims neither at the utopian destruction of the state nor at becoming a new state, nor even at the unification of these aims as in the Reign of Terror, but rather at a new form of political dualism in which a political public sphere would control the public authority of the modern state".[37]

Public spheres are not a mere locus of discussion and debate. The concept of the public sphere is also connected to power and control. The discursive formations of the public sphere implicate the symbolic dimension of the state that Bourdieu emphasized in his definition, as much as the influence of the public spheres on decision making implicate the matrix of power in the state. The public sphere is neither a fictitious locus nor a mere debating society;[38] it is the space in which debates among people, social movements, and human organizations have consequences on policy-making and collective life.

The importance of the mechanisms of communication explains the significance of the media as a battlefield, as well as a means of control, for the understanding of politics. Investigating social movements by examining their systems of argumentation helps reveal the patterns in which the public spheres contribute to connecting the reconstructed cultural identity of the people with the legitimate jurisdiction of the emerging state.[39]

This book is guided by a critique of the ambiguities of the liberal point of view in Habermas's understanding of the public sphere. Only by extending the public sphere debate from one sector of society to the wider public domain, embracing subordinate groups in society, can the complexities of the Palestinian political reality be understood. The Palestinian political experience of state formation involves the efforts of multiple active social forces confronting the authoritarian tendencies of the traditional Palestinian national elite that dominates the national movement and attempts to influence the legal, institutional, and symbolic order in society. In this context, the rise and increase of autonomous public spheres among members of society seeking to influence public policy and generate a broad source for legitimization is a central part of any process of state formation and an important means of democratization.

Methodology

Michel Foucault defined the media space as "a systematic conversion of the power relationship between controller and controlled into 'mere' written words".[40] Opposition groups seek to constitute a public agenda by framing the terms of the debate and providing a means to bypass the limitations imposed by the PA. Therefore, political structures and processes, as manifestations of hegemonic discourse, illustrate the inherent relationship between social structures and discourse structures and how they inform each other interchangeably. According to Fowler, social acts and interactions that are conducted in reality reflect, and are a reflection of, discourse, because discourse is in itself a social interaction.[41] Therefore, language is treated as a major mechanism in the process of social construction and is considered "an instrument for consolidating and manipulating concepts and relationships in the area of power and control".[42]

Analyzing discursive formations can serve as a tool for understanding manifestations of power relations. Discourse analysis is relevant in terms of understanding the power structures and relations between the various political and social players, as a critical analysis of public opinion polls and various types of publications including periodicals, journals, reports, and newspapers will show.

Van Dijk argues that discourse analysis is concerned with "specifying socio-historically variable . . . systems of rules which make it possible for certain statements but not others to occur at a particular time, place and institutional location".[43] Furthermore, Fairclough's critical discourse analysis "aims to systematically explore often opaque relationships of causality and determination between (a) discursive practices, events and texts, (b) wider social and cultural structures, relations and processes; to investigate how such practices, events and texts arise out of and are ideologically shaped by relations of power and struggles over power; and to explore how the opacity of these relationships between discourse and society is itself a factor securing power and hegemony".[44]

Based on this understanding, the different debates between the various political players in Palestinian society are introduced, explaining the ways in which these players utilize discourse to define the future Palestinian polity. Dominant socio-political actors produce specific ways or modes of talking about certain areas "that will define, describe, delimit, and circumscribe what is possible and impossible to say [and do] with respect to it".[45] Therefore, special focus is placed on the modes of legal limitations and discursive censorship apparent in the emerging polity.

Organization of the material

This book is organized in terms of the various theoretical approaches discussed earlier. **Chapter 1** deals with the emerging structure of the PA and the mechanisms, strategies, and forms of power relations. Patterns of institutionalization and differentiation between formal and informal institutions that influence the nature of the emerging regime are explored. In this context, the roles of the dominant founding father – Yasser Arafat – and the hegemonic party are also explored. **Chapter 2** examines the civil sector, and raises questions about the role of NGOs in Palestinian society and politics and their relationship with the central regime of the PA. It also examines the structural and discursive formations used by the civil sector to influence public policy. **Chapter 3** introduces the emerging media regime in Palestine, and examines the structure of the media and the dominance of the central authority in its structuration. **Chapter 4** focuses on one of the better-organized social movements in Palestinian society: the women's movement, and its publications. The different means employed by the women's movement to engender the state through lobbying for equal and just legislation are reviewed. **Chapter 5** investigates the Islamic movement, which forms the main opposition to the PA. The worldviews of two major movements – Hamas and Islamic Jihad – are examined, as well as their attempts to counterpoise the rising hegemony of the PA. Since developments in the peace process exert great influence on internal Palestinian politics, the manner in which Hamas and Islamic Jihad treat the PA and use their weekly newspapers to delegitimize the peace negotiations and set an alternative political agenda are also discussed. The **Conclusion** looks at the achievements and future prospects of each social movement in the framework of the Palestinian polity, and assesses the future for democracy and development in Palestine.

During the period of the formation and power consolidation of the PA (1994–2003), there have been ups and downs in the peace process. Israel has limited the PA from extending its authority over all Palestinian areas in the West Bank and Gaza Strip and visited much harm on the Palestinian process of state formation. Therefore, the examination of Palestinian politics is tightly connected to the regional political framework. The information provided in this study could be appropriated by some to dismantle the Palestinian right for self-determination, or to present the Palestinian people in a negative light. This study, however, is a scholarly work; its objective is to provide a constructive critique of the Palestinian process of state-formation in order to promote democracy, mutual understanding among the different Palestinian political groups, and peace with Israel. Moral or political conclusions reached by the author are clearly stated; those who draw further or conflicting conclusions are entirely responsible for their views: they are not the author's.

❶

Institutionalizing the Political System and the Politics of Control

Under the auspices of the Oslo peace process, and in a relatively short period of time, the Palestinian Authority (PA) has managed to build quasi-state structures. The Palestinian experience follows other postcolonial states by over-inflating its administrative machine. The PA bureaucracy in Gaza alone exceeded 40,000 personnel by 1995.[1] The Gazan civil administration under Israeli occupation, in comparison, employed only 5,000 Palestinians. According to official PA reports, over 110,000 people are employed in its administration.[2] During the transition period,[3] PLO bureaucrats initiated a process of institution building to fill the governance gap created by the pull-out of the Israeli army. The absence of the PLO elite during the *Intifada* influenced the way in which the PA sought to capture political power in the occupied territories and form its political base.[4] The new governmental institutions competed with the existing Palestinian civil organizations and sought to control them,[5] forming what Shain and Linz call an 'interim government' to lead the transition process.[6]

As an interim government, the PA is caught between its endeavors toward independence, and establishing a stable and legitimate regime. It is put under pressure by Israel regarding the borders of the Palestinian state and has to contend with an internal opposition that criticizes its policies. The balance the PA strikes between power consolidation on the one hand, and accountability and public responsiveness on the other, is an indication of the characteristics of the emerging regime in Palestine.

Regime Structure, Institutional Design, and Administrative Power

The Palestinian leadership negotiating with Israel has chosen a presidential political system with an active parliament, thus following political structures utilized in several postcolonial states. Both branches of government were established according to the Israeli–Palestinian Interim Agreement signed in Washington on September 28, 1995. The relationship between the president and his executive and the Palestinian Legislative Council (PLC), founded in February 1996, turned out to be a central stage of Palestinian politics after 1994. The recent changes in this structure, through the introduction of the post of the prime minister while amending the Palestinian Basic Law, is bound to have a major impact on the relationship between the executive and legislative branches of government. Since this change is recent it is hard to assess its impact. Therefore, the analysis that follows is based on the experience of the first eight years of PA history with some reference to recent developments resulting from the outbreak of the second *Intifada*.

Since the viability of state structures is dependent on the strength and character of political institutions formed by the interim government,[7] the relationship between the PLC and the PA president became one of the markers of the way Palestinian political decisions are made. Neo-institutionalists have demonstrated that "political democracy depends not only on economic and social conditions but also on the design of political institutions . . . ". [8] The institutional structures chosen by the Palestinian leadership after Oslo reflected its political calculations. Among the important institutional structures chosen to ensure political stability and democracy were the dominant rule of the presidency, the winner-takes-all electoral system, and the legislative role of the PLC. Although these institutional structures are not solely the result of free choice by the Palestinian leaders, they and the elites generally played a crucial role in determining how institutions function and what goals they seek to serve. A central issue that relates the elite choices to the anticipated regime type is the degree of separation of powers sought in the governmental structure. The Palestinian constitutional system did define clear legal and functional demarcation lines between the different branches of government. Although in some democratic systems the separation of the different branches of government is not always clear and is not a sufficient condition for democracy, a balance between the executive and the legislative is viewed to be a necessary condition if democratic rule is to prevail.[9] In the Palestinian case there has been an imbalance between the executive and the legislative branches; there has also been a lack of any defin-ition of the judicial system. The fact that the head of the PA postponed his ratification of the proposed Basic Law that defines the responsibilities and duties of the different governmental institu-tions, was part of his attempt to manipulate the system for his own ends. The president of the PA ratified the Basic Law in May 2002, almost two years after the outbreak of the *Intifada*, and as a result of external pressures to confine his authority.

The Interim Agreement between the PLO and Israel did not clearly define the formal authority of the Palestinian representative bodies. The agreement commingled the legislative, executive, and judicial powers and responsibilities of the new state institutions. The authority of the PLC was limited by 'existing laws [and] military orders' as well as by the 'legislative powers' of the Ra'ees.[10] According to the agreement, "the Council shall carry out and be responsible for all the legislative and executive powers and respon-sibilities transferred to it under this Agreement."[11] However, the Council is not a sovereign body. It is subject to the Declaration of Principles (DoP) and the Interim Agreement and its authority is confined to areas under PA jurisdiction. Moreover, the agreement states that "legislation, including legislation which amends or abro-gates existing laws or military orders, which exceeds the jurisdiction of the Council or which is otherwise inconsistent with the provisions of the DoP, this agreement, or of any other agreement that may be reached between the two sides during the interim period, shall have no effect and shall be void *ab initio*."[12] Despite these limitations, however, the PLC sought in its initial stages to overcome these obstacles and work as a sovereign representative of the Palestinian population in the West Bank and Gaza Strip.

But the efforts made by PLC members to expand the Council's authority beyond what was agreed upon with Israel were met with rising suspicion on the part of the president of the PA, Yasser Arafat, who sought to gradually undermine its role.[13] Arafat exploited the ambiguous formulation of the Interim Agreement regarding the separation of the legislative and the executive branches of the PA. According to the agreement, "the Executive Authority shall be bestowed with the executive authority of the Council and will exercise it on behalf of the Council. It shall determine its own internal procedures and decision-making processes."[14] The Executive Authority is to be headed by the Ra'ees who is "an *ex officio* member of the Executive Authority".[15] The agreement endows the Ra'ees with 'legislative power' that includes:

1   The power to initiate legislation or to present proposed legis-lation to the Council;
2   The power to promulgate legislation adopted by the Council; and
3   The power to issue secondary legislation, including regula-tions, relating to any matter specified and within the scope laid down in any primary legislation adopted by the Council.

These legislative responsibilities not only blur the principle of separation of powers, but they enabled the president to bypass the formal legislative process by issuing presidential decrees with impor-tant constitutional implications using the authority given to him by the agreement.[16] These decrees are finalized at the presidential office without consulting the PLC. They are non-negotiable and are not subject to any judicial review, for there is no clear constitutional order regulating this issue. Arafat has already issued several presi-dential decrees that have crucial legal implications, without allowing any possibility that the PLC or any judicial institution abolish or limit them. One such decree was issued on February 7, 1995, estab-lishing the State Security Court. This court was established in accordance with American and Israeli pressure, to enable the PA to deal as harshly as possible with violent oppositional activists.[17] Another, issued on November 19, 1998 in accordance with the Wye Plantation Agreement, warned against any provocative activities contrary to the agreement and against racial discrimination. A recent presidential decree was issued to establish the prime minister's post in the PA, which was endorsed by the PLC in March 2003.[18]

The ambiguity surrounding the division of labor between the legislative and the executive bodies harmed the principle of promul-gation.[19] Accordingly, laws passed by the PLC were frozen by the president for an unlimited period.[20] In four years the Council managed to discuss and pass 30 laws, of which the president endorsed only 24.[21] He ignored several laws passed by the Council for long periods of time, such as the Basic Law, and turned the legislative process into a conditional procedure dependent on his political and diplomatic calculations. The Charitable Associations and Community Organizations Law was passed in such a manner, as will be documented in Chapter 3.

Another well-known mechanism that empowers the role of the president *vis-à-vis* the PLC is the tradition established by Arafat according to which there are no independent and separate meetings of the Executive Authority (the cabinet). The weekly cabinet meetings are called 'leadership meetings' and are shared with members of the PLO Executive Committee, members of the Fatah Central Committee, heads of the security services, and the head of the PLC. These joint meetings comply with the aspiration of Arafat to present a broad consensus providing him with political credibility. These 'leadership meetings' eliminate the principle of accountability and create an image, however illusory, of power sharing. The Ra'ees plays on the balance of power between the different political forces, emptying the principle of governmental accountability of any real meaning. Appeals from certain ministers to the president asking that the PA cabinet meet alone were met with outright rejection.

This form of meeting boiled down to eliminating the cabinet as an institution. The marginality of the cabinet leads to two different but interconnected results. First, the president occupies the center stage in Palestinian politics without having to be accountable for his behavior in front of any clearly defined institution. Second, this phenomenon leads to the elimination of the collective responsibility common to democratic governments and empowers the minister as a person. Since there is no cabinet, the minister becomes responsible before the president and himself only. However, because the president is busy and cannot follow each minister every day, this has led to a modern type of "administrative feudalism", in which the ministers have little constitutional power but are administratively very strong. The inflation in employment in the different ministries contributes to this deviant picture. Ministers of the PA, especially those who returned from exile, sought to appoint a maximum number of loyalists to the bureaucracy of their ministry. Family ties were copied into the structures of the PA bureaucracy leading to a situation in which decisions were many times made based on tribal calculations instead of on professional criteria.

Furthermore, the merging of roles in the PA appears to be an even broader phenomenon. The annual reports of The Palestinian Independent Commission for Citizens' Rights (PICCR) in the last several years have demonstrated the lack of clear administrative and procedural rules of enrollment and division of labor in all governmental ministries. Most ministries do not have a clear definition of their authorities and fields of responsibilities. As a result, there are clashes between the different ministries where one ministry seeks to broaden its responsibilities and expand its authorities. Furthermore, there are similar institutions with similar fields of responsibilities in different ministries. In such cases these institutions compete with each other, causing damage to their field of responsibility in general and to specific people in particular. A good example in this context is the responsibility for developing and enacting infrastructure projects. Several ministries such as Local Governments, Health, Agriculture, Sports and Youth, have established their own units for running projects.[22] But the Ministry of Public Jobs claims to be responsible for the development of infrastructural projects. This overlapping leads to competition that ends with several ministries all running similar projects. Another example are the departments of womens' affairs in six different ministries – Culture, Health, Work, Social Affairs, Religious Affairs (Al-Awqaf), and the Ministry of Planning and International Cooperation.

There is a clear functional inflation in all official offices where in many cases more than one person is enrolled for the same position. For instance, in the Ministry of Health there are more than forty General Directors,[23] and in the Ministry of Sports and Youth 40 percent of the employees have the titles of Director or General Director.[24] The overlapping in the functions and positions in the PA is evident with the "magic" job of consultants. There are hundreds of consultants available for the president. The president, based on his own orders, has appointed dozens of consultants who have never been given an exact definition of their brief; nobody knows what their exact job is. These positions are given on personal basis. Looking at the PA's official periodical demonstrates the number of orders issued by the president appointing somebody as a consultant.[25] Among the consultants there are, for instance, several for military and security issues, several for media affairs, and several for economic affairs. These overlapping positions are empty of any real administrative meaning. They only have ritual meaning and serve to enforce the neo-patrimonial control system, which will be addressed in more detail later.

There is another form of functional ambiguity in the PA's administrative apparatus that enforces personal allegiance and reflects the lack of accountability in the governmental bureaucracy. Many PLC members hold official governmental posts, such as adviser to the president, head of a governmental company, or appointed head of a municipality.[26] This confusion of posts deepens the personalization of Palestinian politics, giving governmental functionaries direct access to the legislative process. Many PLC members claim that those who have both positions – as MPs and as government officials – view their executive positions as much more important, for these give them more power and access to decision-making roles. Furthermore, this duality forms a fertile ground for corruption and clientalist politics. PLC members represent their constituency simultaneously as legislators and as executors, thus violating the principle of horizontal authority, that is, the ability of officials of different branches of government to observe each other mutually, thereby preventing the concentration of administrative power in one state institution. Instead of a clear division of labor between the different braches of government, the same officials occupy posts in different branches, emptying the idea of checks and balances of its meaning.

Another example of the powerful impact of informal practices is the lack of clear judicial regulations regarding the legislature's supervision of the governmental budget. The Council has been unable to either monitor governmental spending or force the government to submit a timely budget. Although the absence of an appropriate PA budget is related to the lack of consistent, constant revenues (especially as a result of Israeli delays of the transfer money collected for the PA by the Israeli government) there have been clear internal reasons why the PA executive postponed the introduction of the regular yearly budget. According to a Palestinian political analyst, Ali Jarbawi, "the executive is trying to undermine the Legislative Council by keeping it out of the final status negotiations and by curtailing its ability to hold the government financially and politically accountable."[27]

Two central problems were raised by PLC members: first, not all revenues were reaching the treasury; and second, the PA's public investments were not included in the draft budget.[28] For instance, PLC members postponed for some time their approval of the 1999 budget since problems noted in the preceding year's budget were yet to be resolved. In their review of the budget, PLC members found irregularities in government expenditures: they discovered that large sums of money had not reached the addressed ministries, but were instead deposited in foreign bank accounts for which various people had signatory authority, subject to Arafat's approval.[29] These amounts form discretionary funds placed at the disposal of the president who initially refused to acknowledge the existence of this money. PLC members proposed to legalize these sums by amending the budget law to authorize the executive to build up a reserve that could be spent exclusively by the president. The point was to regularize these expenditures and make them known to the PLC and have them on record. The president refused to regularize these sums of money.

To these irregularities one should add the fact that revenues of the economic monopolies controlled by high-ranking PA officials do not even appear in the budget since they do not reach the treasury. These officials have monopolies over central sectors of the Palestinian economy, such as petroleum, gravel, flour, sugar, and so on. Monopolies operate in a gray area and their revenues are confidentially managed.[30] This pattern enables PA officials to avoid public scrutiny and legal regulation, and forms an easy way to finance activities of the PA that would be heavily criticized if subjected to internal public oversight or external supervision by donor countries.[31] This situation led a Palestinian economist to comment on the PA's *modus operandi*: "The PA's corruption, by now almost universally recognized, and financial mismanagement of donor funds flow from the mentality of a guerilla organization that continues to prevail, wherein the leadership cannot be questioned and operates in secrecy and without accountability. Hence the PA's parallel budgets, one public and one covert, the latter containing hundreds of millions of dollars of public money distributed to buy loyalty for the regime . . ."[32]

This lack of formal regulations regarding the budget makes it impossible for the PLC to effectively monitor the budget and control the government's expenditures. The slight changes in PA economic policies and the establishment of the "Higher Council for Development", which is supposed to coordinate the PA's economic activity, have proven ineffective. The expansion of the PA's payroll represents a clear deviation from the agreed-upon budget.

According to a report of the Ad Hoc Liaison Committee of the PA and the IMF, "PA employment growth in the fourth quarter of 1999 and in the first quarter of 2000 vastly exceeded what had been assumed when the budget was prepared."[33] The report reveals that hiring decisions are made in an unplanned way and that "very few of those recently recruited are in fact for positions envisaged in the budget, thus leaving genuine demands for employment in the judiciary, health and education sectors still to be met . . ." These conclusions expose the executive's disrespect for laws passed by the PLC. Since the PLC has been incapable of instituting respect for budgetary law, foreign agencies had to step in.[34] The PA's deviation from the approved budget is an example of a broader pattern of relations between the executive and the PLC. The head of the PLC's political committee, Ziad Abu Amr, maintained that,

> the PLC is prevented from affirming its authority by the dominant and charismatic personality of Arafat and the multiple sources of legitimacy he enjoys in exercising his individualistic style of leadership. Arafat holds all the strings in his hands. He is capable of suppressing all contradictions and of manipulating them to serve his own interests . . . If the PLC is an embodiment of institutionalization, Arafat's style of leadership is the antithesis of this institutionalization and the concepts of separation of powers and power sharing.[35]

Abu Amr adds that "the political mentality that dominates the Palestinian autonomous areas today is a direct extension of the traditional mentality adopted by the PLO and its leaders. This mentality is far in its basics from a mentality of founding and running a state. This mentality mixes the political–public dimension with the revolutionary–clandestine dimension and it is full of improvisations and total centrality of power." [36] This view is supported by another political analyst, who characterized the relationship between the Council and the Executive as one of marginalization.[37] In his view, "the personality of Arafat, who is elected directly by the people; the fact that he is the historical leader of the Palestinian revolution whose leadership is characterized by total centralization and monopoly over all authorities; . . . [and] the structure of the government, most of whose members are Fatah activists", make the separation of powers impractical.[38]

Therefore, notwithstanding the political circumstances in which the PA functions, one cannot explain Palestinian politics without the impact of Arafat's charismatic personality. According to public opinion polls conducted by the Center for Palestinian Research and Studies (CPRS) in September–October 1996, 72 percent of Palestinians were supportive of Arafat's policies, and 52 percent considered the relationship between the Executive and the PLC to be either "good" or "very good". On the other hand, 60 percent believed that the Executive authority should implement all of the decisions made by the PLC.[39] In January 2000 the positive evalua-tion of Arafat reached 54 percent whereas that of the PLC was 42 percent. Despite the deterioration in Arafat's position among the general public he is still viewed as the symbol of Palestinian national aspirations and would undoubtedly be voted back into office if elec-tions were to be held.[40]

Arafat's position is influenced more by the progress in the peace process than public satisfaction with the performance of the PA's different institutions. An in-depth analysis of the public opinion polls shows that the public differentiates between Arafat and his cabinet, as well as between him and the widespread corruption in the PA institutions. While 76–83.5 percent of Palestinians attribute corruption to the various PA ministries, only 43–48.7 percent believe that corruption exists in the president's office.[41] The polls do not determine, however, the percentage of those who attribute corrup-tion to the president himself. But based on the deterioration in Arafat's image one can conclude that the least accusation leveled at the president would be that he does not work hard enough to reduce corruption and dissociate himself from corrupt people around him.

This pattern, especially the lack of institutional clarity in regard to division of ministerial posts and the absence of economic trans-parency, has been tackled by the administrative reform initiated by the PA after heavy international and Israeli pressure. The appoint-ment of a professional finance minister in mid-2002 and the publication of the "100 Days Plan of the Palestinian Government" based on a presidential decree from June 12, 2002 have promised to bring to some changes in the relationship between the PA presi-dent and his government on the one hand, and the PLC on the other.[42] One clear goal of the plan is to "reinforce the separation of powers, such that the Legislative Council can play its role to the full, as well as the independence of the judiciary and the rule of law". The plan attempts to "restructure the ministries and govern-mental institutions, review their methods of work and create a modern and effective civil service as elements of a reform process that ensures the effectiveness and efficiency of work in the service of the citizen." In the financial domain the plan promised to "deposit all income of the Palestinian National Authority: Taxes, fees, profits from commercial and investment activities, foreign aid in grants and loans, including financial aid extended to projects, in a single account of the treasury, and implement the principle of the accountability of the treasury in the management of public funds". The recent creation of the post of prime minister as part of the administrative reform of the PA was expected to contribute to the implementation of this plan. But, as we know, the appointment of prime minister did not induce serious administrative reform in the PA. The stagnant political situation, resulting from: the besieging the head of the PA in Ramallah, his willingness to relinquish sole control over all axes of power within the PA, and the reoccupation of the Palestinian cities by the Israeli army, has put all reforms in the PA on hold. The resignation of the first prime minister, Abu Mazen, after only five months in office and the fact that the second prime minister, Ahmed Qurei (Abu Ala'a) presented his resignation to the PA president, who rejected it, in mid-July 2004, are further indications that the administrative reform introduced by Arafat in April 2003 has not been fruitful.[43] The death of Arafat on November 11, 2004, has brough about important changes, the most important of which has been the division of Arafat's responsibilities to different people. This major change will facilitate democratic decision-making and transparency.

The Firm Grip of the Founding Father

As the nucleus of an emerging state in a new political reality, PA leaders had to draw upon multiple sources of authority. But because of the fact that the PA was introduced as an extension of the PLO, its legitimacy had to be based on the same symbolic sources. As a result, Arafat, the main source of authority in Palestinian politics, quickly managed to establish his authority as the central figure in the PA. As head of the PLO, the leader of Fatah, and the elected president of the PA, in addition to being a charismatic personality and the symbol of Palestinian nationhood, Arafat had acquired enough power to organize the emerging political system around himself. His official positions enabled him to appoint his 'people' to central positions and intervene at all levels of decision-making.

Arafat silenced his critics, co-opted his enemies, and ostracized dissenters either by integrating them into the government or marginalizing them.[44] His reorganization of the list of Fatah members who had been elected in democratic primaries prior to the first Palestinian general elections serves as a good example of this strategy.[45] Not satisfied with the results of the primaries, he dropped young elected candidates and slated others who had not managed to be elected – intervention that was perceived as anti-democratic and caused much dissatisfaction. Several members who were dropped from the official list ran as independents and were elected to the PLC. Arafat's aim was to marginalize locally popular and partially autonomous Fatah leaders.[46] Sara Roy followed this process of appointing traditional, old-guard types to key positions in Fatah and claimed that "such appointments are at the expense of Gaza's younger Fatah activists, who enjoy substantial grassroots support and who are seen as having paid their dues through long years in prison. Many believe that Arafat's aim . . . is to marginalize Fatah's younger political leadership so as to diminish the challenge they inevitably present."[47]

Arafat's personalization of politics changed the rules of the game in the PA: it de-institutionalized collective action. He tried to empty the structures established by the local political elite in the West Bank and Gaza Strip during the struggle against occupation of any political role in his government.[48] He did not want to commit himself to the existing civil organizational infrastructure and instead promoted the establishment of new institutions connected to himself and led by people who were personally loyal to him. To advance this goal he manipulated the national security discourse, even when the debated issue had nothing to do with the struggle for independence.

Arafat's measures were explained as necessary steps to bridge the gaps between the local and the returning leadership. The returning PLO rank-and-file entered the West Bank and Gaza Strip in accordance with the terms of the Interim Agreement. Their return changed the social fabric of Palestinian society in these areas.[49] The returnees were welcomed with suspicion by the local residents of the West Bank and Gaza Strip, who saw them as representing an authoritarian political culture, and as seeking high-ranking positions within the PA at the expense of the local political elite. The returnees in turn viewed the local population as conservative and provincial.[50] Nevertheless, it was clear to the PLO elite that political survival compelled them to cooperate with the existing socio-political balance of power. Social integration and political consolidation were promoted for political purposes.[51] As a consequence, patronage politics became an indispensable phenomenon.

The establishment of new governmental organizations opened the door for political leaders to create their own circles of political supporters. Since the new political structure had to be established quickly, the patterns of recruitment familiar in Arab society were swiftly utilized. Neo-patrimoniality, where benefits are distributed according to familial affiliation, soon became standard practice. Social groups that did not establish political coalitions found themselves unable to obtain access to public resources or to be part of policy-making processes. As a result, the boundaries of public role and private interest became blurred. Bureaucrats abused their powerful positions and sought private interests using public titles for that purpose. A local lawyer commented on this issue, saying:

> Since the establishment of the Authority most of the big families have begun to reunite themselves in order to operationalize their quantity as quality in order to achieve personal interests and goals. These efforts concentrated mostly around getting as many positions in the PA as possible, overlooking the professional or practical qualities that these positions demand.[52]

The coupling of familial connections with bureaucratic positions was criticized in the Report of the Public Oversight Office and later by the PLC.[53] The Report criticized the inflation in arbitrary employment in high-ranking positions and decision-making roles, pointing out how aristocratic, anti-meritocratic politics was taking hold of the Palestinian political elite.

The administrative reform proposed in the "100 Days Plan" may be able to address some of the shortcomings in the PA. It is a real challenge, especially under current circumstances, when the Palestinian people are living in an area under total control of the Israeli army, to initiate genuine structural changes to the PA. Such changes are hard to achieve because of the internal balances of power within Palestinian society, where familial allegiance plays a major role on the political stage. The impact of the PA reforms on clientalism and patronage politics remain as yet unknown. It seems that until Summer 2004, the administrative reform in the PA was halted by Arafat and his close aides. Arafat has been accused by some people in the West Bank and Gaza Strip of blocking any change in the PA and using the sympathy of the Palestinian people for him, as a result of his imprisonment in his compound in Ramallah by Israel, to justify his reluctance to empower the prime minister of the PA. The stalemate in the PA has led to a deep crisis of trust among the PA top leadership and high-ranking Fatah activists, who dared to target top officials in the PA, such as Ghazi Al-Jabali, head of Palestinian police in the PA. Al-Jabali was kidnapped in Gaza and was released only after his position in the PA was negotiated between PA officials and his kidnappers.[54] Al-Jabali was accused of corruption and after his release he was replaced by Arafat. During this crisis among the leading figures of the reformist camp in Fatah, a previous aide to Arafat, Nabil Amro, was injured when he was shot in Ramallah on July 21, 2004.[55] Minister of communications in the PA, Azzam Al-Ahmad, said that the attempt on Amro's life was aimed at spreading the security instability from Gaza to the West Bank.[56]

The "Awkward Embrace" of the Dominant Party

Neo-patrimonial habits of appointing positions according to familial relations also determined the structure of the PA cabinet. The first PA cabinet was appointed as an interim government in June 1994, based on a decision of the PLO Executive Committee.[57] The cabinet included 16 ministers with full authority to conduct its executive goals as set by the PLO.[58] Returnees, locals, West Bankers, Gazans, members of large and well-known families, and independent personalities comprised this government. Despite the broad social and geographical distribution of the cabinet members, real plural representation is non-existent. Political opportunism and social clientalism were the most common themes, as opposed to inclusive representation of the different social groups. All of the appointed ministers were personally loyal to Arafat, and the Ra'ees entrusted them with a portfolio that rewarded only personal loyalty and allegiance.

Several months after the elections to the PLC, in June 1996, the appointed government was replaced. The five-month delay (the

PLC elections were held in January) was a result of attempts to strike a balance in the new cabinet between those from the PLO apparatus, especially from the Fatah movement who were loyal to Arafat, and prominent local personalities who represented large families or key regions in the occupied territories. The new government represented some changes in the composition of Palestinian politics. Political coalitions in the PLO were affiliated to various factions or organizations, and the seats on the Executive Committee had been divided among the various PLO factions. The new political circumstances changed this form of consensus politics into majority rule. Social, regional, and political background became the main motivation of coalition-building.

The new government, made up of 21 ministers, was endorsed by the PLC by a majority of 50–24.[59] In building the PA government, new social and political factors had to be taken into consideration. First, the absence of any real opposition in the PLC, as a result of the boycott of all opposition parties of the elections that took place in January 1996, prevented the building of a pluralistic political coalition, allowing Fatah supporters to thereby dominate the newly established government. However, Arafat sought to overcome the boycott and reduce its impact. He sought to draw politicians from the opposition into his sphere of influence, especially those who did not agree with the boycott policy.

Second, reflecting the social group tensions of the occupied territories, eleven ministers were Fatah members, while seven others were independents but well known for their close connections with the PLO leadership. Thirteen ministers were members of the PLC and four were members of the PLO Executive Committee. Most of the independents were local residents of the West Bank and Gaza Strip; their inclusion was part of the endeavor of the PA leadership to integrate all the Palestinian social milieux into the governing bodies of the emerging state. They were also a legitimizing factor in according the new government credibility among the local population. Three ministers were appointed who were affiliated with small political organizations that did not have a large constituency amongst the population. They were appointed solely for their support of the Oslo process.

As a result of public accusations of corruption, Arafat was asked to reform his government after one year in office. The General Oversight Office Report, published in May 1997, accused several ministers of misusing and wasting public money. A public debate between the president and the PLC subsequently broke out. The PLC demanded that the president renounce those ministers accused of corruption. Arafat tried to sidestep these demands and sought instead to silence his critics in the PLC.[60] But on August 5, 1998, he finally acquiesced and presented his third government to the PLC.[61] The introduction of the new cabinet was indicative not only of Arafat's ability to out-maneuver his critics, but also to remain above the law. Arafat's new government included all the ministers previously accused of corruption, as well as nine new faces, an increase from the 21 of the previous government to a total of 30 ministers.[62]

Not only did this exceed the number permitted in the ratified draft of the PA's Basic Law, it also failed to clearly determine the ministerial status of some of its members.[63] Several of the nominated "ministers" headed governmental agencies that were not originally established as ministries such as the "ministries" of the environment, administrative supervision, and parliamentary affairs. The president, in order to allow them to serve in a government cabinet, illegally gave the directors of these agencies the rank of minister without adjusting the legal status of their offices. The president took this step after these directors, without any legal basis, hung signs over their entrances announcing them as ministries.[64]

Instead of the required 80 percent of PLC members stipulated by the Interim Agreement, the new government drew only 67 percent of its ministers from the PLC. In addition, Arafat repeated his policy of appointing 4–5 members of the Executive Committee of the PLO as cabinet ministers in order to broaden its base of legitimacy. Sixty percent of the cabinet's ministers were linked with Fatah, and 20 percent were independents historically affiliated with the movement.[65] The dominant role of Fatah was not only reflected in the structure of the government, but was also translated into the balance of power within the cabinet itself. Ministers who did not belong to the Fatah usually "found it more difficult to acquire budgets and other resources or to assert their authority".[66] This phenomenon has to do with the division of labor within the PA, which is based on de facto rather than de jure regulations.

The structure of Arafat's new government invited criticism from several quarters. Many NGO activists accused him of using the government as a device to co-opt opponents and turning it into a mechanism of political and social appeasement.[67] Arafat did, indeed, incorporate the most vocal critics of his second government into his third one, in an attempt to reduce dissatisfied figures by making them part of the establishment structures. By doing this, Arafat discredited his critics, exposing them as greedy opportunists whose criticism was based on personal goals rather than the common good. Furthermore, two successful autonomous ministers of his second government were reassigned to new ministries in the third one. Hanan Ashrawi and Abdel-Jawad Salih, known for their critical positions and wide public appeal, were moved from the ministries of higher education and agriculture to tourism and minister without portfolio, respectively. Both subsequently quit in protest over the lack of qualitative change in the new government, disapproving of the solidification of Fatah's control over the Executive Authority.

Despite the criticism leveled against Arafat's government and the murmurs of dissatisfaction with its composition, 55 PLC members voted in favor of the new government, 28 against, and 3 abstained. Such emphatic approval of the government was a clear example not only of Arafat's hegemony, but also of the impact of the dominant role played by Fatah in the PA. Neo-patrimonial patterns of power proved to be effective in bypassing formal political procedures and emptying them of any substantial meaning.

Arafat's third government resigned in September 2002 following heavy criticism by the Palestinian public.[68] Coming two years into the second *Intifada*, the government had failed to put into practice any political program that could lead to a positive end to the diplomatic impasse. In June 2002, Arafat carried out symbolic measures to reform the PA and correspond to public and international demands to end corruption, but the failure of these measures led to the resignation of the cabinet. Arafat issued a presidential decree on June 9, 2002 announcing government reforms based on proposals first aired in a speech delivered in the PLC on May 15, 2002. According to Arafat, the new government was to be introduced in order to meet the new circumstances resulting from the realities of the second *Intifada*, and would contain five new ministers. Prominent changes included appointing a minister in the Ministry of Interior, a post that Arafat had withheld for himself since the establishment of the PA in 1994. Arafat appointed a prominent Fatah leader to the post, Hanni Al-Hassan, who was brought in to balance the growing internal opposition to Arafat's extraordinary power. At the same time, Arafat announced that Palestinian elections would take place in January 2003; indicating that the current government was only transitional, something that did not happen until Arafat's death.

With these measures, Arafat aimed to ease domestic and international pressure's to reform the PA and end the diplomatic impasse resulting from the second *Intifada*. Arafat also announced the elections on condition of the unilateral withdrawal of the Israeli army from all Palestinian cities occupied during the *Intifada*. This declaration signaled to many Palestinians that, since any IDF withdrawal was highly unlikely, elections would not take place any time in the near future. To increase pressure on Arafat, Fatah oppositional leaders lobbied the PLC to block the approval of Arafat's changes. Since many in the Council opposed Arafat's measures for internal political reasons, it became clear to many ministers in the government that it would be less embarrassing to Arafat if they resigned instead of having to face a humiliating defeat in the PLC. Saeb Erekat, a close aid to Arafat and a cabinet minister said: "The ministers consulted each other and decided for the benefit of the Palestinian people to submit their resignation to President Arafat to enable him to form a new cabinet and to be able to submit it to the council."[69] A leading Fatah leader, Salah Ta'amari, who criticized Arafat's decisions to hand over the Palestinians besieged in the Church of Nativity in Bethlehem and tolerate the imprisonment of PFLP leader Ahmed Sa'adat, based on Israeli–American dictate, admitted that the resignation of the cabinet was the result of "a crisis of trust".[70]

Arafat's announced changes to his government in May 2002 were a clear attempt to overcome Israeli pressure to reform the PA to establish a new political structure that threatened to marginalize him. Following its re-occupation of all Palestinian areas, and having besieged Arafat's presidential compound in Ramallah, Israel stipulated that any lessening of its aggressive policies in the occupied territories could only be achieved by an administrative and political reform of the PA. Beside Israeli pressures, many within Palestinian circles were calling for reform of the PA, and arguing for the establishment of the post of prime minister. Opposition leaders from within Fatah, mainly figures close to Mahmoud Abbas (Abu Mazen), asked Arafat to reform the PA and relinquish some of his responsibilities to a prime minister, who would be in charge of the cabinet and run the daily governmental activities.[71] These calls mirrored the internal split within Fatah between those who believed that any change in Arafat's position would serve Israeli interests, and those who viewed such a reform as a minimal step toward overcoming the political impasse caused by the *Intifada*.[72]

On February 12, 2003 Arafat declared his willingness to appoint a prime minister. The legal and procedural steps to promote this plan were immediately actioned by the PLC. On March 10, 2003 the PLC introduced the legislative changes needed in the Basic Law, the Palestinian constitution, in order to facilitate the creation of the post of prime minister.[73] The PLC defined the responsibilities and the duties of the prime minister, turning this post into a central element in the PA. According to the amendment of the Basic Law, the prime minister is an appointee of the president of the PA; as political power is divided between two people and not focused on one individual, the whole underlying structure of the PA was altered. This change was viewed very positively by Israel, the US and many Fatah leaders who were eager to limit Arafat's authority. But three weeks after Abu Mazen was appointed by Arafat to build a new Palestinian government, it became clear that the prime minister was finding it extremely difficult to overcome the tight grip over Palestinian political life that Arafat held. In spite of the changes introduced in the Basic Law that empowered the prime minister and gave him a free choice in appointing the members of his cabinet, Abu Mazen faced several political manipulations made by Arafat or his close aids designed to prevent certain people from being appointed to the new cabinet.[74] Abu Mazen sought to avoid a direct confrontation with the president, but Arafat made it clear that he was not willing to give up certain issues of central importance, such as the negotiations with Israel, and did not intend to give up direct control of several organs of the Palestinian security forces. He installed one of his close loyalists to the post of the interior minister.[75] The measures taken by Arafat handicapped the job of the prime minister, and prevented him from building his government within the time frame given to him. Despite having the option of a two-week extension to the deadline, Abu Mazen alluded that he would return the post to Arafat instead of asking for more time.[76] But on April 29, 2003, Abu Mazen introduced his government to the PLC. As in the past, his new government also relied heavily on Fatah as the dominant party in the PA.[77] But it did include some new faces that were not close to Arafat, something that boded well for future political developments.

But Abu Mazen's government did not last long. After five months in office, Abu Mazen held his resignation speech on September 6, 2003 at the PLC.[78] He listed several reasons for his resignation, most of which have to do with his inability to mobilize the Palestinian political system based on the basic lines he had presented to the PLC in April 2003. Among the issues he tackled in his speech was the division of labor between him and the PA president, Yasser Arafat. Abu Mazen wished for clearly defined authority to carry out reforms in the PA, which would establish the PA's sovereign control over the means of violence, delineate the authorities of the different ministries and institutionalize the Basic Law as an effective constitution. Abu Mazen addressed the chaos in the security forces and the lack of a clear budgetary policy, which prevents ministers implementing their policy and controlling their employees. He also made clear in his resignation speech that Israeli policies had put major hurdles in front of his government and that the Americans had not intervened enough to support him, despite the fact that he had tried his best to meet the administrative reforms they asked for, Israel had not offered any compromise that would have enabled him to legitimize his policies and face his opponents in the PA and from the Islamist opposition.

Another example of the centralization of power and neo-patrimonialization of politics in the governing bodies of the PA is the monitoring of state local authorities, such as municipalities and local and regional councils. On May 20, 1994 Arafat issued a decree stating "the laws, regulations, and orders that were operational before June 5, 1967 in the Palestinian territories will remain in force until they are standarized."[79] This decree invalidated Israeli military regulations that had been issued since the occupation of the West Bank and Gaza Strip. Simultaneously they reactivated Jordanian and Egyptian law in the respective areas, according to which, the West Bank and the Gaza Strip are divided into administrative districts.[80]

The Minister of the Interior is responsible for all internal affairs and has an administrative body to fulfill his directives. He can also appoint governors, who constitute the highest legal and political authority within each of the different districts. As the representatives of the executive branch of government, the governors are supposed to implement its policies. Furthermore, their authority has two administrative dimensions: one is connected to public services, and another is related to public order. Consequently, the governors are in charge of all the municipalities, the administration of the central government, and the district police.[81]

In appointing the governors, the interior minister, technically, has to consult with the head of the state, but as matters stand the head of the PA – Arafat – is himself the interior minister; therefore Arafat is in complete charge of this powerful governmental apparatus. Disturbingly, there are no clear credentials that prospective governors must have in order to acquire the position according to the law, and indeed, many of them are Arafat's political cronies. The PA areas were originally divided into twelve districts, with a governor for each district. Although appointed by law and despite personal differences between them in terms of power and influence, the governors turned out to be efficient agents of control in the hands of the president.[82]

The governors' offices became a central channel through which the local population could communicate with the central authority. The dominant roles of the governors have personalized politics and re-established the power of extended families and kinship groups, a development conditioned by the fact that most governors are foreigners in their own districts. In most cases of the nine West Bank governors are returnees.[83] These governors, who came mainly from the Western District of the PLO which was in charge of Palestinian resistance against Israeli occupation in the West Bank and Gaza, had to establish a new power base in an unfamiliar social environment. To ensure the effectiveness of their position, and to make sure that their authority was respected, they tried to legitimize their power by co-opting the dominant families in their regions. Patronage and the exchange of allegiance for posts in the administrative apparatus emerged as a successful mechanism for all parties.

Since governors coordinate all the activities of the official offices of government, they are central personalities in their districts. As a result the governor becomes the mediator in every local conflict, be it between citizens, between citizens and officials, or between the different governmental branches. The governors become the main point of address for most conflicts in that particular society, and arbitrators in familial and tribal conflicts. The centrality of their role enabled the president to become involved in local issues, in extreme cases, as the supreme judge.[84] As a result, the governors' offices became merely another structural tool that strengthened the central government and weakened independent civil organizations. This mechanism of control was one of the tools used by the PA president to reach the public directly, bypassing the fundamental representative institutions such as the PLC. The power and control of the role meant Arafat remained opposed to relinquishing the post of interior minister. Arafat also insisted that the appointed prime minister, Abu Mazen, could not entrust anybody with the post without the prior approval of Arafat, hence the reason that Abu Mazen kept the post unfilled in his government, introduced to the PLC on April 29, 2003.[85]

The political patterns described above all served to diminish the maneuvering room for modern civil and political agents, such as parties and non-governmental organizations. One should note that, at this stage, the elections for the local councils and municipalities were constantly postponed, with Arafat instead appointing his loyalists to office in the large districts in the West Bank and Gaza Strip. In one particular case, the appointed head of a central city in the West Bank is also a member of the PLC and the PLO Executive Committee, which conflates his legislative role with his executive positions.[86]

Such a flagrant conflation of authority is even more severe when we look at the security forces and the interventions of the Minister of Justice in the court system. Since its establishment, the PA has functioned without a clear constitutional order.[87] The laws applied in the PA areas in its early stages are rooted in different legal sources and periods – Jordanian law, Egyptian law, British Mandate law and Israeli law. As a result, until the enactment of the Palestinian Basic Law there has not been a one united and clear legal order in the Palestinian areas.[88] Consequently, there have been cases in which the security forces have arrested citizens without any order being issued by the Attorney General's office.[89] The forces have also refused to release certain prisoners, despite the fact that the court has ordered their release. This phenomenon is especially evident in the cases of political prisoners arrested for being members of opposition movements or criticizing the work of the PA. Detainees were held in police custody for long periods without charges, despite decisions made by courts to release them.[90] Many Palestinian detainees were denied the opportunity to speak with their lawyers, and were also denied representation in court.[91] In the period 1994–99 more than 21 prisoners died of torture in Palestinian jails.[92]

The lack of judicial independence has led the Minister of Justice to intervene in the judicial system, which is in contravention of the legal rules and regulations of the PA.[93] The Attorney General has also confirmed the intervention of the Minister of Justice in budgetary matters of the court in order to exert pressure on it.[94] The Minister has, furthermore, forced judges to resign, or sent them for early retirement without consulting the Chief Justice or any other judicial authority.[95] The intransigence of the executive regarding judicial decisions has discredited the judicial system in the eyes of the population. This has, in turn, led to the expansion of informal protection systems based on personal connections and allegiances.[96] Therefore, the public's evaluation of the judicial authority and court system has been in steady decline.[97] Many residents have turned their backs on the official judicial system and have returned to traditional forms of problem solving. Customary law, which is based on a long tradition of rules and norms accepted in Arab Palestine, has become a common ground for many Palestinians, who recognize its effectiveness relative to state courts.[98] The PA, which had an active role in promoting this process, encouraged patronage, clientalism, and corruption, while emptying official institutions of any real legitimacy and independence. This affected the perceived reliability of the official judicial system and consequently had a negative impact on the universalization of the rule of law.[99]

Electoral System and Party Design [100]

The new political structure established after 1994 raised public expectations and exhibited, in the eyes of many, a clear indication of the increasing prospects of democracy in Palestine. The high turnout for the first Palestinian elections reflected such public expectations.[101] The first Palestinian elections, based on the Interim Agreement, were important for Israel as a procedural act that legitimized the PA as a partner in the peace negotiations. They were important for the Palestinian leadership as a source of its authority and support for its policies. The electoral system had been determined in general terms in the agreements with Israel; the election law was ratified by the PA Executive in December 1995, and followed the guidelines set out in the peace agreements. The presidential form of government chosen by the Palestinians created a mixed election system, with separate voting for the presidential post and for the parliament. For the presidential elections, the West Bank and Gaza Strip are considered as one area in which all citizens over eighteen are eligible to participate in the direct elections. The elections for the Parliament were determined as 'general, direct, and free' and would take place in 16 different districts. Each district would send between one and twelve representatives to the Parliament (in proportion to its number of residents). The elections first took place in January 1996, with 75.86 percent of the eligible population taking part in them. Yasser Arafat was challenged by only one other candidate, Samiha Khalil, and won by a landslide vote of 88.1 percent, while Khalil won 9.3 percent of the legible votes. The elections led to the constitution of the first elected Palestinian Parliament where 88 members were elected, out of 725 candidates in total.[102]

The division of the West Bank and Gaza Strip into 16 districts tipped the scales in favor of the large families and tribes. In a district-based, winner-takes-all electoral system this led to the consolidation of their power in the new political system, shutting out political parties that would have won up to six seats in the parliament had the PA chosen the proportional representation system. The PA therefore managed to organize a highly homogeneous parliament consisting of local Fatah leaders, PLO activists, young Fatah candidates, notables, members of the business community, and tribal representatives, thereby ensuring support for Arafat on almost every issue. If it is true that the elections marked a new era of democracy in Palestinian political history, then it is equally true that the electoral system reduced the chances of proportional democratic representation and eroded the possibility of a change of leadership. On the contrary, the first-past-the-post electoral system allowed the consolidation of power of the dominant Fatah elite in a coalition with the dominant families.

The fact that the elections were a result of the peace agreements between the PA and Israel led opposition parties to boycott them. The three main opposition political groups – Hamas, the PFLP, and DFLP – did not take part in the elections. They viewed the elections as legitimizing the peace agreements with Israel, which they opposed. Furthermore, the chosen electoral system did not leave any doubts regarding the efforts made by the PA leadership to marginalize their role and prevent any chance of them winning enough seats in parliament. The PA leadership had no wish, evidently, to continue the quota system that had historically characterized PLO politics. The political boycott also contributed to the disproportionate representation of the candidates in the different districts and helped secure the easy triumph of Fatah.

Among the candidates, a large majority was independent and unaffiliated with any political party. The second largest group of candidates represented new ad hoc political parties that were established solely for the elections. Of 130 candidates who were affiliated with existing parties, 75 were affiliated with the Fatah. Fatah won 77 percent of the seats in the Parliament, such a high proportion that it essentially undermined the role of the parliament as a genuinely representative body. The Fatah hegemony became one of the main forces that paralyzed the ability of the parliament to control the executive and form a key source of public legitimacy.

The first elections led to the establishment of a stable, but unbalanced, party system in the PA. The secular opposition parties that boycotted the elections were marginalized. As a result, Fatah lacked any serious political challenge and today totally dominates the formal political system. The fact that the elected president is the head of the dominant party turns the majoritarian decision-making system into a stagnant majority rule.[103] This combination, in a highly personalized political system, constitutes fertile soil for clientalist relations that in many cases lead to institutionalized corruption.

The elections in 1996 marked a regression in the role of political parties in Palestinian politics. Despite the fact that a high percentage of Palestinians participated in the elections, the boycott of the opposition parties harmed the principle of representation and turned the formal political system into a partial player in the wider political field. The Islamic opposition, especially Hamas, began to exert tremendous influence on political developments that eroded the formal political process of much of its meaning. The decision of Hamas's leadership to boycott PA institutions on the one hand, and to carry on with its military struggle against Israel on the other, coupled with the inability of the PA to stop this militancy, have all served to undermine the Palestinian process of state-building. Hamas's boycott left Fatah as the dominant party in the PA. Hamas's military strategy gave Israel the excuse it needed to use its military power to disrupt the Palestinian project of national reconstruction. The Israeli government elected after the failure of the Camp David talks in July 2000 has used to the full the military operations and the terrorist attacks conducted by Hamas and Islamic Jihad to promote its disruption of the peace process, and this has led to the reoccupation of all Palestinian territories. This development has halted the process of state-building in Palestine. Israel has, ultimately, destroyed the institutional and civil infrastructure of the PA. For that reason, any Palestinian attempt to resume the process of national reconstruction has to start from scratch. The Israeli policy of destruction is related to the administrative reforms imposed on the PA. Israel's policy aims at reshuffling the whole Palestinian process of state building so that it meets its own visions and interest. This policy has been coined as *Politicide* by the Israeli sociologist Baruck Kimmeling, who claims that the proponent of this policy is Ariel Sharon.[104] It aims at eliminating any prospects for the establishment of a Palestinian state by eliminating leaders, reducing land spaces and increasing the number of Jewish settlers in the Palestinian areas.

❷

Deconstructing Autocracy

NGOS AND THE POLITICS OF CONTENTION

The establishment of the Palestinian Authority created a new set of circumstances to respond to for the acting non-governmental organizations (NGOs). Prior to Oslo, such NGOs operated under Israeli restrictions and without the authority of an overarching legitimate Palestinian body behind them. With the advent of the PA, the NGOs could now operate within a framework of Palestinian state legitimacy. The Palestinian civil sector under occupation constituted an interesting example of the gradual development of a civil society that has no state.[1] Because Israeli rule was seen as illegitimate, many NGOs operated illegally and were not registered with the proper Israeli authorities, as required by law. Most of these organizations – which are predominately financed by donations from Western and Arab countries – delivered relief and development services, thereby helping Palestinian society to lessen the hardships of occupation.

But the establishment of the PA altered the geopolitical landscape in which the NGOs operated. The increased level of access to Gaza and the West Bank that the Interim Agreement with Israel granted to the Palestinian people's national leadership created a new set of political circumstances for Palestinian society in general, and for the civil sector in particular. Consequently, the social network of Palestinian society has undergone serious changes.[2] The return of many Palestinians from abroad has taken place in parallel with the new legitimacy given to the PLO leadership. The rapid growth of the non-governmental civil sector will be charted in this chapter; indeed, it would not be inaccurate to claim that hundreds of new civil organizations were established following the start of peace talks between

Israel and the PLO in the early 1990s, and again after the establishment of the PA in 1994.[3] Naturally, the NGO sector has had to reorganize and adapt to the new social and political reality. Whereas prior to the Oslo Accords most NGOs conceived of themselves as the spearhead of resistance to Israeli occupation, the creation and legitimation of the PA changed the way NGOs saw themselves. A central question that many NGO activists began asking was, What will the nature of the PA be, and what kind of relationship will develop between the civil sector and the new Palestinian regime? Another question raised by many in the civil sector was, What role should they take in the coming stage of development in which the occupation partially retreats from Palestinian territories, yet while a Palestinian state still does not exist?

The years since the establishment of the PA, especially the most recent years, have witnessed many fluctuations in the relationship between the PA and the non-governmental civil sector; many of the questions raised above remain unanswered. There have been many misunderstandings between the PA and the civil sector, such as the space of maneuverability given to the civil sector in the emerging Palestinian regime. Civil organizations expected a large degree of freedom to act, as is the case in a functioning democracy, but still taking into consideration the unique political circumstances in Palestine.[4] However, the PA displayed a high level of suspicion toward the civil sector, and in a number of cases sought by administrative or legal means to limit the financial and political support NGOs received. These clashes have led to several measures taken by both sides which altered the nature of the relationship between them (although, in the final instance, the PA has always enjoyed the upper hand in terms of power relations).

The focus here is on one type of civil organization, namely those which are politically oriented. These civil organizations are mainly concerned with the nature of the political order in Palestine, and therefore focus on matters related to the rule of law and human rights. The reason for this limited treatment of the civil sector is twofold. First, the field of politically-oriented NGOs are also those to which the central regime is most sensitive (which is unsurprising as they deal with the nature and policies of the political regime and the state), and therefore, they face serious challenges. One test for this sector lies in its ability to protect itself *vis-à-vis* the expanding central authority as well as against the rising power of traditional social structures, such as tribalism, sectarianism, and clientalism. The extent to which the political NGOs influence the emerging political regime in Palestine and the mechanisms such organizations use to influence policy-making will also be examined. The second reason for limiting our treatment of the civil sector to political NGOs is because these NGOs illustrate an important dimension of the emerging Palestinian public sphere that has often been overlooked in other studies. The aim is not to provide a full analysis of all aspects of Palestinian civil society, but rather to explore the impact of civil organizations on the process of state-building and especially on decision-making. Service-providing NGOs often fall outside this remit and as such are only briefly discussed here.

The rest of this chapter is composed of three sections. First, a brief historical background is provided on the forms of civil organizations that operated under Israeli occupation. Second, the changes that took place in the civil sector as a result of the establishment of the PA are addressed. In this context, a distinction is made between two main periods: the "initial years", from 1994 through to the introduction of the Law of Charitable Associations and Community Organizations in February 2000; and the second "present", beginning after the ratification of the law. The third section deals with the "identity" of the political organizations and their discourse, followed by an analysis of the role of these organizations in the broader context of the PA and the extent to which they are able not only to sustain their existence, but also exert some degree of influence on political developments in Palestine.

Historical Roots and the Organizational Structure

The process of nation and state building in Palestinian was interrupted on several occasions by the intervention of external political powers. During the British Mandate, the Palestinians had to fight for independence against two enemies: the ruling British authority, and the Zionist movement. Despite, or more likely as a result of this struggle, many Palestinian unions, clubs, and other civil organizations soon developed that had modern as well as traditional elements.[5] Although these organizations were essentially tribal in nature, there was an attempt to transcend local borders and include other families, villages, and communities. One such example can be found in the Christian–Muslim committees that united members of both religions in order to achieve common goals. In many cases, these organizational forms were utilized in order to widen the family networks and strengthen their influence, with the aim of gaining political power as well as to occupy social and political positions.[6] This process of organizational expansion, which increased during the 1930s, came to an end in the late 1940s with the establishment of the State of Israel.

After 1948 the Palestinians were confronted with a new situation: they became dependent on Arab regimes that had little or no interest in an independent organization of Palestinians.[7] This led to the adoption of two forms of organization: (1) organizations that tried to reconstruct traditional forms of living in which the family was of central importance – for example, in the refugee camps, families that were torn apart reunited in order to rebuild a social network;[8] and (2) professional and student unions that represented the specific interests of their respective members. In most cases these organizations developed outside of the refugee camps, especially among the Palestinian middle class, which included many Palestinians who were active in the national movement prior to 1948 and intellectuals who understood the importance of the institutionalization process for political mobilization.[9] These unions were later co-opted by political organizations and functioned as the organizational infrastructure of the Palestinian liberation movement. Beginning in the 1960s, the Palestine Liberation Organization (PLO) dominated those civil institutions that defined, as their priorities in the fight for national liberation, the representation of the interests of their members. Thus, the PLO's civil infrastructure played a major role in rebuilding the Palestinian national identity and in the remaking of a coherent Palestinian society.

Institution Building and Civil Resistance

The "normal" life-style of the typical Palestinian changed dramatically following the June 1967 war. The isolation of Palestinians living in the occupied territories from the rest of the Arab world, coupled with the daily strain of living under Israeli military occupation, fuelled the military conflict. The inhabitants of the West Bank and Gaza lost their administrative center, and the PLO – only recently founded – lost its direct and immediate contact with the Palestinian population, which was subsequently split into pro-Jordananian and pro-PLO camps. As a result, a new conflict over Palestinian loyalty was created. Jordan was able to maintain contact with the Palestinian population and enjoyed the extra benefit of political influence as well because of its arrangements with Israel concerning the territories, as the Hashemite kingdom continued to pay the salaries of the public servants and financed religious organizations in the West Bank.[10] The PLO, meanwhile, used its "authoritative and allocative" power to mobilize the population for its own aims. The PLO's main concern was to be recognized as the sole and legitimate representative of the Palestinian people, and therefore to have the ability to mobilize the population to resist the Israeli occupation in order to establish a Palestinian state.

Pressures exerted on the Palestinian population by the PLO, Jordan, and Israel initiated the politicization process and the subsequent crystallization of nationalist, Islamist, and traditionalist streams. This led to a decrease of traditional forms of rule in the occupied territories and the start of the development of new organizations which represented more than one social, local, or family interest, and were thus better equipped to adapt to the changing political context. The non-governmental organizations that developed in the occupied territories can be categorized into two main ideal types: (1) non-governmental organizations and associations that function as a civil voice and framework for the promulgation of democratic cultural values; and (2) service providers.[11] Type (1) NGOs are those autonomous NGOs formed by the convergence of private sector voices calling for a resistance to the occupation in the name of democratic values, such as national self-determination, equality, and human rights. Many of the civil organizations, for example, were affiliated with political parties such as the Fatah, the PFLP, the DFLP, and the Communist Party. They were mobilizing agents leading resistance against the Israeli occupation. Some of these organizations are supporters of socio-economic development and advocates of democracy. Type (2) category of NGOs refers to those organizations developed in order to supply public services not provided by the occupying power. These were task-oriented organizations that formed a quasi-public sector. In practice, however, this crude form of categorization fails to capture the sheer variety and different composition of the NGOs. As a result of the occupation, various NGOs took different forms in order to manipulate the Israeli authorities and ensure their existence in the future. This influenced the structure of the civil sector that emerged after the establishment of the Palestinian Authority.

The Initial Years of the PA: Manipulating the Civil Sector

With the establishment of the Palestinian Authority, the new institution sought to control all aspects of public life in Palestinian society. As part of a comprehensive "national reconstruction" and the building of the foundations of the future Palestinian state, government institutions began to limit the space of maneuverability for existing civil organizations. A new era of power centralization began, aimed at transferring the authority over daily life in Palestine to the growing PA bureaucracy. The administrative power of the PA grew rapidly within a short period of time, despite the limitations set on it by the peace agreements with Israel. The PA bureaucracy sought to control most aspects of social reality in areas under its jurisprudence and to meet expectations set by the peace process. This process of power centralization was not a smooth one. Many civil organizations feared, and were suspicious of, PA policies. The cleavages in Palestinian society resurfaced and influenced, positively as well as negatively, the new process of political and social structuration. The shift away from a strategy of liberation to that of state-building has been accompanied by significant changes in the political orientations of all the actors on the Palestinian political stage. The focus on state-building required the adoption of new political strategies as well as a break with the hegemonic ideological legacy. However, since this change of objective was a result of a disputed political deal with a party still considered an enemy (Israel), not all the political and social actors were willing to adapt themselves to the new stage. As a result, several long-held cleavages began to emerge and assert themselves as the main characteristics of Palestinian political dynamics.

One such cleavage emerged between the returning national elite and its allies in the occupied territories and local elites who were critical of the Oslo agreement. The authoritarian tendencies of the PA and the dominant role of returning leaders in the process of national reconstruction infused fear in the hearts of many local leaders of oppositional parties in the West Bank and Gaza Strip. Ali Jarbawi, a university professor and a well-known commentator on Palestinian society, described this process:

> The claim that assimilation or unification now exists is an illusion. Those who have returned are not part of the 'inside,' and this is especially true of those who have not been given senior posts. I would say that there is a worrying, but not yet explosive, trend. No, we are not about to witness an explosion, but these issues will certainly be components of future internal explosions. On the very same day on which our symbol of unity, 'the glue' that holds us together, Abu Ammar (Yasser Arafat), will vanish, all these problems will come to the surface and will undoubtedly lead to chaos. The relationship between the returnees and the people of the homeland is a relation between a group of influential returnees who came back for reasons of self-interest and to govern the locals.[12]

These observations are validated by Jamil Hilal's well-founded study on the political sociology of the new regime in Palestine[13], which demonstrates how the PLO elite and their allies in the occupied territories have dominated the entire political system. Since Hilal's observations the situation has become less pronounced, but this cleavage has been institutionalized into the PA structure and continues to play a role under different guises.

Another split, which has surfaced as a result of the Oslo Accords, occurred along the Islamic and national lines. Since the Islamic movements exert the most effective political power in the opposition and the secular national factions have lost most of their constituencies, this cleavage tends to be situated along the Hamas, Islamic Jihad and Fatah lines. Both Hamas and Islamic Jihad opposed the peace process in general and the Oslo Accords in particular.

The national elite became the leading force within the PA. It centralized its authority in compliance with the peace process. The PA elite also sought to achieve the internal pacification of Palestinian society by finding ways to control all security forces in its areas of control and prevent a situation in which militias carry guns in the streets. These attempts, in addition to differences regarding realms and borders of political activity, have led to misunderstandings that ultimately led to violent actions, such as in November 1994, when 14 Hamas activists were shot dead by Palestinian police for failing to comply with orders issued to the

public. The PA has also waged several attacks on the social, political, and welfare infrastructures of the Islamic movement in an
attempt to weaken its support base. Many Islamic leaders and journalists were imprisoned for transgressing the PA-defined legitimate
space for political and journalistic maneuvering.[14] During the
current Al-Aqsa *Intifada* the differences between these two players
have mainly been suppressed, but mistrust continues to define their
relationship.[15] The Islamic movement has accused the PA of not
being serious about the *Intifada* and seeking to stop it by reaching a
deal with Israel, as demonstrated by the killing of several Hamas
supporters in the Jabalya refugee camp by Palestinian police in
December 2001.

State–civil society relations were also exacerbated by the establishment of the PA. This cleavage resulted from the Palestinian
Authority's attempts to centralize its authority; it believed that, as
the central government, it had the right to regulate the civil sector as
part of its efforts to assert its power on the ground. However, both
elites, that of the PA and those in the civil sector, came from similar
socio-economic backgrounds, and therefore the split between them
is less exacerbated. Nevertheless, two major differences between
them remained. First, whereas the PA elite is composed primarily
from returnees, local Palestinians make up a large portion of the civil
sector elite.[16] Second, the dominant majority of senior political figures in the PA came from the Fatah movement; in contrast, many of
those active in the civil sector – who eagerly sought to maintain their
freedom – were either independents or linked to left-wing political
movements such as the Communist Party, PFLP, DFLP, or other
small factions. Coupled with the contrast in political culture between
returnees and locals, which was influenced by their past experience,
these two disparities have led to major misunderstandings.

The PA sought several demands from the NGOs:[17]

1   NGOs must be legally registered;
2   the activities of NGOs must be officially supervised;
3   NGO spending must be properly monitored;
4   NGO funds must be audited on a regular basis;
5   NGO sources of income must be made public;
6   NGOs must publicly declare their loyalty to the Palestinian
     cause.

The PA's establishment has led to polarization and differentiation within the civil sector.[18] Many NGOs and civil activists perceived their role as temporary and awaited the establishment of an official Palestinian authority in order to be integrated into it. After the PA was established these NGOs quickly became part of its structure. Another group of civil institutions sought to maintain its autonomous structures and function independently. A third group of organizations did not adopt either position at the time and still fluctuates between dependence and independence.

Despite the disagreements within the civil sector, many NGOs were assertive about their right to protect their freedom of action as part of their endeavors to promote democracy and a liberal political culture. NGOs that sought to safeguard their control in the face of the PA's expanding power and the growing administrative and legal demands made by the latter's institutions found themselves caught in a serious dilemma. On the one hand, most of them struggled for Palestinian independence and were loyal to the PLO as well as to the PA. On the other hand, the NGOs' attempts to maintain their autonomy were viewed by PA officials as defying the PA's authority and resisting its control. The NGOs' debate with the PA, as a result of the lack of coordination between the PA's different ministries, was complex.

The PA adopted several measures to curtail the active civil sector and restrict its operations. One of these policy measures was to compete with NGOs for the same sources of funding. In this regard, the PA demanded that all funds given by donor countries to the civil sector be transferred to a central PA-controlled account from which the monies would be distributed to each of the NGOs. This demand increased the tension between the PA and independent NGOs, with the latter concerned about the allocation of funds. The Palestinian Non-Governmental Organizations' Network (PNGO), which is a coalition of more than 80 service-providing NGOs established in 1993 and among the most active players in the regulation of the relationship between the PA and the civil sector, has voiced concerns regarding attempts by the Ministry of Planning and International Cooperation to seek any means possible to influence donor states and organizations and divert their support to governmental organizations.[19]

Thus, it was in an atmosphere of mistrust that the two sides negotiated their relationship and sought solutions to the disputes between them. The competition over donors' money led the World Bank, in 1998, to establish a trust fund handed to a Swiss-based NGO, which manages some of the money that donor countries contribute to the state-building process.[20] Notwithstanding the steps taken by the World Bank, active NGOs affirmed their position, stressing the importance of including the non-governmental sector in decision-making processes and the necessity for mechanisms outside the PA for controlling the project.[21] The attempts of many NGOs to protect their autonomy *vis-à-vis* the PA has led many governmental officials, ministers, and bureaucrats to accuse the civil sector of opposing the state-formation process and of serving the interests of foreign donors.

The attacks on the independent NGOs began in September 1995, when the Ministry of Social Affairs introduced a draft law proposal to regulate the relationship between the PA and the civil sector. The draft law concerning Charitable Societies, Social Bodies, and Private Institutions, which soon reached the press, was heavily criticized by a wide spectrum of institutions in the NGO sector. Arguing against the proposed law, Mustafa Barghouthi, the head of the Union of Palestinian Medical Relief Committees, said:

> The individuals who formulated the law completely disregarded the unique role played by NGOs, choosing instead to treat them the same as charitable societies. One of the major controversial issues is that in order to obtain a permit, you must first obtain the approval of several ministries, including the ministry most involved – such as the Ministry of Health in the case of health NGOs, or the Ministry of Education in the case of those NGOs involved in education – in addition to the Ministry of Social Affairs and the Ministry of Interior. Then, the registration must be renewed every year, because the law states that there should be annual elections, and in the event of the death or resignation of a member of the board, he can only be replaced following the approval of the minister concerned. In addition, in order to obtain external funding, the NGO must again obtain the approval of the ministry. Moreover, it is not allowed to retain funding for certain projects for more than one month after the project has ended or to possess funds that are not transferable, such as property and the like. If the NGOs protest, the Authority says that they do not want transparency or to operate according to terms of reference.[22]

The terms of the law were unacceptable to NGOs that wanted to protect their freedom of operation. The draft law provided proof of the PA's attempts to establish complete control over the civil sector, as is the case in other Arab countries, such as Jordan, Algeria and Syria.[23] The NGOs waged a major lobbying campaign against the law both among the wider Palestinian public and within the PA itself, contacting ministries and PLC members, trying to solicit support for their positions. Furthermore, they appointed lawyers to conduct a comparative study of NGO laws throughout the world, and to prepare an alternative draft law according to the demands of the NGOs. This proposal was presented to officials, ministers, and PLC members with the hope that they would adopt it and approve it as law instead of the previous proposal. Several NGOs even complained directly to the donor countries in order to win their support.

As the debate over the proposed NGO law drafts continued, extreme pressure was exerted on the civil sector in general, and on several NGOs in particular – primarily those that waged the lobbying campaign against the PA. Despite the conflicts of interest, some understandings were achieved and most NGOs managed to carry on functioning. In this context, it should be made clear that there were, and still are, differences between the NGOs themselves in terms of their leadership, public engagement, and field of activities, which influence the relationship between the PA and each specific NGO.

As the PA was still in its initial stages of development, it was incapable of providing all the necessary services to the local population. The NGOs that provided services in such fields as health, education, welfare, and agriculture were therefore no less necessary to the PA than to the people running them. The PA was caught between either frustrating these service-providing NGOs by seeking to control them and limiting their space of maneuverability, or legalizing them and thereby legitimizing their existence. The support that these NGOs received from the wider Palestinian public and the relationship they have established with major sectors of society, combined with the bad name attributed to the PA and the accusations of it being authoritarian and corrupt, operated in favor of the service-providing NGOs in particular and the entire civil sector in general. Nevertheless, the relationship between the PA and the civil sector remained tense. Although the Ministry of Justice modified the draft law proposal in October 1995, the amended draft retained most of the provisions of the original draft.

The PA did not cease its attempts to limit the NGOs' freedom of operation. Toward this aim, the PA utilized its intelligence and security forces in order to monitor the NGOs' activities and thus ensure their subordination to a PA-endorsed political environment. At the peak of the PA attack on the NGOs, the General Palestinian Intelligence distributed two questionnaires requesting detailed information about those involved in the NGOs' activities. NGO activists were asked about their families and friends as well as about their political affiliation and activities. This form of questioning, whereby civil organizations are asked to supply information for what the security forces called the "security of the institutions", became standard procedure, and was a clear means of surveillance by which the PA sought to penetrate the civil sector and control its activities. In a few cases PA security used force in order to obtain information about important NGOs. In September 1997 the Security Forces searched the offices of many charitable organizations accused of being affiliated with Hamas. For security reasons several of these NGOs were ultimately closed.[24] The attack on these NGOs was part of a policy intended to weaken the Hamas infrastructure, in compliance with Israeli–American demands to take measures against terrorist organizations. But the PA's submission to Israeli pressure did not end with the attack on the Hamas-affiliated NGOs. On October 25, 1998 Security Intelligence forces illegally broke into and ransacked the Fatah offices in Ramallah. In response, Fatah – the largest political party in the territories – organized a public protest during which one teenager was shot dead.

The PA also initiated a policy to establish a government "union" to manage the NGOs. On January 7, 1997 a meeting headed by Fatah Central Committee and Legislative Council member Hakam Bala'wi[25] was convened in order to elect a commission for the NGOs in the West Bank. The goal of the commission, according to Bala'wi, was to restructure the NGO administration and uncover corruption and patronage.[26] The creation of such a commission reflected the PA's attempts to bring the NGO sector under its control. As a result, the PA did manage to create a broad civil sector that operates under its surveillance and competes with the autonomous NGOs for funding. The Ministry of NGO Affairs, established in June 1999, came to monitor the civil sector and coordinate the NGOs' activities, mandate, and budgets. The decision to establish the ministry was made during the height of an official and public campaign against the autonomous civil organizations, who were accused of exploiting public funding for private purposes.[27] The role of the new ministry was not clearly defined, since it was established by a presidential decree that declined to list the ministry's responsibilities. Consequently, ministry officials took steps to create their own place in the PA power structure and to define their own responsibilities.

Many NGOs faced great difficulties in dealing with the Ministry of the Interior, which is in charge of their registration and controls all security forces according to the peace agreements with Israel. To escape the heavy hand of the Ministry of the Interior and its security apparatus, many NGOs had to turn to the Ministry of NGO Affairs for help. Thus, many NGOs found themselves cooperating with the new ministry in order to overcome obstacles created for them by other PA ministries. This pattern of conduct, which many NGO activists considered to be intentional, has quickly established the new ministry's status as an integral player in the civil sector; it has become an arbitrator between the NGOs and the PA ministries and is able to monitor – at least indirectly – the activities of the civil sector.[28]

The PA's interventions in the civil sector and attempts to control its activities are illustrated by the experience of Tamkin, an NGO that assists in the functioning of other NGOs and which is supported by the US Aid organization. The PA published an official advertisement in Palestinian newspapers declaring Tamkin illegal. When asked by the heads of Tamkin about the decision, the Ministry of NGO Affairs claimed that the organization was not legally registered. As a result, the Tamkin heads turned to US Aid for help. After protracted negotiations, the PA made Tamkin's reopening conditional upon being involved in setting the priorities of the organization's aid to other NGOs. Tamkin had little choice but to agree to making the PA a full partner in setting its policies.

The PA's policies have led to reductions in the NGOs' resource base. Donor organizations based in the West – such as the United States, Norway, Holland, and Denmark – wanted no part in the conflict between the PA and the NGOs, and preferred a "muddling through" policy, whereby they redirected part of their assistance to NGOs run by the Palestinian Authority. The donor countries justified their policies as an attempt to assist the PA to establish its power as the central legitimate authority in the territories. These developments – in addition to the PA's need for service-providing NGOs –

have led to growing interdependence between the NGOs and the PA. In the health services, for example, the PA has sought to create cooperation with the NGOs, which has led to the sharing of responsibilities in some fields. The civil sector today runs 62 percent of primary health services and operates some 123 clinics in the West Bank and Gaza Strip, 35 percent of the total number of clinics in Palestine, serving approximately 250,000 people.[29] The civil sector also provides 90 percent of the professional education services in which 100 organizations are engaged and approximately 3,000 people are employed. In the field of rehabilitation for disabled and released prisoners, the civil sector runs five programs that give services to 25,000 persons at 200 different locations. Furthermore, in the field of pre-school education, the civil sector provides nearly 100 percent of the services given in some 1,200 kindergartens in which 40,000 children are taught. There is also extensive activity in the agricultural sector, with 13 civil organizations active in this field providing aid across 433 different sites, employing around 600 people.

All of these services, provided by the civil sector, have prompted the PA to examine its developmental role. Consequently, a few PA ministries cooperated with, and even provided some support to, several NGOs, especially those responsible for essential services that the PA cannot supply. For example, the Palestinian Ministry of Health declared that it has "adopted a vision that identified the roles of both the government and the non-governmental health care sectors as partners in health care delivery".[30]

Between Law and Praxis: the Power of Lobbying

Notwithstanding the growing cooperation between the PA and the NGOs, their relationship has remained tense. PA ministries' treatment of developmental NGOs that supply essential services contrasts starkly with the attitudes toward empowerment of organizations that focus on educational, legal, gender, and human rights issues. This tension was realized in the legal-juridical field and concentrated in the PLC, where the proposed law to regulate the civil sector was introduced for legislation. In November 1996 the PNGO and the Palestinian General Union of Charitable Societies (PGUCS) submitted a draft law outlining their vision of how the civil sector should be regulated. This draft law reflected two major issues that characterized Palestinian politics during the transitional period. First, there was a growing trend of strong lobbying by civil organizations to influence the PLC to adopt liberal and democratic legislation. The PNGO as well as other civil organizations, such as women's organizations have established a tradition of advocacy and lobbying to influence public policy. The civil sector protested extensively for a Civil Status Law, the Law of Charitable Associations and Community Organizations, Independence of Judiciary Law, Health Insurance Law, and the Labor Law. This wide spectrum of laws reflects the civil sector's broad interests and desire to contribute to the formation of a democratic Palestinian society. Second, the democratic role that the PLC sought to play *vis-à-vis* the Executive Authority, which has historically been dominated by Yasser Arafat, has also become a contentious issue.

Many PLC members were close to the civil sector in their worldview, despite the fact that many of them belonged to Yasser Arafat's Fatah faction, the dominant party in the Council. The PLC's political committee received the submitted draft law for NGOs and promised to promote its legislation. During this period many discussions and contacts regarding the law took place between PLC members and civil activists, which sometimes included representatives from the various PA ministries. The task was to formulate an appropriate draft law acceptable to all parties. However, the Ministry of the Interior (headed by Arafat) and Dar Al-Fatwah Wal-Tashri'a (The Legislation and Religious Orders Office), which is part of the executive authority, were not satisfied with the proposed law. Therefore, two documents for the same law were submitted to regulate the civil sector.

The PLC's legal committee was caught in a dilemma: which proposal should it support? Since the Council backed national understanding and reconciliation (in principle) the legal committee decided to come up with a new draft partly based on a combination of the previous two proposals. The PLC then introduced this new draft to the concerned parties. The PNGO examined the law and found that it neither reflected its own original draft, nor accurately represented the compromise formulations that had previously been reached between the PNGO and representatives of the different ministries. Because the PGNO found many defects and weaknesses in the new draft, a new round of negotiations was held in which the civil sector and the government put pressure on the Council to adopt a version that more closely reflected the demands of each. The legislation process was postponed several times due to a number of factors: more time was needed for a mutual understanding to develop between the PA and the civil sector; the civil sector was waiting to exert the necessary pressure to promote democratic legislation; and the emerging confrontation between PA President Yasser Arafat and the PLC, have all delayed matters. Because the PNGO was concerned that the PLC might submit to the President's wishes, it called on all civil organizations to participate in the debate over the proposed law.[31]

On December 12, 1998 the PLC passed the third reading of the Draft Law of Charitable Associations and Community Organizations. However, this final version was not one of the drafts presented by the parties involved in its discussion, but rather a compromise that failed to meet the full expectations of any party. According to Palestinian Basic Law, the President has one month to ratify any law passed in the PLC. The President also has the right to introduce changes to any law produced by the PLC before it becomes effective. The President's reservations or changes must be introduced to the PLC within 30 days from his reception of the draft law. In cases where the President introduces changes or reservations, the draft law is returned to the PLC for another, "third" reading in order to be finalized.

In the instance of the Draft Law of Charitable Associations and Community Organizations there have been reservations raised over the law in the form in which it was passed by the PLC. However, the modifications introduced into the draft law were not introduced by the President of the PA; they were in fact formulated by his government and sent to the PLC in its name. Moreover, these reservations were not returned to the PLC within the time limit set by the Basic Law. Nevertheless, the PLC discussed the draft law on May 25, 1999 and subsequently passed it in a third reading by a proportional majority without taking into consideration the proposed changes.

This prompted a legal discussion among its members, who were divided into two camps. The first claimed that the voting procedure in the PLC, which ratified the law, was illegal and demanded an absolute majority to validate the draft law. The second camp claimed that a proportional majority of the voters was sufficient to pass the law after it was returned from the President's office.

However, the dispute between the two camps concerning the voting procedure in the PLC was not merely a legal and procedural one. The camp that called for an absolute majority supported the changes introduced by the government and wanted to invalidate the vote in the PLC by relying on procedural regulations. In contrast, the camp that supported proportional voting rejected the changes introduced by the government and wanted to use procedural regulation to promote its own views. Eventually, the voting procedure in the PLC was declared valid by a legal recommendation of the Palestinian Independent Commission for Citizens' Rights (an official PA organization). Nevertheless, the draft law was returned to the Interior Committee of the PLC, which then reintroduced it with the proposed changes to the PLC once again, as the President and his supporters wished. The final version of the law included the changes proposed by the government.[32] In February 2000 the President ratified the "final" version of the law and it was published in the PA's official newspaper. Thirty days after its publication, the legislation became an obligatory law that regulates the relationship between the PA and the civil sector, and the Interior Ministry gave NGOs nine months to regulate all their administrative and financial matters accordingly. The outbreak of the second *Intifada* interrupted this procedure.

Several civil activists admitted that, notwithstanding the long legislation and political process, the civil sector was satisfied with the law, provided the PA ministries respected its spirit.[33] However, it soon became apparent that the PA had not given up its efforts to control the civil sector and its activities. For example, in regard to the registration of NGOs, the Interior Minister set regulations based on his own interpretation of the legislation, distorting the original meaning of the law. The new directives go far beyond the law's intent and seek to introduce restrictions that were not imposed in the original documents, but not excluded from its proviso, either. Based on these instructions, the Ministry of the Interior also issued new questionnaire forms, which were sent to registered NGOs in Gaza, which asked about the personal and political activities of their members, including questions regarding past detentions or imprisonment and the reasons behind the circumstances.[34] The PNGO asked its legal consultant to prepare alternative regulations and instructions based on the NGOs' understanding of the law. These proposals were introduced to the Non-Governmental Sector Ministry, headed by Hassan

Asfor.[35] The PNGO and the ministry subsequently entered into new negotiations based on these instructions.

The Constitutive Power of the Legalist Liberal Civil Discourse

The experience of the civil sector law clearly demonstrates the manner in which the legislation process takes place in the PA. It also acts as a kind of microcosm of the general interaction between the PA and the civil sector. The PA – which should be understood as a series of interacting and interdependent institutional structures, procedures, and behavioral norms, not as a unitary entity – has been eager to establish its authority on the ground by subjugating all realms of Palestinian society to its control. As a result, clear autocratic tendencies have become common features of the PA's authority (witness Arafat's hegemonic role and his involvement in every dimension of the PA's emerging political structure).[36] The autocratic–authoritarian tendencies that have characterized Palestinian state-building processes are also influenced by regional and local circumstances, including developments in the peace process. External pressures, especially Israeli, to curtail the opposition and prevent incitement have added to the rise of autocratic and neo-patrimonial political structures, which serve the interests of those involved in the peace process.

The same legislation process reflects the level of freedom that civil organizations are granted to influence public policy and lobby for democratic values. The civil sector has had a major influence and unique impact on most of the laws passed by the PLC, an impact that has been built over the last decade and prompted by the establishment of the PA. A growing discourse of civil organizations in the fields of law, politics, education, and human rights, has, since the 1990s, sought to influence the processes of national reconstruction and state building. This discourse, while neither homogeneous nor always cohesive, has been growing and expanding into the different realms of Palestinian collective life, spreading liberal and democratic values that put special emphasis on the rule of law and human rights. This legalistic–liberal discourse, which is rooted in the resistance to Israeli occupation, has paid greater attention to the internal Palestinian political developments, convinced that what transpires during the transitional period and the term of office of the interim government will largely determine the nature of the future Palestinian regime.

Notwithstanding these observations, the legalistic–liberal discourse has been gradually becoming more salient in the Palestinian public arena. Human rights organizations, institutions of law and public order, women's groups, research institutions, and academic forums are among those shaping the institutional infrastructure and constitute the discursive power of the legal–liberal dialogues. Their role is manifested in a variety of ways which include periodical publications, newsletters, reports and memorandums in newspapers, and other media, promoting democratic values such as freedom, equality, social justice, public transparency of governmental institutions, rule of law, accountability, pluralism, human rights, and active citizenship. This discourse connects these values with the development of society by claiming that constructing a modern society is only possible when Palestinian society as a whole, especially its political regime, respects these values, not only in theory but also in practice. Social justice and human rights have thus become among the most central collective values sought by the civil sector. However, according to the proponents of this discourse, social–societal development is not limited to merely the economic aspect of public and private life; it also includes the political welfare of the individual. Therefore, despite the fact that many of the NGOs that are part of the PNGO deal with agriculture, health, and other forms of development, other NGOs focus on the development of what they call "human power". The various publications of legal organizations (*Al-Haq* ["Justice"] and *Al-Qanun* ["The Law"]), human rights organizations (*Al-Damir* ["Consciousness"]), and research centers (*Muwatin* ["Citizen"]) clearly illustrate the content and the extensiveness of materials that address public order and basic freedoms. Furthermore, a wide range of publications target the different sectors of Palestinian society, hoping to reach all types of people in order to encourage citizens to be both critical and self-conscious.[37]

The liberal–legal discourse displays significant suspicion toward traditional social structures such as tribalism, familialism, and sectarianism. As a modern national discourse, the discourse views Palestinian society as a national one that should behave as a nation if it wishes to achieve sovereignty. In this context, those individuals involved in promoting these values and ideas see their contribution to the national resistance against occupation as centrally important and support the PA's efforts to reach a peace settlement with Israel complicating the relationship between the civil sector and the PA; it is neither one-dimensional nor antagonistic. The liberal–legal discourse formulates a clear link between the resistance against occupation and the demand for national self-determination with the freedom of the individual. This does not mean that all civil organizations call for an individualistic society, but most of them do favor the reconstruction of a modern society composed of equal and free citizens living in a democratic state. They view the PA as the legitimate political entity representing Palestinian interests, and despite the PA's lack of sovereignty, demand accountability and respect for the rule of law.

The Palestinian Independent Commission for Citizen's Rights (PICCR)

PICCR was set up in 1993 by a number of independent Palestinian public figures. It became an official organization as a result of a presidential decree specifying the creation of an independent institution charged with "monitoring and working toward the integration of human rights into Palestinian legislation and institutions".[38] Since its inception the Commission has issued several annual reports, the first of which was published in 1995. PICCR's main work revolves around receiving and pursuing citizens' complaints with the aim of ensuring the proper application of the relevant law. PICCR also strives to raise public awareness of citizens' rights. Palestinian citizens usually submit complaints directly to PICCR's offices or to field workers throughout the entire West Bank and Gaza Strip. PICCR also initiates cases independently when an issue of public interest is concerned and deals with any case of an alleged breach of the law by official Palestinian bodies.

Based on the information in PICCR's newsletters, the organization conducts training workshops for a wide range of participants, including teachers, medical personnel, and workers. The main aim of the workshops is to raise public awareness of citizens' rights. The Commission also has various publications, including an annual report of all known human rights violations committed by the PA or Israeli authorities, published in Arabic as well as in English to allow access to its information to as wide an audience as possible.[39] The report addresses all dimensions of citizens' rights. It sheds light on all branches of government, lending special attention to the administrative, procedural, and decision-making aspects. The report is supported by other subject-oriented publications and is usually divided into several parts including an entire section (of special concern to this chapter) that deals with human and citizens' rights in the PA.

The first three chapters of this report deal with the functioning of the three branches of government – legislative, judicial, and executive – and focus on the efficiency and effectiveness of these institutions and their compliance with the rule of law. In most cases the report points out the shortcomings in the operations of these institutions and suggests ways to overcome them. In the final report for the year 2000, PICCR put a special emphasis on the crisis in the Palestinian judicial system and the court system in particular. The report explained the implications of these problems for the status of citizens' rights in Palestinian society and for the rule of law.

The report also gives special attention to violations of citizens' rights committed by the executive authority as well as the selective application of the law and the subsequent rulings handed down by the courts. The executive authority in the PA is considered the primary axis in the work of PICCR, because it dominates the judicial and legislative branches of government, and has been given powers that are normally the responsibility of the other two branches. The report addresses all issues related to the executive's functioning, such as the budget and the lack of regulations curbing its expenditures and income; or the absence of any law that organizes and defines the operations of the security forces; and the PA's employment policies, which create an atmosphere of clientalism and familialism within the PA structure.

The fourth chapter of the report addresses violations of human and citizens' rights committed by the PA authorities. The report includes the number of prisoners who have died in PA jails: 23 between 1994 and 2000. It also addresses the manner in which the security forces sometimes forbid public gatherings, which is a violation of the right of assembly as stated by law, and discusses methods of torture used by the security forces in Palestinian jails and other places of imprisonment. Furthermore, the report exposes all known cases of politically motivated detention or imprisonment and the brutal imprisonment of citizens for civil or criminal reasons. PICCR has devoted a special report to the issue of political imprisonment in addition to its treatment of the issue in the annual report.[40] It defines political imprisonment as "the imprisonment enacted by the authorities against individuals and groups based on oppositional political positions or on the background of organizational or political affiliation to opposition groups but which does not violate international law regarding human rights".[41] This definition emphasizes the differences delineated by the Commission between three types of prisoners: (1) individuals imprisoned by the PA because of their affiliation with Islamic or leftist political organizations that oppose the peace process with Israel; (2) individuals imprisoned for their critical comments against the PA; and (3) those imprisoned for cooperating with Israel. The Commission does not consider the last type of imprisonment as political in nature since Palestinians who cooperate with Israeli security forces violate Palestinian law.

The PICCR's annual report documents hundreds of cases of violations of basic citizens' rights involving both individuals and groups, suggesting that there is a particular pattern to this conduct. The Commission also presents recommendations and proposals to improve the efficiency of the governmental institutions as well as to promote the status and importance of human rights in the PA. The Commission usually pursues an in-depth follow-up of special cases that attract wide public concern, published in special reports added to the Commission's periodical (published four times a year, summarizing its activities).[42] These PICCR publications, workshops, and lectures, and appeals to the media in cases where the authorities do not cooperate with the Commission, have an impact on the public in general and the authorities in particular. This comprehensive type of work is conducted by many other human rights organizations operating in areas under PA control, whose publications are similar to those of the PICCR. These organizations' publications and monitoring work are having a cumulative effect, as most human rights organizations report a distinct improvement in the PA's human rights record accompanied by an increased willingness among PA institutions to cooperate with human rights organizations. However, this does not mean that violations no longer occur, or that these improvements meet the minimum standards a democratic society demands. Based on the Commission's report, many issues are still in need of improvement. The executive authority, for example, still ignores the appeals of human rights organizations, violates the law, and does not adhere to Palestinian court rulings. Nevertheless, the publications and their (albeit slight) impact are an indication of the importance of the legal–liberal discourse in Palestinian society.

The Palestinian Non-Governmental Organizations' Network (PNGO)

The PNGO unites many human rights and legal organizations as well as others that supply social, health, welfare, and agricultural services. The PNGO has been coordinating the work of these organizations and their common efforts *vis-à-vis* the PLC and the PA ministries. It is therefore illustrative to focus on the Network, and especially on its publication *Al-A'mal Al-Ahli* ("Civil Work"), which is published monthly in Arabic and distributed with the daily *Al-Ayyam* newspaper. This supplement, which is part of the PNGO's public outreach program, began appearing in mid-1998. According to its defined goals, the supplement "aims to strengthen relations between the PNGO and the local Palestinian community and to promote the most important issues and challenges that face civil work in general".[43]

The PNGO has been a central coordinator between the civil sector and the PLC, investing energy in raising awareness amongst the Palestinian population of the importance of democracy to the national reconstruction process. Among its first priorities is the PNGO's "advocacy and public education program". In this context the Network declared that it "will continue its program of advocacy and public education *vis-à-vis* the Palestinian Legislative Council and will continue its regular documentation of PLC sessions through its Advocacy and Public Education Coordinator. The sessions are documented in order to expose happenings in the Council to Palestinian NGOs and NGOs might wish to respond to them."[44]

The PNGO has also sought to be a force on the issue of the right of assembly – one of the most important and basic rights in a democracy. Several Network members have organized public gatherings, education days, and appeals to the High Court against violations of the right of assembly. An example of the latter is the group's response to the order given by the Police Chief, Ghazi Al Jabali on February 29, 2000 forbidding a public rally organized by the Al-Damir organization, as well as any other public gathering without his authorization. As a group belonging to the Network, Al-Damir appealed to the High Court to cancel the Chief's order. Khalil Abu Shmaleh, the head of Al-Damir in Ramallah, said that "denouncing the rally was a matter of principle and the controversy is basically on the form of speech. The police ask us to formulate our application in such a way that includes a sort of a plea and requesting which is not the spirit of the law."[45] In addition to the PNGO appeal to the High Court, many other human rights organizations and political parties went to the High Court and also sent an appeal to President Arafat, PLC head Abu Ala'a (Ahmed Qurei), and PLC members explaining the danger of Al-Jabali's order which violates the 1998 Law of Assembly and other basic democratic values.

The NGOs' Network has sought to deepen the public's understanding of the civil sector's importance and the positive role that this sector can play in promoting the interests of the Palestinian people. For this purpose the Network placed special importance on the use of the local and international media to inform the public of its activities as well as "issuing occasional press releases or public statements in response to incidents, or related to issues concerning NGOs and civil society".[46] Furthermore, the Network organized debates and discussions between Network members and PA officials regarding public issues and held conferences to attract public attention to those issues it considered to be of great importance to democracy in Palestinian society. The Network has thus managed to penetrate the public sphere and become influential in shaping public policy and to represent certain Palestinian publics which otherwise might have remained silent and unheard.

NGOs are in part responsible for generating the public debate and refusing to accept non-democratic behavior by the executive. The PNGO believes it is crucially important to reach out to the public declaring, "it is essential to create public awareness on vital issues that affect people's lives and the well-being of society as a whole."[47] The Network also believes in building strong ties with various sectors of the Palestinian public. This is another reason for the publication of 8,000 copies of *Al-A'mal Al-Ahli* ("Civil Work").

The newspaper supplement focuses on different issues of central importance to the Network's activities and to the Palestinian public. The network also addresses civil and community work provided by the NGOs. Senior activists publish their opinions on the civil sector's priorities and agenda. These opinions are part of the informative campaign that the PNGO wages to raise public awareness of the civil sector's central role in a democracy and help deepen public understanding of the concept of active citizenship, in terms of taking responsibility for one's own life and actions. Central activities of the Network's member groups are usually publicized, either on a special activity organized for the public (such as a study day), or as workshops, educational seminars, and legal activities (such as appeals to the courts carried out by one of the legal organizations). The newspaper supplement relates to the Network's general activities and publishes its policy position regarding public matters. These positions are usually published within the framework of the supplement's editorial, as each supplement focuses on a different issue. In addition, there are articles published by Network activists articulating their opinion on public matters.

The collection of subject matters published in each issue reveals to the public the various civil and community work being done. *Al-A'mal Al-Ahli* seeks to achieve the central goal of lobbying and mobilization among the wider Palestinian public, as part of its strategy of drawing public support for the NGOs, which in turn enables it to confront the authorities more effectively. The newspaper supplement also serves to meet one of the most common demands raised *vis-à-vis* NGOs in general, that is, to be transparent and open to public scrutiny.

Conclusion

There is a wide range of civil organizations that deal with different realms of public and private life in Palestine. These organizations vary in their subject matters as well as in their forms of organization. According to studies published *in Al-A'mal Al-Ahli*, the civil sector is active in 450 locations in Palestine and serves some 1.5 million people, employing about 25,000 people.[48] A wide range of publications exist that form a discourse that can be referred to as legal–liberal because of its focus on the rule of law and human rights in Palestinian society.

The historical roots of the civil and community organizations can be traced back to the period of the British Mandate, but they became more politically active under Israeli occupation. With the establishment of the PA, the civil sector has undergone tremendous changes. The PA became the first central Palestinian political authority of self-rule. The new regime sought to take control of all civil services provided to the public, which under Israeli occupation had been supplied mainly by civil organizations. This development has led to confrontations between the PA and the civil sector over spheres of influence. The confrontations have focused not only on the range and form of the activities that the civil sector could provide, but also over the actual existence of an independent and autonomous civil sector. Senior PA officials such as the Minister of Justice waged a public campaign against the civil sector and accused its organizations of corruption and of wasting public funds on large salaries and expensive cars.[49]

Two questions arise in this context: the extent to which the civil sector manages to maintain its autonomy from the emerging state structure, and the extent of its influence in the public policy arena. Regarding the first question, we have shown that a clear division of labor between the PA and the civil sector has not been established. Nevertheless, the latter has proved its ability to protect itself from the central authority's designs for absolute control. A dynamic and pluralistic civil sector exists in Palestine that has developed its own realms for action and discourse, but its influence on public policy remains unproven. No clear mechanisms of cooperation and consultation as yet exist between the PA ministries and the civil sector. Any cooperation is sporadic and dependent on the personalities responsible in each ministry and NGO. As witnessed with the Law of Charitable Associations and Community Organizations, the civil sector was able to bring about some changes in the law despite the will of the government, although the latter has not yet given up its efforts to limit the civil sector and designate very narrow parameters for it to function within. This does not mean that these attempts will necessarily succeed, but it is clear that the democratic cooperation between the civil sector and the PLC, as well as the active role of the NGOs in setting public policy, are conditioned by the priority of security issues and the superiority of the institution of the presidency in the PA's political structure. The cooperative relationship between NGOs and PA ministries has sometimes set limitations on the NGOs' freedom of maneuverability. Being bound to the PA ministries led to major restrictions in the NGOs' ability to serve as a counterweight to the government and criticize its policies.

One also finds constitutional limitations on the civil sector's advocacy and lobbying activities in Palestine. The PA's agreements with Israel placed a greater emphasis on security matters than development and transition to a democratic society. In many cases Israel viewed the free hand of civic organizations as a threat and accused the PA of allowing incitement. The fact that the peace process has not resulted in Palestinian independence has led to the regulation of NGO activities, confining them within clear geopolitical and legal boundaries. The current Al-Aqsa *Intifada* has deteriorated the situation in the region to an almost complete and unrestrained confrontation between the Israeli army and the Palestinians. Consequently, this situation has influenced the civil sector's priorities to be refocused on resistance and welfare rather than efforts for stable development and democratization.

In terms of the effect of the current conflict on legislation, the PLC has been effectively neutralized in the last four years. Unable to convene regularly as a result of Israel military occupation of all PA areas and its veto on all Palestinian national activities within the institutions of the PA, it has only been allowed to meet on rare occasions when the decisions made have met Israeli demands and dictates, such as in the case of appointing a Palestinian Prime Minister in early 2003.

A serious problem that the Palestinian civil sector faces on a whole is the instability in terms of sources of financial support. Most, if not all, Palestinian NGOs rely on foreign financial support. The donor countries and organizations therefore play a major role in setting the Palestinian civil sector's policies and priorities. The Palestinian civil sector has not yet managed to generate its own financial resources from within Palestinian society, which means that it will have to depend on foreign support for the foreseeable future. There is no doubt that this situation influences the civil sector's nature and that the NGOs' activities are limited according to what the donors view as appropriate.

Another weakness of the Palestinian civil sector lies in its public outreach and its own internal ideological accountability. Despite the fact that most civil organizations in Palestinian society provide services to the public, it is unclear whether the civil sector believes that the public is sufficiently aware of the vital connection between the developmental and national tasks the NGOs fulfill. The extensive efforts made by the PNGO and other civil organizations to promote themselves in the public domain reflect two important points. First, the civil sector does not have enough public support for its endeavors to protect its "space" of maneuverability *vis-à-vis* the PA. Consequently, the civil sector seeks to reactivate public involvement and to encourage voluntarism not only for the sake of the general public good, but also for the sake of strengthening the relationship between the public and the civil sector.[50]

These complex problems are connected to the philosophical and valuational foundations of the civil and community service in Palestinian society. In closing, it is worth mentioning the questions raised by George Giacaman, a political philosopher and prominent activist in the Palestinian civil sector.[51] Giacaman asked himself and his colleagues about the amount of time they devote to verifying and explicating the meanings of the values for which they all claim to be working. For instance, he asks about the meaning of social justice in the era of globalization and late capitalism. Most civil organizations, especially the PNGO, list social justice as among their major goals, but what is the meaning of this expression and to what extent do the different organizations agree on a meaning? Giacman claims that, if it means "reducing poverty" or "small projects" as it does in South America, then the civil sector will be protecting the dominant socio-political order *vis-à-vis* globalization. As a result, civil projects will become partners in expanding globalization, drifting away from the mission of encouraging development and social justice. The lack of definitions for the valuational and philosophical foundations of the civil and community services has led to an effort in the civil sector to focus energies on aspects perceived by the public as of secondary importance. For instance, human rights organizations have tended to focus on abstract political rights, but Giacaman argues that many people see the rights to health care and humane treatment in hospitals as more important, or at least more urgently needed than gaining full political rights. This does not mean that political rights are not of central importance, but Giacaman's comments reflect the current, out of touch emphasis in the civil and community work and the urgent need to broaden the scope of thinking on these major issues, and perhaps to address more immediate, material concerns. Giacaman's comments also point to the causes for the lack of a satisfactory level of public awareness, appreciation for the services provided by the civil sector, and the critical need for change.

3

The Constitutive National Press

MECHANISMS OF THE PALESTINIAN MEDIA REGIME

This chapter examines the role of the media within the Palestinian Authority and evaluates the space the regime afforded for freedom of expression. The media's methods of framing attitudes and setting the public agenda are also investigated. The outbreak of the second *Intifada* changed the whole Palestinian political arena; when Israel reoccupied all Palestinian cities it destroyed the PA's institutional infrastructure. Nevertheless, the experience of the Palestinian media with the PA reveals several central characteristics of Palestinian politics, and is relevant for evaluating future prospects. An examination of the relationship between the PA and the media will enable us to designate the media's place on the spectrum between being an autonomous public sphere, open for free argumentation and deliberation, or being a mouthpiece of state imperatives, assisting in shaping public imagination, a tool of manipulation.

Examining this relationship will also touch upon the emerging patterns of administrative, procedural, legal, and discursive means that define what is permissible and forbidden, possible and impossible, and worth or not worth saying, writing, or broadcasting in the emerging Palestinian polity. Four categories of mechanisms – administrative, procedural, legal, and discursive – exist that promote or limit freedom of expression and enable or restrict the publication of certain materials or information. The four categoriese examined here constitute what is called a "media regime". This regime determines what is published and what is not, determines the rules of publishing, as well as how and why the particular rules are set. The importance of the media in processes of transition to statehood and democratization, and the role it could potentially play in promoting them as an open public sphere, are discussed below.

Media Regime and Mobilization Structures

The media has always played an important role in Palestinian national politics, and has been a significant mobilizing tool in the hands of the elites. Despite the limited number of readers as a result of low literacy rate in Palestinian society before 1948, several newspapers were published in Palestine.[1] Journalism played an important role in propagating Palestinian nationalism.[2] Political leaders and, later, parties utilized newspapers to promote their views and express their positions in different fields that concerned the contemporary social elite. A major issue that drew the attention of journalists, and was covered extensively in newspapers, was the Jewish immigration to Palestine and its influence on Palestinians. As Rashid Khalidi demonstrated, the media of the 1930s warned of the political, social, and economic implications of the Jewish immigration and journalists sought to direct public awareness to the need for the opposition to British policies toward Jews.[3]

In the post-1948 period, and especially after 1967, the media became a central player in Palestinian national strategy. The PLO established an extensive information infrastructure as part of its attempts to enter the diplomatic arena and institutionalize the Palestinian right of self-determination. For this purpose the PLO established radio broadcasting in cooperation with different Arab regimes. The Voice of Palestine, broadcast from Cairo or Baghdad, was well known among Palestinians.[4] Newspapers, weeklies, and monthlies became part and parcel of the PLO public relations campaigns in different Arab states. The efforts invested in the Arab and international media reflected the importance of communicating the Palestinian problem to the world. The PLO acted as a nation-state in regard to constituting a Palestinian imagined community despite the structural state of dispersal in which most Palestinians lived.[5]

The PLO introduced its media organs into the occupied territories in the early 1970s.[6] It financed weeklies and daily newspapers in order to influence Palestinian public agenda in the face of Israeli and Jordanian control of the education system in the West Bank and Gaza Strip. The media was utilized as a "state ideological apparatus" to promote PLO interests among the rising national elite.[7] The main two media organs, *Al-Fajr* and *Al-Sha'b* newspapers, promoted a blunt, unsubtle PLO political line and conspired against Israeli and Jordanian attempts to encourage a political course independent of the PLO's influence.[8] Israel moved to censor the Palestinian media and intimidated journalists who did not adhere to its strict control of media contents.[9] The PLO, for its part, did everything possible to maintain continuous connections with national journalists, who operated as agenda setters. The PLO managed, through mobilizing financial and human resources, to strengthen its influence on media outlets and sometimes even to dictate editorial policies. The growing power of the national elite in the occupied territories turned the pro-PLO national worldview into the dominant ideology in the area. Journalists were among the most active nationalist forces supporting the PLO and opposing Israeli occupation.

The signing of the Oslo Agreement and the subsequent establishment of the PA marked a major shift in the Palestinian media landscape and affected all the PLO's newspapers, weeklies, and periodicals. It also signified the creation of new media forms that had been prohibited under Israeli occupation. This period of development following Oslo was characterized by an increase in the number of newspapers, weeklies, and periodicals. Prior to that, the PLO had had to invest the major part of its information campaign efforts in the mobilization of Palestinian society for the struggle against Israel, a policy that had to be revised as a consequence of the Oslo Accords. However, the winds of change in PLO information policies could be felt several months prior to the signing of the accords. This change was illustrated by the closing of the PLO's main publication, *Filastin Al-Thawra* ("The Palestine Revolution"), which was published by the PLO Information Center. The monthly *Shu'un Filistinia* ("Palestinian Affairs"), which was published by the Palestinian Research Center, was also closed.

In addition, financial problems in the PLO prompted the closure of other publications it had funded in the occupied territories. It withdrew its financial support for *Al-Fajr* ("The Dawn") and *Al-Sha'b* ("The People"), two of the main dailies in the occupied territories, which ultimately led to these papers' closure. In addition, the financial crisis in the PLO following the Gulf War (1991) led to the closing of other newspapers and weeklies, such as the privately owned *Al-Biader Al-Siyasia* ("The Political Fields"), which represented the political views of Fatah.

Perhaps the most interesting point in regard to this wave of newspaper closures was that the closures of *Al-Fajr*, *Al-Sha'b* and *Al-Biader Al-Siyasia* passed virtually without reaction in the Palestinian street. This silent response reflected the average Palestinian's lack of concern due to the artificial nature of these newspapers; but it also reflected the psychological readiness of the Palestinian public in the occupied territories to move on to a new phase of hope for a political settlement to be attained in peaceful negotiations following six years of *Intifada*.

According to public opinion polls conducted in 1993–4, the majority of Palestinians in the West Bank and Gaza Strip supported the Oslo agreements, indicating that they viewed the peace process as a way out of their miserable situation.[10] The newspapers that remained in operation until the institution of new media agencies several months later, *Al-Quds* and *Al-Nahar,* adopted different editorial lines of coverage during this period. The pro-Jordan *Al-Nahar* criticized the PLO for compromising on fundamental issues and thus "selling out" to Israel. It also criticized the way in which the Oslo agreement was reached and the fact that the PLO did not coordinate its steps with other Arab countries, especially Jordan. This viewpoint led directly to the closure of the daily. On July 28, 1994, the management of *Al-Nahar* was informed that the paper could no longer be distributed in the areas controlled by the PA. Although the newly-established Palestinian Ministry of Information provided technical reasons for the closure, claiming that the paper did not apply for a permit to distribute in the autonomous areas, the real reason was the paper's political line.[11] In contrast, *Al-Quds* adopted a more cautious approach. While the paper gave the PLO its unconditional support, its pages included the opinions of writers with dissident viewpoints.

Both dailies tried to reflect the public debate regarding the state-building process and the future characteristics of the sovereign Palestinian society.[12] The newspapers' editors strived to adopt a liberal policy of reporting through which they hoped to examine the margins of tolerance of the newly-established Palestinian Authority as well as to reflect their hopes that the end of occupation would also mark the end of censorship and the authorities' intervention in freedom of the press issues. However, this dual position did not last long. After the closure of *Al-Nahar*, the editors of *Al-Quds* avoided printing any content that could be interpreted as direct criticism of the PA. Their caution went so far that they did not even report the closure of *Al-Nahar*. A deviation from this policy by one of the paper's prominent journalists, Daoud Kuttab, led to his release from the daily's editorial board. The owners of *Al-Quds* therefore sought an accommodative editorial line that would not harm their economic interests and hence refocused the paper's attention on the public mood regarding occupation.

The establishment of the PA created a new socio-political reality in the West Bank and Gaza Strip. In response, the new political structure mobilized different social forces that sought to influence the shaping of this new reality. The political discussions between Oslo supporters and rejectionists conditioned the mode of action of the different political forces, with each party seeking different means to win public support and mobilize the population for its specific goals. Civil organizations exploited the fluidity of the new political reality to consolidate their influence in Palestinian society. A widespread expectation among civil activists in the West Bank and the Gaza Strip was that their institutions would form the basis of the emerging Palestinian state. Consequently, many of the existing civil organizations cooperated with the corresponding PA ministries, as they expected, ultimately, to become part of the latter. Other civil organizations sought to protect their autonomy and secure their independence, prominent among them human rights, legal, and media organizations, which attempted to guarantee their status in a legitimate civil society. On the other hand, the PA sought to expand its authority and influence in all aspects of social life – even in areas beyond its control. The Palestinian elite that returned from exile to assume the leadership positions in the PA was well aware of the complex socio-political reality on the ground, and aware of the impact of communication technologies on shaping public opinion and mobilizing the public for political purposes. The centrality of the media's role was related to the fact that Oslo did not mark the end of the national struggle for independence; the PA leadership soon realized that the media could play an active role as a mobilizing agent in the fight for a Palestinian state. Two PA officials – Nabil Amro, a former PLO ambassador to Moscow, and Akram Haniya, a close consultant to Arafat – introduced two different newspapers into the Palestinian market. The first appeared in November 1994 in Gaza under the name *Al-Hayat Al-Jadida* ("The New Life"). This newspaper, which soon became the mouthpiece of the PA and was distributed for free to government offices, "replaced" the official PLO weekly *Filastin Al-Thawra* and set about creating new expectations among the Palestinian public about what the future held. *Al-Hayat Al-Jadida* reflected the position of the PA in all aspects; patronized by the PA, it became highly politicized. The second new daily began appearing in December 1995 and introduced new printing and layout technology. *Al-Ayyam* sought to become the central newspaper in the PA-controlled areas. It employed a collection of professional journalists who successfully turned the daily into a model for Palestinian journalism. The newspaper included a large amount of space for editorials and commentary, which consequently turned it into a very political daily. Its nationalist editorial line has transformed *Al-Ayyam* into a mouthpiece of official Palestinian nationalism, despite occasional criticism (an issue to be addressed below). Akram Haniya, the editor of *Al-Ayyam*, formerly served as the editor of *Al-Sha'b* until the mid-1980s when he was deported to Tunis by Israel, and this legacy has played a role in shaping the worldview constructed by the newspaper.

The new dailies all reflected the official position on the emerging political reality in the Middle East. Since names and icons have always played a major role in Palestinian national politics, the shift in the newspapers' names from *Filistin Al-Thawra* ("Palestine the Revolution") and *Al-Fajr* ("The Dawn") to *Al-Hayat Al-Jadida* ("The New Life") and *Al-Ayyam* ("The Days") reflects a journalistic passage, from the stage of revolution and mobilization toward the stage of administrative centralization, internal pacification, and state-building. However, although the new dailies heralded a shift in the political history of the Palestinian people, they did not reflect a fundamental change in the media's role in public life. PA leaders manipulated the press into a new role that ties it better to the national project. The newly-established newspapers formed a challenge to the already existing *Al-Quds*. Each daily, in its own way, has adopted a kind of mediator's role in which it attempts to explain PA policies to the public and at the same time express the public's demands to the PA. This role is reflected by the fact that both newspapers have emphasized a national responsibility approach to the role of the press, rather than freedom of the press driven by the economic forces of the market. The press-as-mediator concept was evident in the newspapers' nationalist discourse and their clear adherence to the official political line of the PA. A brief review of their editorials over the last several years clearly demonstrates patterns of framing news items, and reveals a hidden agenda close to the PA's official line. The dailies' selection of subjects worthy of coverage and their methods of priming help to promote the PA's national agenda and frame public attitudes in favor of official policy making. This does not necessarily mean that these newspapers do not criticize or question policies adopted by PA ministries and officials, but one needs to differentiate between the newspapers' conservative-national editorial line and the more critical approach when it comes to (un)covering questionable behavior of officials, inefficient policies, or other acts of misconduct by PA institutions. A distinction should also be made between *Al-Ayyam* and *Al-Hayat Al-Jadida* in regard to the degree of readiness to address issues in a more in-depth manner and from a critical point of view, with *Al-Ayyam* demonstrating greater courage in presenting a more comprehensive and profound brand of journalism. But a comparison of the respective editorial lines of the nationalist newspapers with that of the Islamic newspapers (addressed below) shows a shared high degree of conservatism in regard to the socio-political reality in the PA.

It is therefore appropriate to say that the major Palestinian daily newspapers under the Palestinian Authority adopted the PA's political line and defended the strategy of peace propagated by its elite. In this regard the three dailies made a clear effort to emphasize and justify the peace strategy of the PA. One Palestinian journalist managed to capture the new political line of the press when he wrote:

> The language and the subject have to adapt themselves to their location and timing, which are loaded with politics. The strange circumstances that led the "terrorists" to return to their homeland and enter into a dialogue with the "Zionist enemy" imposed a parallel transformation in the concepts and values, far from direct mobilization and competition. The language and the subjects had to adapt to the new reality. This has led to a new form of journalism where the echo of fired bullets is not heard and where the conflict is replaced by peace and the enemy becomes a partner.[13]

In addition to the new dailies, Yasser Arafat established the

Palestinian Broadcasting Corporation (PBC) in order to manage the official broadcasting of radio and television. The importance the Palestinian leadership attributed to these media is expressed by the fact that Arafat created the PBC even before his arrival from exile to Gaza in July 1994. It is also important to note that Arafat appointed Radwan Abu Ayyash, a former head of the Arab Journalists' Association, as head of the PBC. Abu Ayyash was, and continues to be, a Fatah activist and is deeply loyal to Arafat. By appointing a *bona fida* professional to this post, who at the same time was loyal to Arafat, the Palestinian leader showed political sophistication.

Official Palestinian radio broadcasts (Voice of Palestine) began from Jericho on July 1, 1994. By January 1996, 38 percent of Palestinians listened to the station.[14] Only one year later public opinion polls showed that 44.5 percent of Palestinians said they trusted the Voice of Palestine most as compared to Jordanian radio and Israel's Arabic-language broadcasts. Opinion polls conducted in August 1998 and October 1999 further showed that Palestinians had come to view the Voice of Palestine as their most reliable source of radio news, although only slightly fewer people trust Israel Radio's Arabic-language service and Jordanian radio.[15]

The official Palestinian television station began broadcasting from Gaza on November 15, 1994 under the leadership of Hisham Mickey, a close aid to Arafat.[16] Broadcasting lasted three to four hours a day and mainly comprised Palestinian-produced news as well as entertainment programs provided by other Arab stations, primarily in Egypt. Over time this changed and the station began to develop and produce its own programs.

Despite the fact that there are separate Palestinian television stations broadcasting in the West Bank and Gaza, the main decisions concerning news events and how they are to be interpreted by Palestinian television are made in the basement of Arafat's headquarters in Gaza, where the television station's offices are located. The national struggle against Israel is one of the major themes broadcast and the national discourse of the PA is reflected in most news programs. But, according to Farid Abu Dhair from Al-Najah University, "Palestinian Television does not mirror Palestinian reality, despite the fact that it seeks to achieve this goal. It reflects more the worldview of the upper classes . . . This does not mean that these classes necessarily watch the broadcasted programs. They rather think that these programs are what the audience should see. Thereby they reflect their paternalistic views on the public."[17] The entertainment programs and films broadcast are still very often imported from neighboring Arab countries.

In addition to the newspapers and the PBC there is a long list of Palestinian weeklies and other periodicals that are published in the PA areas. The foremost group of publications in this context is that of the opposition parties, Hamas and Islamic Jihad. Hamas's weekly, *Al-Watan* ("The Homeland"), which was edited by Sayed Abu Musameh, was closed after a series of suicide bomb attacks carried out by Hamas activists at the beginning of 1996 in Israel. The Hamas-affiliated Islamic Salvation Party (Khalas) was established in 1995 and received a license to publish the weekly *Al-Risalah* ("The Message") in Gaza, which began to appear on February 13, 1996 and is edited by Dr Ghazi Hamad. Salah Bardawil is the chief editor. *Al-Risalah* reflects the position of the party and criticizes the PA for its policies of peace and accommodation *vis-à-vis* Israel. Islamic Jihad also publishes a critical weekly, called *Al-Esteqlal* ("Independence"), which combines the party's ideas with heavy criticism of the peace process and the related policies of the PA. It is edited by Ibrahim Nagar whom the PA arrested on several occasions as part of its sanctions against Islamic Jihad. Its chief editor is Ala'a Saftawi.

Media Consumption and the Centrality of Media Frames

The existing data regarding media consumption in Palestinian society is very limited. Our knowledge of media consumption patterns prevents us from drawing conclusions about the influence of the media on the public agenda. Nevertheless, some groundwork has been done that potentially reveals some interesting pointers about Palestinian media consumption. The Palestinian Central Bureau of Statistics published a media survey conducted in June–July 2000 which included 8,276 households in the West bank and Gaza Strip. The survey indicated that 89.7 percent of Palestinian households own a TV, and 45.4 percent percent own a satellite dish, enabling them to receive TV broadcasts from neighboring countries. The findings of the survey indicated that the Palestine TV channel is the most viewed terrestrial channel (36.7%), and found that 29.8 percent of Palestinian households view Palestine TV on daily basis, although this is true for fewer in the West Bank (16.2%) than for those living in Gaza (56.2%). The main explanation for this gap is that Palestine TV has a poor transmitting reception in the West Bank areas. Al-Jazeera is the most popular satellite channel (35.1%) among those households that have satellite a dish. Sixteen percent of those interviewed listen to the Voice of Palestine on a regular basis and 46.9 percent listen occasionally. When it comes to the printed press, only 10.9 percent of households receive daily newspapers each day.[18] The percentage of households enjoying access to weekly and monthly newspapers amounted to 8.3 and 0.6 percent, respectively. These numbers could be misleading if we consider the fact that most people do not subscribe, but rather purchase the newspaper on daily or weekly basis. When the number of households was calculated based on method of receiving the daily newspaper, weekly newspaper, or magazine, the survey revealed that 4.2% subscribe, 74.2% purchase, 15.6% borrow, and 6% get them free. The same survey demonstrates that, whereas 3.8% of those who read newspapers receive them based on subscription, 78.6% of newspaper readers purchase them, and 12.9% borrow them. The survey also revealed that 16.7% of males and 6.3% of females read daily newspapers on daily basis, while 37.5% of men and 31.8% of women read the daily newspapers only sometimes. When those who read the newspaper were divided based on section of newspaper they read and on gender, the survey found that the most read section is the local section (males 91.4% and females 86.6%). The second most read section among males (87.5%) is the political section, followed by the religious pages (73.9%). Among females the second most read section of newspapers is the religious (82.2%), followed by the social (81.9%). These details show the centrality of the religious sections among newspaper readers. The economic section, for instance, comes in tenth place for both men (49.1%) and women (29.8%).

When it comes to the weeklies, only 5.3% of males and 2.1% of females read weekly newspapers on a regular basis; 12.1% of males and 8.7% of females read weeklies sometimes; 82.7% of males and 89.1% of females do not read weekly newspapers at all. This data illustrates the gap between readers of daily newspapers and readers of weeklies, although it confirms the notion that there is a weekly newspaper readership. Most of the readers of weeklies probably belong to social groups that are targeted directly by these newspapers (feminist or Islamist audience).

Only 5.4 percent of persons age 18 years and over have access to the internet.[19] This percentage varies between males and females – 7.9% and 2.8%, respectively. The findings of the survey indicated that the place of work or study constitutes the most common setting for internet utilization among persons aged 18 years and above (37.7%). In this age group, 56.1% of the individuals normally use the internet for work, research, and knowledge purposes.

Furthermore, a survey conducted by the Jerusalem Media and Communication Center (JMCC) in August 1998, questioning 1,192 people, found that only 21.7% buy a newspaper on daily basis, while 25.9% buy a newspaper at least once a week.[20] In another survey conducted a year later in October 1999, 27.8% of 1,200 people sampled said that they buy the newspaper daily.[21] Another 22.2% answered that they buy the newspaper at least once a week. These surveys correspond with the data revealed by PCBS, showing that, although the number of newspaper readers is not very high, it is still higher than one may think, since many of the readers are not subscribers and some of them borrow the newspaper from others. The survey conducted by the Palestinian Center for Public Survey and Research (PCPSR) in July 2001 also contributes to this argument.[22] The survey found that 21% of the respondents read one of the three daily newspapers everyday; 55.4% answered that they read one of the papers between 1–4 times a weeks.

Although these numbers do not provide an accurate picture regarding newspaper consumption in Palestinian society, they give an estimate of newspaper reading patterns. When it comes to reading weeklies, and especially Islamist weeklies such as *Al-Risalah* and *Al-Esteqlal*, the picture becomes less clear. One public opinion survey conducted in August 1998 by JMCC related to the newspapers of the opposition; it asked the sample group if they knew of any newspaper related to the opposition. Whereas 25.2% of the respondents said that they did know, 58.6% gave a negative response. Among those who know about the newspapers of the opposition 37.7% named *Al-Risalah* as the newspaper they were familiar with, and 14.3% named *Al-Esteqlal*. More people knew about these newspapers in Gaza than in the West Bank: 55.8% from Gaza versus 15.6% in the West Bank for *Al-Risalah*, 18.2% from Gaza versus only 9.6% in the West Bank for *Al-Esteqlal*. These numbers clearly indicate that the circulation of the Islamist newspapers, while not very high, is still prolific in the Palestinian society and that they are recognized as having different opinions than those expressed in the daily newspapers. Furthermore, in a society where cash is very scarce and 15.5 percent of the people confess that they read a paper that others have bought, the number of people exposed to news-paper influence might conceivably be higher than the above numbers indicate.

The Search for Homogenization: Between Consent and Coercion

Faced with the double problem of having to act under the watchful eyes of the Israeli authorities while also facing the Islamic opposi-tions' growing power in its territories, the PA leadership sought to build a strong centralized authority. This policy was underwritten by the foreign donor states that preferred to strengthen the PA rather than back the civil organizations, based on the belief that this approach would best serve the peace process.[23] The PA's efforts to create a centralized source of power were evident in the structure created in the security services. Within a relatively short period of time, Arafat managed to build no less than nine different security services to control Palestinian society and satisfy Israeli security demands.[24] The security forces subsequently exploited the vacuum of political authority that resulted from the time gap between the withdrawal of Israeli forces in May 1994 and the establishment of the PA two months later. During this period Yasser Arafat's secu-rity forces asserted their control over the already existing power structures – political parties, civil administrations, jails, police stations, etc.[25] Although their role was reduced to implementing the PA's decisions subsequent to Arafat's arrival in Gaza in July 1994, their fierce presence is still strongly felt. This process of power centralization was expanded to the realms of freedom of speech and publication, with the PA seeking a policy of patronization, politi-cization, and national reinforcement *vis-à-vis* the media.

The first sign of this policy was articulated by the formation of a Ministry of Information to coordinate all matters of information, media and press in PA areas. The Ministry "was formally estab-lished by virtue of a presidential decree . . . on June 25, 1994"[26] and was assigned the task "of drafting media policy for the newly-born Palestinian state to cope with the transitional period of the peace process". It became "primarily preoccupied with initiating the broad foundations for the rights of free press and expression to prevail".[27] In response to a question about the role of the Palestinian media, Minister of Information Yasser Abed Rabbo said:

> We do not deny that there is a common cause among all the sectors of Palestinian society and all the institutions in Palestinian society – including media institutions – with the Palestinian National Authority. We have the same cause: attaining our own independence, our self-determination, and building a state. But if you are referring to interference of the state in directing the media or telling them what they should and should not do, I think there is a lot of exaggeration there. Even on our TV and our broadcasting stations, which are controlled by the state, the TV takes a position of criticizing different aspects of our life. And there is no censorship on the TV at all, by the way. On TV you can express yourself on political, economic, social matters, about any issue you would like.[28]

The minister's comments establish the limitations imposed by the Palestinian media regime. Although there is no formal censorship in the PA, there is a common national cause universal to all Palestinians, and it is the PA that defines it. The cause of independence is by far the first priority, and makes all other disputed issues, including the character of the emerging regime, secondary. As a result, the media is expected to take part in the national efforts to attain independence. Internal Palestinian policies in such areas as health, education, planning, and others, are ignored; achieving independence is paramount. According to Abed Rabbo, these issues have to wait. The minister's argument that television is uncensored is irrelevant since access to Palestinian television and radio is limited and subject to a stringent system of control, led until recently by Arafat's assistant, the late Hisham Mickey. Mickey was the most powerful figure in Palestinian television and his influence on the content and programming far exceeded that of the PBC president, Radwan Abu Ayyash, who presides from Ramallah.

The Ministry of Information has dealt with many difficulties faced by Palestinian journalists. This ministry, however, is not only an active player, determining the centralized media regime in Palestinian society; it is also subject to the regime, as set by President Yasser Arafat, who is directly involved in most decisions made by the PBC. As a result, the "official" rules of the game in the field of broadcasting and publication are subject to informal rules based on the system of patronage established over the last several years.

In June 1995 the Palestinian Press Law was issued in order to replace the Israeli military regulations in the occupied territories and define the relationship between the newly-established Palestinian Authority and society as a whole. The fact that the Press Law was among the first laws issued by the PA reflects the sensitivity and importance Palestinian officials attributed to the freedom of expression. The law is liberal and democratic in its general spirit and characterizes the transitional phase of the PA, which lacks sovereignty and is still subject to negotiations with the occupying power. In comparison with similar situations in which a state is in the process of creating institutions and laws, the Press Law does create some open space for freedom of expression.[29] It also laid the groundwork for legalizing a pluralistic media system that includes privately as well as publicly operated media. For example, according to Clause 2 of this law:

> Press and printing are free. Furthermore, every Palestinian individual is entitled to freedom of opinion. Every individual attains the absolute right to express his opinion in a free manner either verbally, in writing, photography, or drawing, as a different means of expression and information.

The reality is much more complex than this seemingly positive and sound statement about freedom of the press. Clear structural pluralism exists, which is expressed in the number and variety of Palestinian newspapers, weeklies, and other print media. In addition, besides the official PBC, there are more than twenty different local privately owned cable television stations in the Palestinian cities under PA jurisprudence. This plurality reflects a certain extent of tolerance *vis-à-vis* the Palestinian population's aspirations and needs to express itself in a variety of manners and means. The PA's *expressed* policy is that freedom of the press is a central issue that the Palestinians will not surrender. In most interviews about the Palestinian regime, President Arafat has always made it clear that the Palestinians have a free press that can criticize him and his government, that a free press is a part of the Palestinian experience, and will continue to be so, because he believes it is a crucial part of his power and part of democracy. This policy was also made clear by a top Ministry of Information official with respect to the local cable stations, who said:

> We support the idea of private civil stations in Palestine that form plurality of stages allowing people to express themselves in matters concerning their daily life. The Authority should not monopolize information about cultural, intellectual and political activities. This deepens democracy and public freedom and creates a large space for argumentation between different ideas. There should be private stations beside the official broadcasting agencies in order to create positive competition and constructive dialogue. However, these stations must be professionally competent and well equipped in order to attract interest as sources of culture and art.[30]

Despite the spirit of the Press Law and the decisive language from Arafat and his officials, a large gap exists between these declarations and the reality on the ground, which proves to be far more complex than the law's theoretical intentions. Foreign observers and Palestinian watchdog groups have commented that the new Palestinian Press Law "prohibits publication of everything from security secrets to immoral or blasphemous material".[31] Many clauses in the law are formulated in a vague language that could be subject to virtually any interpretation. A good example in this regard is Clause 8 of the law:

> The pressman and all persons dealing with this profession, should fully respect the rules and morals of this career which includes abiding to the following obligations:
>
> A— Respecting the individuals' rights and their constitutional freedom, and non-interference in their private lives.
> B— Presenting press material in an objective, integrated, and balanced form.
> C— Striving for accuracy, integrity, and objectivity in commenting on news and main events.
> D— To refrain from publishing that which may ignite violence, fanaticism and hatred or invite racism and sectarianism.
> E— Non-exploitation of the press material in commercial advertisements with the aim of increasing or decreasing the value of certain product.[32]

The obligations of this clause are open to a wide range of interpretations by officials, who could use them in an opposite and limiting way. Standards of objectivity are difficult to meet, especially when the subject matter is news. What is classified as "accuracy, integrity, and objectivity" when commenting on the news, and who decides when reporting encourages violence and hatred? These questions illustrate the problems stemming from the Press Law's general language and the overwhelming power given to authorities to enforce it.

Therefore, a number of administrative, economic, regulatory, and other forms and measures constitute the Palestinian media regime. These mechanisms transform the relationship between the emerging state and the existing media into an antagonistic one: they turn the spirit of the law and the liberal declarations made by PA officials into mere lip service when it comes to the reality on the ground. To illustrate this tension between the media and the state, the different mechanisms that ultimately result in some kind of censorship of the Palestinian media are explicated below.

Administrative Mechanisms of Consent

Any person interested in opening any institute related to information dissemination – be it newspaper or radio, television station, or bookstore – must obtain permission from the Ministry of Information and from the Ministry of Interior. From the onset, this requirement deters some people from entering the field of information in any capacity. The Ministry of Information has designated a special department "responsible for providing licenses for newspapers, magazines and private broadcasting and TV stations" (PA website – www.pna.net). This department enables the PA to control all news agencies and to set limits on their work. Examples of such limitations are evident in the revocation of licenses issued to newspapers and television stations. On several occasions the ministry has revoked the licenses issued to the weeklies of Hamas and Islamic Jihad. The Hamas-affiliated weekly *Al-Watan* lost the ministry's approval in 1996 when it embarrassed the PA after several suicide bomb attacks in Israel carried out by Hamas members.

The same policy was enforced when the Ministry of Information, on February 16, 1998, ordered eight owners of cable television stations in the West Bank to close their offices and stop broadcasting. The order came as a surprise because, until then, more than twenty television stations had been operating in the West Bank.

These local cable stations are usually private enterprises that lack basic equipment and professional qualifications; the main aim is simply to earn money by entertaining their audiences. However, the wide variety of stations, both in terms of their character and content, has provided an effective forum for discussion and debate of Palestinian issues. This plurality of stations has enabled different political, cultural, and social groups to express themselves and hence influence the public space.

The private cable TV stations are an important phenomenon in the Palestinian media regime. Despite their low-budget, low-tech nature, some of them are viewed by large numbers of people.[33] For instance, Assalam TV is viewed by 55–69 percent of TV-owning households. Amwaj TV station is viewed by 40–54 percent in Nablus, Ramallah, Al-Bireh, Jerusalem, Salfit, and in North Gaza. Al-Majd TV is viewed by 70 percent of the households in the Gaza Strip.

Although the status of these stations was never formally legalized, the Ministry of Information has permitted them to exist. There are more than 30 local cable TV stations in the PA areas. A document sent by the Palestinian police chief to the northern district chiefs of police stated that: "all stations must sign a written agreement not to broadcast any news dealing with illegal marches and demonstrations, and to stay away from news that lead to excitement."[34] This order, direct from the Ministry of Information, was related to broadcasting coverage of Palestinian marches and demonstrations against American policy toward Iraq in February 1998, at a time when the crisis between UN weapons inspectors and the Iraqi government had led to a critical situation in the Gulf area, with the US, supported by Britain, threatening to use force if Iraq did not open presidential sites for inspection. The intensification of the situation led many Palestinians to protest against what they viewed as a hypocritical American position, in which the US insisted on applying all UN resolutions on the (Arab) state of Iraq, while closing its eyes to Israeli violations of human and national rights of the Palestinians in the West Bank and Gaza Strip. Many Palestinians participated in marches, demonstrations, and rallies during which American and Israeli flags were routinely burned. This display by the Palestinian population embarrassed the PA leadership and put it in a delicate position. Not wanting to repeat the mistake of 1991, when the PLO expressed its support for Iraq during the Gulf War, the PA chose to preempt the problem altogether by issuing the order to close those cable stations covering the events in Palestinian cities. To justify the order, the PA accused these stations of committing incitement that placed a burden on "central Palestinian interests".

One of the stations shut down – Open Wave – had managed to reach a broad circle of listeners in the greater Bethlehem area. The station broadcast a series of interviews with Palestinians who had demonstrated against "American provocations" in Iraq and expressed sympathy with the Iraqi people. (These demonstrations came before the closure order.) This incident prompted the Palestinian police to close the station, occupy its offices, and arrest two of its employees on charges of inciting the public and organizing demonstrations.[35] The police issued an order on February 9, 1998, forbidding demonstrations and protests in connection to the crisis in the Gulf or the public expression of support for the Iraqi people.[36] Whereas supporters of Fatah, the main party within the PA, were allowed to demonstrate against US action in Iraq, the PA withheld permission for opposition groups to organize public demonstrations against US foreign policy.[37]

A technical detail sheds further light on the centrality of local cable television stations for many Palestinians, especially in the northern areas of the West Bank: the public transmission of official PA stations does not reach all Palestinian areas. Therefore, cable television stations provide the public with services that enable people lacking private dishes to receive the transmissions of different Arab stations, including those included in satellite broadcasts. Consequently, closing local cable televisions results in completely cutting many Palestinians off from any television service whatsoever. Therefore, the PA's silencing of the private cable stations was not only a violation of the owners' freedom of expression, but also had negative repercussions on a significant portion of the Palestinian public.

Restricting distribution and blocking access to governmental data are other means by which the PA exerts administrative control over the media. Such measures were applied against the newspapers *Al-Nahar*, *Al-Quds*, and *Al-Risala*. *Al-Nahar* was the first to be subject to administrative measures restricting its distribution in the PA-controlled areas.[38] Despite the fact that in July 1994 the PA formally controlled only the Gaza Strip and Jericho, the paper was forbidden to be distributed in *all* Palestinian cities. The PA's official position was that the paper had not applied for a permit from the Ministry of Information. Its pro-Jordanian editorial line, however, was the PA's real reason for clamping down on it.[39] Despite the fact that *Al-Nahar*'s editor, Othman Hallaq, met with Yasser Arafat 36 days later and got permission to publish, the paper failed to regain the circulation it had lost in the interim and was forced to close. The harsh example made of *Al-Nahar* did not go unnoticed by other Palestinian newspapers, which avoided any mention of the incident in their pages.

Al-Quds was faced with a similar reaction by the PA after the newspaper's editor, Maher Al-Alami, failed to comply with requests by the Preventive Security Forces to publish a flattering story and photograph on a meeting between Yasser Arafat and the Christian Orthodox Patriarch. Al-Alami was summoned to the offices of the Preventive Security Forces in Jericho where he was detained for five days. One month later, on August 19, 1995, the PA revoked *Al-Quds'* license to be distributed in the autonomous areas in the West Bank and Gaza Strip. The PA's withdrawal of the paper's license was enough to prompt the owners to dash to Gaza in order to meet with Arafat. After the meeting, the paper changed its editorial policy and began to cover the President's travels around the world, prominently displayed on the front page, and reported solely on the positive dimensions of PA policies. While the paper does still publish (indirect) criticism of PA agencies, this is usually done in a modest fashion with only a brief mention on *Al-Quds'* inner pages.

The Hamas-affiliated Islamic daily *Al-Risalah* also claimed in the early stages after the paper's founding that it was subject to a boycott by PA officials and that it was not granted access to government data. An examination of *Al-Risalah*'s contents today reveals that this boycott does not exist anymore, if it ever existed at all. Administrative policies are increasingly used to restrain the maneuvering space of the newspaper, as will be demonstrated in Chapter 6.

The effects of these formal regulations on the Palestinian public are reflected in various opinion polls. In a December 1996 poll by the Palestine Research and Studies Center (CPRS) in Nablus, 52 percent of the Palestinian population admitted that they could not criticize the PA without fearing its reaction. This data was almost identical to the results of a previous poll in June, in which 49 percent expressed their opinion that people fear the PA. This fear is rooted in the PA's reaction to those who criticize its policies or personnel. The results of opinion polls conducted by the Jerusalem Media and Communications Center (JMCC) in August 1998 and October 1999 support the view that most Palestinians think that the Palestinian media is not independent. Nevertheless, 73 percent of Palestinians believe that having an independent press is a vital factor in promoting democracy while 81 percent think that the press should have an impact on government.[40]

In summary, despite the Palestinian Press Law, PA administrative policies have seriously restricted freedom of expression and have reduced the maneuvering space of journalists and editors. A study of the daily *Al-Quds* has found that, since the establishment of the PA, there has been a significant decrease in the number of reports dealing with such public issues as politics, social policy, NGOs, and social problems.[41] In addition, the detention of journalists and the violation of the freedom of expression by administrative means limited the media's role and led to the practice of self-censorship, a subject that will be addressed later.

The Power of Economic Procedures

Economic dependency is a central condition affecting the mass media in the Arab world; the brief Palestinian experience does not deviate from this state of affairs.[42] The low national and private incomes, as well as the population's low literacy rate, play a major role affecting the economic independence of the mass media. Harsh economic conditions for most Palestinians, and especially the high rate of unemployment, make newspapers and magazines a luxury. According to Hanna Siniora, publisher of the English-language newspaper *The Jerusalem Times* and the monthly *Palestine Business Report*, every newspaper purchased is read, on average, by eight different people.[43] Consequently newspaper publishing in the West Bank and Gaza Strip is not a particularly profitable business venture. Newspapers report heavy losses each month, a situation that makes publishers and editors vulnerable to political manipulation. In several cases the PA has subsidized newspapers that, as a result, became easy targets for manipulation.[44] A well-known method of subsidization is the bulk purchase of subscriptions. *Al-Hayat Al-Jadida*, for instance, is delivered "free of charge" to governmental offices. Although the paper suffers tremendous financial losses every month, they are more than offset by the financial support provided directly by Arafat's office.[45] According to an internal report of the Palestinian Legislative Council's budgetary committee, 68 of the daily's employees receive their salaries directly from the PA.[46] *Al-Ayyam* also benefits from the supportive policies of the PA.[47] For example, all PA school textbooks are printed by *Al-Ayyam*.

Palestinian journalists themselves are also subject to a variety of means of economic manipulation. According to Said Ghazali, "most of them live below the poverty line".[48] Being "powerless and without respect by their editors", journalists "are not allowed to write critical stories". As a result they are easy targets for accepting gifts offered by high-ranking officials. Daoud Kuttab was fired from his position at the *Al-Quds* newspaper after signing a petition protesting the arrest of *Al-Quds* editor Maher Al-Alami. The newspaper's owners felt they could not tolerate Kuttab's behavior, which could endanger the future of their paper, and therefore they got rid of him. The head of the newspaper claimed that the paper should function like any other economic enterprise, and that any obstacle to the financial interests of the paper should be removed.[49] The poor economic conditions in which journalists live, as well as the lack of support they are given by their editors, create fertile ground for a culture of patronization. Bribery is a well-known method for discouraging Palestinian journalists from reporting news deemed by official figures to be less than positive. Journalists sometimes withhold critical news pieces about PA policies from being published until the misdoings are corrected, and even then they are reported in such a manner as to praise the commendable actions of the authorities in dealing with the issue.

Legal Regulatory Frameworks

Central obstacles to the freedom of the press are the formal and informal regulations regarding content. A prominent expert on censorship, Scammell argues that regimes make use of limitations on the freedom of expression "as an instrument to assist in the attainment, preservation or continuance of [their] power".[50] Regimes thus extend their physical power "into the realm of the mind and the spirit". Any examination of censorship must go beyond technical obstacles placed before the media, and explore cultural and moral surveillance and control. Censorship in this context is not a collection of separate incidents but a behavioral pattern.[51]

Despite the liberal connotations of the Palestinian Press Law, the law itself enables the PA to limit freedom of expression and publication based on a variety of informal measures. Clause 37 of the Palestinian Press Law demarcates boundaries of what is allowed and what is forbidden to be published, thereby defining the frames of reference and perimeters of freedom of expression:

A–   It is strictly prohibited for any print media to publish the following:

1. Any secret information about police and security forces, its armament, locations, movements or military drills.
2. Articles and materials harmful to the religion and doctrines guaranteed by law.
3. Articles that may cause harm to national unity or incite acts of crime or plant seeds of hatred, dissension, and disunion, or stir up trouble and sectarianism among the members of society.
4. The minutes of the secret sessions of the Palestinian National Council and the Council of Ministers of the Palestinian National Authority (PNA).
5. Articles and news aimed at undermining confidence in the national currency.
6. Articles and news which are apt to infringe upon an individual's dignity, personal convictions and liberties or cause harm to their personal reputation.
7. News, reports, letters, editorial, and pictures that do not fit accepted morals.
8. Drugs, medical products, cigarette advertisement and similar items unless the advertisement has been approved in advance by the Ministry of Health.

B–   It is strictly forbidden to import any publications from abroad if it contains materials prohibited for publication by virtue of this law.[52]

Such vague, obtuse standards leave the door open far too wide to questions of interpretation, thus enabling the authorities to easily accuse journalists of "violating" the law. These standards can be easily interpreted and manipulated in order to allow for means of administrative surveillance and control. In this situation, PA officials have a broad maneuvering space *vis-à-vis* the media. The demands set by Clause 8, combined with these standards, mean that virtually any piece of information can be deemed to be illegal.

Using respect for religion, morals, and national unity as a standard for freedom of publication raises many questions for any journalist who must consider the punishment he or she could receive for violating the law. What is the definition of national unity, and whose morals are being used to set the standards? These questions are left for officials to answer. In a situation where the judicial system is unable to withstand challenges to the rule of law, these standards come to constitute a plain infringement upon basic rights and freedoms, which results in censorship of whatever material governmental officials do not like. With arguably hyperactive security forces charged with the task of enforcing the rule of law, journalism becomes a hazardous job under the Palestinian Authority. Several clauses of the law were formulated in order to engineer mechanisms to encourage the rise of a loyal media that would rely upon official versions of the truth. Besides major incidents in which newspapers were closed or subject to sanctions, many journalists have been arrested, detained, and even tortured for "violating" the spirit of the law.

Even in modern Western democracies, military censorship has been used in various ways in different periods of time.[53] But in most cases, censorship in Western liberal democracies was enacted for a limited period of time, especially in times of war or other exceptional situations that have been perceived as a state of emergency. Past or present censorship is not perceived as a means for exerting constant administrative control over freedom of the press in a liberal democratic state. In contrast, the formulation of the Palestinian Press Law is universally applicable, with no limits set on its time or scope. Therefore, the law is a control mechanism that enables the authorities to consistently censor the media.

Despite the fact that the PA is still in the midst of a battle for national independence, the cases in which the spirit of the law was imposed demonstrate the authoritarian mode in which the law was interpreted. The detention of Iyad Sarraj, the commissioner-general of the Palestinian Independent Commission for Citizens' Rights, is a good example of this. Sarraj was detained on December 5, 1995 for "criticizing the PA", and detained again on May 16, 1996 for nine days for a quote attributed to him published in the *New York Times* in which he confesses that he was freer to write his opinion during

Israeli occupation than he is under the PA. Sarraj was released as a result of pressure from foreign diplomats and was subsequently accused of having "dubious connections" to the West and was depicted as a traitor.

Using national unity as a criterion for freedom of expression also raises questions about the true intentions of those who formulated the law. It is well known that several regimes in the Third World have utilized a narrow and strict interpretation of the concept as a means for silencing the voices of the opposition.[54] The spirit of the law reflects the regime's lack of faith in the public's ability to denounce extreme ideas that endanger national unity. It does not leave the public space for self-reflection and imposes an overly strict conception of the role of the press.

In a similar fashion, PA officials use the ambiguity of the Palestinian Press Law to silence the opposition, as witnessed in closure by the PA police of the weekly *Al-Risalah*, affiliated with the Islamic Salvation Party, an offspring of the Hamas movement, the main political opposition group and the greatest political threat to the PA. *Al-Risalah* is a popular socialization mechanism for Hamas, which has criticized the PA and sought to compete with it for the loyalty of the Palestinian population in the West Bank and Gaza Strip. To this end, the weekly emphasizes two central themes that constitute the pillars of Hamas's ideology. The first is related to their objection to the peace process and the negotiations with Israel, while the second has to do with Hamas's criticism of the PA's secular political, social, and moral policies. Despite the fact that the weekly does not emphasize its affiliation to the organization, it nevertheless expresses the Hamas world-view. Therefore, the closure of *Al-Risalah* was an attempt to sever the connection between Hamas and the Palestinian public, and to limit the movement's ability to communicate its oppositionary positions. In addition, the timing of the publication's closure clearly illustrates the PA's vulnerability to external pressure. *Al-Risalah* was closed on several occasions that were dictated by the international relations of the PA, especially Israeli and American pressure in connection to the desire to make progress in the peace negotiations.[55]

PA officials also utilized the nationalist discourse as a tool against the Islamic opposition as a means to accuse it of betraying the interests of the Palestinian people. Hamas's critical position and rejection of any reconciliation with Israel have put the PA in a difficult situation, for, while allowing Hamas to continue its critique of the peace process was viewed negatively by Israel and the US, closing *Al-Risalah* was criticized as undemocratic and a clear violation of the freedom of expression. Furthermore, the PA's attempts to tame Hamas and include it in the Authority via constructive dialogue, turned the publication of Hamas's weekly into a good tool to co-opt the movement. However, the PA's policy *vis-à-vis* Hamas was dependent upon external circumstances, especially in regard to progress of the peace negotiations with Israel. Unable to maneuver effectively between the criticism of human rights agencies and Israeli pressure, the PA tried to delegitimize the two major Islamic movements – Hamas and Islamic Jihad – by accusing them of serving foreign interests and cooperating with the enemies of the Palestinian people. The PA policy in this area has led to severe violations of basic rights of Hamas activists.[56] This particular PA policy is especially problematic if we consider the political and communicative lines that the weeklies of the two Islamic organizations follow with regard to the PA. *Al-Risalah* and *Al-Esteqlal* (the latter is the mouthpiece of the Islamic Jihad), adopted quasi-autonomous editorial lines; both provided some space on their pages for the secular opposition and tried to reflect on those issues of concern to the wider, including secular, Palestinian public. The two newspapers sought to present themselves as an alternative public space and debating forum, disconnected from the PA and critical of its policies. Hence they pose a challenge to the three major secular dailies, which were forced to change their editorial lines to fit in line with the official policies of the PA.

The three national dailies – *Al-Quds*, *Al-Ayyam* and *Al-Hayat Al-Jadida* – differ in their editorial lines from *Al-Risala* and *Al-Esteqlal*. The former are restricted in their editorials, and occupy similar positions, lying between autonomy and subordination.[57] Among the characteristics shared by the national dailies, one could emphasize the following:

1 *The three newspapers share and articulate the national discourse dominant in the PA that promotes the worldview of the national movement in general.* The newspapers focus on national issues such as the struggle for independence and peaceful negotiations with Israel. Most of the front-page headlines, as well as the editorials, address the efforts of the national elite to achieve a suitable solution for the Palestine question. This is translated into lengthy and detailed descriptions of the diplomatic and political efforts being made to achieve a real breakthrough in the peace negotiations. Therefore, the communicative message of the dailies serves to legitimize the PA as well as to serve functions of articulation, mobilization, and conflict management. They determine which political demands in society should be aired and which should be muted. The dailies also define the limits of freedom of expression and set restrictions based on the necessary and permissible regulations established by the political leadership, especially the president. They grant value to specific issues by priming them *vis-à-vis* other issues, thereby serving the hegemonic political, economic, ideological, and moral order.[58]

2   *The PA's political agenda is fully reflected in the discourse adopted by the newspapers.* The framing of Palestinian reality is subjugated to the efforts to achieve independence. The peace strategy is not questioned; instead there is a clear focus on Israeli violations of the agreements reached with the PA. From this vantage point, many editorials address what is perceived to be the true intentions of the various Israeli governments and the biased American position toward the peace efforts made by Israel. In this context, many articles address internal Israeli politics and the dominant Zionist ideology and how both block progress in the peace process. Such an attitude has become extremely apparent following the failure of the Camp David Summit in July 2000 and the outbreak of the second *Intifada*. The editorials of the newspapers, especially in *Al-Ayyam*, demonstrate Zelizer's theory that journalists are an interpretive community.[59] The cumulative effect of this community is evident in media coverage, with a constant focus on the nature of Israeli policies and the militaristic approach Israel has adopted over the last several years in order to promote an enforced solution that meets its interests. This coverage emphasizes the role of the right-wing parties, and especially the settlers in the West Bank and Gaza Strip, in blocking any realistic solution.

3   *The three dailies devote a substantial amount of space to advertisements, which reflects the newspapers' place in the emerging Palestinian capitalist economic system.* Being part of the Palestinian economic reality and seeking to survive in a difficult situation, the dailies have to adhere to the rules of the market. As a result, their interests are deeply tied to the dominant economic elite that has emerged in the PA. Sharing the same socio-economic background

as well as the same political worldview with the dominant economic and political elite leads to similarities in the way political events are interpreted and framed. In this sense the Palestinian dailies do not differ from newspapers in other nation-states. They are patriotic, and vacillate between being a free expression of autonomous positions and conveying loyalty to the hegemonic political order. In this manner, the dailies demonstrate a significant degree of social responsibility and serve a functional role in the central authority's efforts to gain public consent.

4 *The three newspapers pay much less attention to PA policies on internal affairs than one would expect from the national press.* Differences in language and layout notwithstanding, the three dailies systematically deal with social, cultural, and economic conflicts in Palestinian society. Their treatment of these issues occurs from within the dominant national discourse. As a result, their critique serves to expose the deviations from what is thought to be the national interest. *Al-Ayyam* is the most liberal and addresses issues of national importance even if they disclose internal social or political disputes. Nevertheless, the newspaper remains rooted in its national discourse, and in most cases its criticism stems from a patriotic point of view (as expressed by the editorials and the articles written by the senior editors of the newspaper). One example that illustrates this point of view is the report and the editorials written after twenty Palestinian figures signed and published a leaflet on November 27, 1999 criticizing the PA for corruption and "selling out the homeland". The three dailies devoted much attention to this topic. They presented both the critique of the Palestinian Authority and the PA's reaction to the criticism. An examination of the reports published in the days immediately following the leaflet's publication reflects the loyalty of the editorial lines of the newspapers to the official nationalist discourse: while they discussed the critique directed at the PA, they gave priority to promoting the point of view of the PA and its supporters. Examining the space devoted to the opposition, as well as the discourses utilized, demonstrates the national underpinnings of the language used by the newspapers. The editorials of the newspapers, especially in *Al-Ayyam* and *Al-Hayat Al-Jadida*, fully endorse a nationalist point of view.[60] The twenty individuals who published the leaflet were criticized for not having any political or popular credibility, which had the effect of delegitimizing their point of view, without even addressing their claims.

Conversely, the positions of PA officials and Fatah leaders were given priority and their reliability was presented as being beyond doubt. The reaction of the PA, especially the subsequent detention of several authors of the leaflet, was not questioned, even if the detentions themselves were criticized. Those responsible for the leaflet were framed as violators of accepted norms of political maneuvering in Palestinian society; they were accused of exploiting the freedom of expression given them in order to disseminate inaccurate information.

Generally, the three dailies cover, first and foremost, the President of the Palestinian Authority in most of their front-page headlines. Unless there are urgent and crucial developments in the political and diplomatic arena, Arafat is usually the main topic of the news. Moreover, internal affairs are covered from the same national vantage point, with problems and disagreements framed in order to contribute to the national endeavors for statehood. Violations of human rights committed by security forces, corruption of PA officials, and the lack of accountability in the different PA agencies, receive little attention.

According to one Palestinian journalist, coverage of corrupt behavior of PA officials is largely dependent upon the particular official's level of power in the political hierarchy. News items published in this area are either an indication of the lack of an official's power or the manipulation of the media by powerful politicians intended to embarrass a rival or enemy.

There is seldom a critical view presented of the educational, social, economic, and health policies of the PA ministries. In cases where these issues are raised, the coverage tends to be descriptive in nature. The Palestinian newspapers base their reports on the different ministries' policies as presented in briefings given by PA officials. The papers tend not to conduct their own investigations, nor do they provide the public with independent information, despite the occasional appearance of coverage of issues based on investigative journalism.

5 *The three dailies avoid covering human rights violations perpetrated by the security forces of the PA.* Whereas much attention is devoted to allegations of human rights abuse by the Israeli authorities, which is legitimate according to Palestinian norms of journalism, much less attention is paid to infringement of privacy, freedom of assembly, freedom of expression, and political impris-

onment that takes place within the PA. If covered at all, such incidents are modestly reported and are usually hidden deep inside the newspaper.

6 *Little attention is devoted to social movements such as the women's movement, opposition parties (the Islamic parties), and the non-governmental sector. Furthermore, there is little attention given to the activities of the Palestinian Legislative Council and its members.* Coverage of information that reflects the Council's criticism of the activity of the PA executive is usually nominal. Furthermore, the activity of the media is given little space in the general coverage of the newspapers. Another incident involving Daoud Kuttab highlights the restrictions imposed on journalists. Kuttab, a well-known Palestinian journalist and winner of the 1996 International Press Freedom Award, heads the Communications Center at Al-Quds University. His independent television studio had been broadcasting sessions of the PLC. On Tuesday, May 19, 1997, Kuttab had covered a session of the PLC during which the PA was subjected to severe criticism that included charges of alleged corruption. At 11 p.m. the following day, the telephone rang in Kuttab's home. On the other end of the line was a police officer who summoned Kuttab to the police station in Ramallah. Kuttab went as he was asked to do, and did not return home that night. The following day, the Palestinian police denied holding him both to the media and Amnesty International. Allegedly, the live broadcasting of PLC sessions was the main motive behind Kuttab's arrest; the PA was not interested in allowing the allegations to be leaked to the press. According to Palestinian journalist Walid Batrawi: "Daoud Kuttab was arrested because a few members of the Council were against live broadcasts because of a number of scandals that were taking place that they did not want people to know about."[61] This incident suggests that the PA fears open critique, especially the exposure of corruption within its ranks to the public, which could undermine its authority. Although similar information is usually published in English and Arabic by Palestinian human right agencies, they are tolerated because their publications do not reach the wider Palestinian public, although the people in charge of these institutions have also encountered similar treatment at the hands of the PA security services.

7 *The three dailies publish nearly identical information and virtually mirror one another.* This is supported by an in-depth content analysis of the three newspapers. The three dailies repeat the news of the news agencies, especially the official Palestine News Agency (WAFA), rarely introducing changes based on their own investigations. Furthermore, the three newspapers partially repeat news items from the Israeli press. The contributions of local Palestinian journalists to these newspapers are limited, and never take the form of in-depth investigations of issues of concern to the public. This phenomenon can be explained by the policies of self-censorship adopted by local journalists, as we shall discuss in more detail later.

Political affiliation is another example of the way regulatory frameworks impact on the role of the media. The interdependence between politically affiliated individuals and media agencies serves as an effective mechanism of control. The editors of two central newspapers in the PA have close connections with President Arafat: Nabil Amro and Akram Haniya once had influential positions in the PLO apparatus and are still affiliated with prominent figures in the PA. Their work as editors of daily newspapers is certainly influenced by their political affiliation and personal connections. The positive dimension of this situation is the access they have to government figures, official sources, ministries, and other agencies, which allows them to provide more information and a better interpretation of PA policies. *Al-Ayyam*, for instance, is a more daring newspaper as compared to *Al-Quds*, and provides greater coverage of the PA's internal and external affairs. Its quasi-liberal policy is based on the ability of its editors to sense the margins of freedom allowed; their close ties to the PA do not allow them merely to go beyond the veils of secrecy set by the security services, but also enable them to sense what news items the authorities will ignore, and what will be deemed a provocation. The negative side of such an affiliation is the one-sided nature of the press, which is transformed into a seismograph that has to sense the attitude of the authorities and publish accordingly.

The creation of the PBC in 1994 in order to operate a public radio and television station illustrates the impact of political affiliation on the independent position of the press. The appointed president of the PBC, Radwan Abu Ayyash, is a veteran journalist, but his appointment was based on political allegiance, and being a prominent Fatah activist was a crucial criterion. The subsequent attempts of the PBC president to develop autonomous broadcasting policies were countered by severe policies from Arafat. Despite the fact that the PBC's headquarters are located in Ramallah, they receive only one-third of the amount of money allocated to the PBC in the PA budget.[62] The rest of the funds go to the PBC offices in Gaza, where the main broadcasting and program decisions are also made. The control room of Palestinian television is located in the same building as Arafat's offices in Gaza. The Gaza division has transformed the headquarters in Ramallah into a merely symbolic presence. Broadcasting and personnel decisions are made in Gaza, mainly by Arafat's communications advisors. An authoritarian regime in control of the PBC is in place, and is subject to the personal rule of the PA President. This form of control is illustrated by the fact that the radio and television stations transmit news that invariably opens with items about Yasser Arafat's activities.[63] In addition, all programs that deal with political issues reflect the standpoint of the PA and promote compliance to its orders. Such programs are expressions of a televised monopoly on meaning and the monitored setting of the public agenda. Journalists, editors, and managers do not have any sense of autonomy in their work – they are appointed on personal grounds and lack almost any authority[64].

A study of PBC coverage during the first Palestinian elections for president and the legislative council in January 1996 exposed the discrepancy between the airtime given on Palestinian television to Fatah candidates, and that given to candidates of other parties.[65] In the period December 15–25, six different parties appeared on the televised election commercials. Fatah obtained two hours and 22 minutes of screen time, while Hamas only managed 31 minutes. The even smaller parties barely reached the public at all, their screen time totaling around ten minutes. The large gap in party coverage reflects the domination that Fatah has over the public space, which gives it a much better chance to influence public opinion. The same pattern repeated itself in the PBC coverage of the elections of independent candidates – composed of Fatah sympathizers and other candidates – to the Legislative Council.

The Discursive Power of Self-Censorship

Subsequent to several incidents in which the PA reacted severely to the media, newspapers began to establish their own means of censorship. As such, self-censorship has become a common phenomenon among Palestinian journalists. In addition to the traditional Israeli restrictions on Palestinian press freedoms – closure of newspapers, detention of journalists, denying journalists essential press cards or travel permits – under the PA new methods of control have found their way into newspaper rooms and journalists' minds. These methods of self-censorship are clearly expressed in the words of one Palestinian human rights activist:

> There are no "censorship officers" standing threateningly over editors' heads, ordering them what and what not to print. Yet, "a mean-looking officer" lurks constantly in each journalist's mind; a continual nightmare that forces every conscientious journalist to choose between bearing the full consequences of his "follies and smartness" or betraying his conscience by demonstrating national responsibility.[66]

A long record of intimidation and ambiguous wording in the Press Law made journalists unable to anticipate how the PA would respond to coverage of certain issues. This is especially true in the case of national unity. In the words of the journalist Walid Batrawi:

> If the law says that nothing should be published against Palestinian unity, or national unity, but they do not give a definition of what national unity means, I start thinking when I begin to write that maybe this sentence might harm the national unity. Ultimately, it leads you to self-censorship which is an extremely dangerous thing. The PA does not ask you to submit your articles to the censor, but in one way or another, the Palestinian press law restricts you.[67]

A list of sensitive subjects that journalists shy away from in order to avoid detention, harassment, or custody, include the following:

1 Any material that reflects negatively upon the PA President or his family;
2 Criticism of the PA patronage system, especially favoritism and corruption;
3 Any subject concerning the lack of political, administrative, or financial accountability of PA officials;
4 Criticism of social and immoral behavior in society having to do with clan-relationships, religious discrimination, or gender problems.

According to Palestinian journalist Said Ghazali, "Most Palestinian journalists speak in soundless, hushed voices about the bad treatment they have been subjected to. Most of them are aware that their Union is a political platform and cannot defend their rights."[68] As a result of such conditions, journalists' reporting becomes a mere repetition of what had been said by this and that politician. Journalists admit that they "can only call politicians to get their political comments" and "attend meetings and seminars and write about their achievements".[69]

Sovereignty, Democracy, and the Media

The different forms of censorship directly and indirectly exercised by the Palestinian Authority are not completely disconnected from the overall political circumstances in which the PA operates. The pressure exercised by Israel and the US on the PA concerning the opposition Palestinian movements raises another dimension of the freedom of expression in the PA. The PA's lack of sovereignty puts it in a position where it must violate the democratic right of freedom of expression and move against opposition movements in the hope that it will thereby advance the chances for progress in the peace process. The relationship between the PA's dependency on Israeli and American generosity and violations of freedom of expression is illustrated in the Authority's policy toward the cable television stations.

The PA's behavior with regard to the cable stations reveals its dependency on the support of foreign powers. The PA had to restrict the freedom of expression of its population and close several cable stations in order to avoid clashes with the US or be accused by Israel of supporting terror. The Gulf crisis in February 1998 unveiled the fragility of freedom of expression within the PA and its secondary position in relation to the Authority's interests in the regional and international arenas. Public debates among different Palestinian social or political agents must correspond with national interests as defined by the PA. Due to the "imbalance" of power between Israel and the PA, the latter's leadership is caught between the need to prove its ability to control the population under its jurisprudence, and the public demand to respect freedom of expression. For the sake of ensuring the continuation of negotiations with Israel, the PA was willing to violate basic human rights. The Wye River Agreement even institutionalized this arrangement by holding the PA responsible for reducing incitement against Israel in the Palestinian press.

Consider the PA's handling of the Islamic press: the PA has come down hard on the Islamic press when it dared go beyond what has been defined as tolerable; criticism of the peace process in general, and Israel in particular, by the two major Islamic weeklies has led, on several occasions, to their closure or the detainment of their editors.

American and Israeli influence on human rights and freedom of expression within the PA can also be found in the creation of the State Security Court by Arafat, based on a Presidential decree issued on February 7, 1995. In its report dated April 16, 1995, Amnesty International disclosed that:

> The establishment of the State Security Court followed pressure by the Israeli and US authorities on the Palestinian Authority to act against those believed to be carrying out or supporting acts of violence against Israelis. In this context the independence and functioning of the judiciary has been compromised in the interest of political expediency.

A State Security Court, characteristic of authoritarian regimes, symbolizes the PA's efforts to reach not only internal pacification but also to establish hegemony over Palestinian society. The Court reveals the willingness of the PA leaders to exceed any legal limitation in order to avoid occasions that may embarrass the PA in front of Israel and the United States. The Executive Authority of the PA, as a means of overcoming the shortages of the regular court system, and as an efficient mechanism to respond to pressures from the Palestinian public in special circumstances, has transformed the State Security Court into a regular court that can deal with cases involving civil charges. The Palestinian Independent Commission for Citizens' Rights has pointed out in one of its reports that in three cases in Gaza, President Arafat responded to pressure from the public, especially from tribal leaders, and ordered the Security Court to discuss those civil cases that ultimately resulted in the death penalty being handed down and carried out after Arafat confirmed the sentences.[70]

The creation of the Court violates the 1994 Cairo agreement between Israel and the PLO which states: "Israel and the Council shall exercise their powers and responsibilities pursuant to this Agreement with due regard to internationally-accepted norms and principles of human rights and the rule of law."[71] Nevertheless, Israel and the US saw its establishment as a crucial step toward implementing the PA's commitments to fight radical movements in Palestinian society.[72] The PA granted the State Security Court special status and turned it into a tool to deter the opposition. Predictably, most of those brought before the Court were not given the opportunity to properly defend themselves. In many cases the suspects were arrested and brought to the Court without being made aware of the charges against them, and without having had a lawyer appointed to properly defend them. The allegations were, in most cases, not revealed to the suspects and the Court's ruling was given after only one meeting. In some cases suspects were adjudicated in secret without a possibility of appeal to a higher court.[73]

Conclusion

Said Ghazali, the Palestinian commentator, perhaps best summarized the Palestinian media regime when he remarked upon the May 20 arrest of Dauod Kuttab. He said that this case served "to send a message to increasingly outspoken Palestinian journalists who dare to step over the red line".[74] The Kuttab case, as well as similar incidents, symbolized the ongoing process by which the Palestinian media is being tamed by the PA according to its priorities. Many cases of violations of the right of expression by the PA police have been justified in the name of the national interest, or by patronizing certain traditional values and concepts of Palestinian society, such as honor.[75] The Palestinian Press Law is an ambiguous, obtuse law that has the potential to be used to advance democratic values. But it can, equally, provide a means to suppress dissidents. Despite minor changes in the PA's policies toward the media and journalists, the method has been proven effective. Difficulties in the peace process, combined with Israeli and US pressures on the PA regarding Palestinian opposition groups, only tighten the grip on the freedom of expression within Palestinian society.

Nevertheless, a large space for maneuvering remains, and there are indications of structural pluralism existing within the PA. The transformation of this pluralism into a real free public sphere, in which the media plays a significant role, depends not only on the PA's behavior, but also upon the determination of the media itself to play a major role in defining the characteristics of the future

Palestinian society. The PA must accept that a critical media is not necessarily anti-nationalist, and should allow (or even encourage) the media to play an active role without it being accused of betraying national interests. However, the media cannot expect to receive its freedom on a silver platter. If freedom of the press is to be a guiding principle for a democratic Palestinian society, editors and journalists have to accept the fact that they will inevitably come into conflict with the regime, just as is the case in Western democratic states.

4

The Deconstruction of Gender Regime

THE WOMEN'S MOVEMENT AND THE PREDICAMENT OF EQUAL CITIZENSHIP

The Palestinian women's movement came of age within the confines of the larger national struggle. As a consequence, the national movement has conditioned women's involvement in the political struggle; the primacy of the nationalist discourse made any discussion of women's rights secondary.[1] As an exilic movement, the aspiration of the PLO – to territorialize its power base – has produced patterns of power relations that rendered the interests of women the lowest priority of the national movement.[2] Palestinian women were therefore ideologically defined to suit the PLO's official priorities, portrayed as "mothers of the nation". As such, they were encouraged to concentrate on grassroots, domestic activity and leave the main military and political battlefield to the "real soldiers".[3]

The women's movement was the first to begin reorganizing itself and alter its discourse to suit the new emerging post-Oslo political reality. Women's organizations became more engaged in lobbying for greater involvement and representation of women in decision-making processes. The attempts made by several women's organizations to bring feminist issues to the center of the public debate has led to a fragmentation among women's rights activists, and to direct confrontation with the various social and political forces seeking to undermine their efforts. Following the establishment of the PA, the Palestinian women's movement found itself caught in a kind of Gordian knot in which, the wider the scope of the women's struggle for gender equality, the greater the fragmentation within the woman's movement became, and the broader the resentment to its efforts.[4] Clear differences grew between the different women's organization regarding the best post-Oslo strategy, under the emerging PA state apparatus. The counter-response to women's efforts was mainly led by the Islamic movement, which sees all attempts to promote feminism as political.[5]

Although the PA is not exclusively responsible for constructing gender divisions within Palestinian society, these divisions cannot be seen only in the context of any of the PA's specific mechanisms: it is centrally implicated in gender relations and constitutes a definitive gender regime. According to Connell, states are "the center of a reverberating set of power relations and political processes in which patriarchy is both constructed and contested".[6] Each state has its own combination of institutions, apparatuses, and arenas, each of which has its own histories, contradictions, relations, and connections, both internally and externally. Between them, these interrelationships play an important role in constituting gender inequalities. Kandiyoti claims that states "may appear just as constraining as the tyranny of more primordial loyalties to lineage, tribe or kin, the differences being that such demands are enforced by the state and its legal administrative apparatus rather than individual patriarchs".[7] Therefore, to understand the Palestinian women's movement's attempts to overcome social barriers and assume an influential position in the various levels of state building, one must examine the structures of domination in which women's identities and social differences are produced.[8]

The PA's new institutional structure mirrors the dominant national discourse and thus contributes to the construction of a clear gender regime.[9] Through a fusion of what Hill-Collins called the "matrix of domination" [10] and the sexual division of labor, new mechanisms of gender relations emerge which exclude women from positions of authority. The PA has played a major role in forming and re-forming prevalent social patterns. The women's movement on its part, developed different strategies to overcome political–legal and cultural–religious barriers, which undermined women's equal participation in defining the cultural and political model that a society is based around. This chapter will examine changes in the women's movement over the last decade, investigating two main fronts in the struggle for women's rights: the democratic (appealing to the PLC), and the media based (publishing feminist newspapers).

The struggle, and lobbying, for liberal legislation in the PLC concerns the personal status law. State law is a discursive field that consists of competing ways of bestowing meaning on the world and of organizing social institutions and processes. It is therefore an ideal field in which to examine the status of women and the source of their deprivation without overlooking the complexity of the women's movement itself.[11] As Weedon maintains, "Differences between competing views of justice within the field of legal discourse are articulated in language and in the material organization of state institutions which control the meaning of justice, punishment, compensation and rehabilitation."[12] That is, state institutions define justice in ways that serve particular values and interests. Since discourses, their meaning, and political significance are rarely fixed, there exists a struggle between competing values hoping to feed the institutional system in society. The legal administration embodies the hegemonic ideological discourses, which have the power "to establish authoritative definitions of social situations and social needs, the power to define the universe of legitimate disagreement, and the power to shape the political agenda".[13] Therefore, the examination of the law as a discursive field enables us to come to grips with the related issue of socio-cultural hegemony, and helps us explore the contest between hegemonic and counter-hegemonic definitions of social situations.[14]

Approaching the gender regime in the PA in this manner complements neo-patriarchal theories of the state.[15] As an overarching theory, patriarchy tends to overlook the complexity of social identities[16] and homogenizes women as a singular group on the basis of shared oppression.[17] Despite the patriarchal features of Palestinian society,[18] however, Palestinian women are not just passive recipients and non-participants in the determination of gender relations.[19] Neo-patriarchal explanation, as Judith Butler claims, turns culture into destiny.[20] Therefore, the text presented below will go beyond dichotomous conceptualizations, but remain aware of the fact that women's oppression is endemic and integral to social relations regarding the distribution of power as well as material resources.[21] The other branch of women's action that will be examined is the attempts of some women's organizations to set a feminist public agenda by disseminating their worldview through publishing a feminist newspaper. The discursive structure of the newspaper will be examined in order to illustrate women's efforts to counter the prevailing valuational order in Palestinian society and politics and establish a more liberal alternative to that order.

Gender-Regime and the Politics of Identity and Difference in Women's Action

Within the confines of the Palestinian national struggle signs of a new feminist discourse began to emerge at the beginning of the 1990s. The urgency to push for a women's agenda intensified after the signing of the Oslo agreement with Israel and the constitution of the PA. Many women came to believe that failure to take action during the transitory period, promoting a women's agenda and ensuring their active participation in shaping the character of the future Palestinian state, would mean the loss of the potential benefits of their long struggle for both national and equal rights.[22]

Women became aware that their popular image as subdued and passive had changed as result of their involvement in the *Intifada*, but they were conscious that these changes "did not result in significantly modifying the cultural–traditional role of women in Palestinian society".[23] Therefore, many Palestinian women became determined to directly confront and remove obstacles and restrictions that had been the cause of women's issues being sidelined in the ongoing political debate. One important feature of the new consciousness among Palestinian women was that they began assessing and examining previous activities as part of an all-inclusive process of seeking strategies and effective ways of organization for a new comprehensive campaign. Newly-established women's centers were the pioneers in this campaign. These centers, established at the end of the 1980s and beginning of the 1990s, are run by educated women who utilize social science methodologies to explore the sources of discrimination.

The various women's centers collected data regarding the number of women in the different public institutions in the PA. One study conducted by the Women's Studies Center in East Jerusalem aimed at providing "scientific data on women's status in society to be provided to policy-makers". The study examined the status of women in six PA ministries. The findings were not surprising. The study demonstrated that a negative correlation exists between position and women's representation in the six ministries – the higher the position, the fewer the number of women.[24] Whereas nearly half of the lower-ranking positions in PA institutions are occupied by women (46 percent), women fill only 14 percent of the higher positions.[25] The study concludes by arguing that "women will stay out of the decision-making circles as long as a comprehensive social change based on developmental orientation does not take place."[26] The conductors of the research indicated "women's issues are not a priority neither for the PA nor for the supportive and opposition political parties."[27] The study also criticized existing structures of distribution of resources and exposed the material determinants underlying women's deprivation.

A central initiative of the new women's centers was to establish the Women's Affairs Technical Committees (WATC). WATCs were set up in 1992 as part of the attempts made by women to assist the Palestinian negotiating teams in preparation for the peace negotiations with Israel. The committees were soon transformed into a framework for coordination and cooperation between women organizations. WATC became a coalition of six women's study centers, five women organizations affiliated with political parties, human rights organizations, and many politically independent and professional women. Its plural composition was a major source of its power, and was translated into extensive lobbying and educating initiatives.

The establishment of the WATC reflected the conviction among Palestinian women activists that a strategy of cooperation and coordination between the various women's NGOs would best promote women's issues. It also reflected the belief in the need to run an organized campaign that had wide support within the women's movement for the purpose of promoting their goals. WATC declared that the different women's centers "work together for the realization of the abolition of all forms of discrimination against women, thereby assisting in the creation of a civic democratic society characterized by equality and social justice".[28] They aimed at "bringing women's issues to the forefront in all spheres of life in Palestine".

Among the first initiatives promoted by WATC was agreeing on a common charter that summarizes the principles of women's rights. The charter was issued at a conference convened in Jerusalem in August 1994, and was based on the equality provisions included in the 1988 Palestinian Declaration of Independence, the Charter of the United Nations, and the Universal Declaration of Human Rights. The fact that the General Union of Palestinian Women (GUPW) in Tunis joined in issuing the charter marked the growing coordination between women's organizations that belonged to the PLO and women's NGOs established in the occupied territories. The charter called upon "all women and forces of democracy in Palestinian society" to unite "in an effort to eliminate all obstacles that hamper women's equality with men, hand in hand towards a democratic society that achieves total national independence and social justice and equality".[29]

Despite its clear feminist emphasis, the charter was formulated within the framework of Palestinian national aspirations. It called for the elimination of all forms of discrimination, and demanded that women be included in all political, civil, economic, social, and cultural rights in the "constitution and legislation of the independent state of Palestine". The framing of women rights within the national narrative came to facilitate the women's movement's efforts to influence the drafting of the Palestinian Basic Law, a process that had begun in Tunis, before the PA was established in 1994. The first proposed Basic Law draft did not include any provision on gender equality.[30] Therefore, the women's charter demanded:

> To grant the woman her right to acquire, preserve or change her nationality. Legislation must also guarantee that her marriage to a non-Palestinian or a change of her husband's nationality while married, will not necessarily change the citizenship of the wife . . . Women should also be granted the right to give citizenship to her husband and children, be guaranteed the full freedom to move, travel and choose her place of residency . . . [31]

The charter's formulation mirrored the attempt made by the women's movement to promote women's rights without confronting the national elite and its political discourse. The charter attributed existing discrimination against women to the colonial legacy imposed on Palestine, reinforced by prejudiced customs and traditions.[32] The structure of the national movement and *its* contribution to the discrimination of women are not mentioned.

A debate erupted within the women's movement regarding the nature of the official ties with the PLO and the PA. Whereas prominent GUPW (General Union of Palestinian Women) figures that had returned to the occupied territories favored coordinating their efforts with the emerging PA, the WATC preferred to preserve its independence and follow its own course of lobbying and mobilization. This debate exposed the rising tension concerning the relationship between state and civil society in general within the new Palestinian institutional structure,[33] with the PA leadership favoring the subordination of civil organizations for the good of the national struggle.[34] To this end, efforts were made to co-opt women into the emerging national structure. Non-governmental women's organizations were caught between protecting their independence and their wish to have positive contacts with governmental institutions for the sake of influencing policy-making.

Internal Women's Differences

The emerging socio-political reality in the occupied territories and the establishment of the PA led to the rise of three schools of thought within the women's movement. The first consisted of the traditionalists who accepted the *shari'a* – the applied Islamic law – as the legal basis for personal status and the main moral code to regulate family life in Palestinian society. This school of thought is affiliated with the Islamic movement and opposed the national discourse adopted by other women's organizations. Organizations that identified with this approach did not view themselves as part of the women's movement and operated within the confines of the Islamic movement. Since this stream did not establish its own independent mobilization structures, following its patterns of operation is almost impossible.

The two other schools of thought that began to emerge within the women's movement, although interconnected and mutually supportive on many levels, differ in how they essentially understand the women's situation, and over the most effective strategy to overcome discrimination and improve the status of women in Palestinian society.

One school can be described as accomodationist in nature and willing to consider the current social, political, and economic circumstances that lead to discrimination against women as temporary conditions that will change after independence is achieved. Adherents to this perspective not only accept acting from within the PA's institutional structure, hoping instead to influence its policies from inside; they are also less critical of the PA's policies. They view affirmative action as the ultimate strategy for achieving women's rights and direct their efforts toward promoting women within the emerging official political and economic institutions. Through networking, campaigning, media work, and training women for better posts in decision-making institutions, supporters of this strategy believe that the creation of change *inside* the existing political and economic structures will lead to a redistribution of material and human resources, thereby creating equality for women.

Several of the women's organizations that support this school are affiliated with political parties active within the PA. Consequently, their positions are, to a large degree, determined by the policies of their "mother" parties.[35] These women's groups seek to overcome the inequitable outcomes of the existing social arrangements without undermining the underlying framework that generates them while at the same time striving to promote women's issues without disrupting the existing social structure. Despite their critique of the reality Palestinian women face, followers of this school of thought subscribe to and prefer gradual solutions conditioned by the national goals of the Palestinian people.[36]

The third school, in contrast, is more confrontational in its feminist world-view, for it attempts to address and restructure the underlying frameworks which are responsible for women's deprivation. Although its adherents accept affirmative action as a short-term policy, they do not view it as a satisfactory solution for the deprived status of women in society. They have designated the engendered socio-political structure as the main obstacle to women's equality, and therefore envision, in the long term, a total transformation of this structure as the only satisfactory solution for women. They target governmental policies, procedures of legislation, and cultural traits in order to promote this objective. Supporters of this school criticize the PA's economic and social policies, which are in line with instructions from the World Bank and the International Monetary Fund.[37] These policies support increasing privatization and the shrinking of government expenditures in social, medical and educational programs.[38] One of the advocates for this school of thought claimed that "There is a need to exert pressure on the PA to follow for more just policies that include all sectors of society." [39] Toward that end, she maintained that a need exists "to link economic growth with development based on basic pillars such as equality, social justice and the rule of the law. Real development conditions sovereign political decisions and development of the productive sectors that enable self-reliance and let internal democracy to come out and express itself in an atmosphere of pluralism, mutual respect and democratic dialogue."[40] This school also claims that a wide variety of factors contribute to the formation of the terrain of citizenship including "ideologies of nationalist entitlement; networks of political patronage; changing social, political and economic relations; the formulation and implementation of new policies and changing patterns of political participation, as well as the limits of the Oslo agreement".[41] According to this approach, the women's movement must develop a comprehensive strategy to deal with all these issues if it is to achieve its goals.

Attempts are therefore made to expose the cultural, political, and economic dimensions behind the engendered institutional order which discriminates against women. One of the issues that adherents to this school emphasize is the dominant cultural discourse in which women's subjectivity is constituted. Consequently, this school targets the implications of the legal system for gender issues as well as the prevalent value system in Palestinian society by exposing the "contradiction between rights in civil/constitutional law (public rights) and rights in personal status law".[42] In addition to legal reform, advocates for this approach call for broad educational and socialization programs in order to transform the wider social context. In recent years, this new women's discourse has become more daring in its language, engagement, and practice; and while the national Palestinian cause was not ignored, it takes the controversial precedent of placing women at the center of the socio-political analysis.

The differences between the two latter schools – that is, between party-affiliated and non-party affiliated women's groups – were demonstrated in the debate regarding a quota for women in the 1996 elections for the Palestinian Legislative Council. Party-affiliated women's organizations were influenced by the position of their respective parties. Some followed the position stated by a leftist party leader that those individuals most likely to generate the most votes would be selected to appear on candidacy lists irrespective of their gender. Other women's groups called for a 30 percent quota for women in the PLC, knowing that without it only a few women would receive the necessary votes. The proposed quota system would have been a precedent, and consequently would have established a platform on which to protest other relevant issues in the future.[43] The women's groups rejected a proposal to create a women's secretariat to be attached to the Palestinian presidency that would promote women's issues as well as the formation of a Ministry of Women's Affairs.[44] Instead, they were more interested in incorporating women's issues into all the PA ministries based on objective qualifications that would enable female candidates to compete on an equal footing with male competitors. The data supplied by women's centers regarding women's affiliation and deprivation, in addition to their stated position toward adequate public sector representation, reflected the emphasis on political–economic injustice. According to supporters of this school of thought, social equality demands the restructuring of polity and economy. Therefore, they demanded reorganizing the division of labor, subjecting investment to democratic decision making, and setting objective and transparent criteria for public positions.

Since such a total structural overhaul was unfeasible, they decided to promote the idea of a quota system as a temporary strategy in the initial stages of the national reconstruction process.[45] Women who supported the idea were aware of its negative implications: affirmative action reinforces the image of the woman as a victim and makes the location of women in the social, economic, and political structures the main focus of struggle, instead of addressing the inherent problems contained within these structures. Based on this line of thought, a quota system may be subjected to the same patriarchal mentality that is the source for the exclusion of women from the public sphere.[46] These women's organizations claim that, among the basic obstacles to women's equality, are the patterns of conduct where private patriarchy takes on public dimensions in the process of state-building.[47]

The Art of Lobbying and the Model Parliament

Since the changes in the political situation in the territories precipitated by the Oslo agreement and the creation of the PA took place, the legal status of women has become one of the main discursive fields addressed by women's centers. The women's movement was well aware of the state's power in transforming legal reality.[48] Despite the cautious position adopted by progressive Palestinian women, they came to consider legislation and its implications on women's status as one of the central fields to be contested and altered. The PA's transitive status, combined with the lack of a uniform application of the law in Palestinian society, made it ripe for an attempt to influence the constitution of the emerging state. Supporters of this stream of thought insisted that "the fight for national independence and the struggle for women's rights can and should go hand in hand".[49] This conclusion was drawn based upon the experiences of other women's movements in the Arab world, especially in Algiers, where the women's movement was marginalized after independence.[50]

Until the creation of the Palestinian Authority in 1994, the Palestinians themselves did not legislate any of the laws that ordered their private and public life. As part of the Ottoman Empire, personal status law in Palestine was based on the Islamic *shari'a*, which was also the main source of legislation. Under Ottoman laws, women were deprived of almost any civil rights. Their role was determined by family law, an outgrowth of the Ottoman "Millet" system,[51] according to which each religious community regulates its matters related to family status according to its own religious beliefs. Such a system is still in place today in Israel.[52] In the West Bank and the Gaza Strip, which until 1967 were under Jordanian and Egyptian rule, respectively, *shari'a* remained the main source of legislation. Even during Israeli occupation, the Jordanian personal status law of 1976 and the Egyptian Family law of 1954 were applied in Muslim religious courts in the West Bank and Gaza Strip. Similarly, Christian denominations have their own religious courts for the Christian community.

The PA became the central political authority after its establishment in parts of the occupied territories; its influence grew as the peace process progressed. But the PA's authority was not absolute, as the supreme responsibility for the territories remained in Israeli hands. Nonetheless, the PA was depicted as being responsible for the internal affairs of the Palestinian citizens living under its jurisdiction. The 1996 elections to the PLC prompted a public discussion regarding the PA's constitutional status. As one of the most well organized social forces, the women's movement viewed the PLC as a fitting avenue through which women's rights could be institutionalized via legislation. Despite the restricted role of the PLC, women's organizations seized the new opportunity that the process of legislation opened for promoting women's rights. They exploited the rising debates within the PLC and Palestinian society regarding the state-building process and the constitutional dimensions of the emerging Palestinian regime to promote their worldview. Women's organizations were aware of the powerful gender constructs in every national project. One of the main issues targeted by women was the definition of citizenship.[53] Most women's organizations were opposed to the patriarchal implications of citizenship as it was formulated in the Basic Law. Women's groups lobbied against this understanding in a comprehensive public campaign called "The Model Parliament: Women and Legislation" (MP).

This initiative was an attempt to open new public avenues in which different people could engage in debating issues, such as women's labor, social welfare, education, and criminal and public law. As defined by the initiators, the model parliament

> is the culmination of the national campaign for legislation that guaran-
> tees equality and human rights for Palestinian women. It is a public
> gathering that provides a democratic and free stage for official and unof-
> ficial people from different social groupings and different parts of the
> homeland. It is shaped in the form of parliament and parliamentary
> discussions in order to discuss several proposed amendments to the
> existing laws. This seeks to achieve equality, abolish women's oppres-
> sion and to eradicate their discrimination in the law as well as to
> formulate and adopt the amendments for the sake of women's rights and
> the good will of the family and society.[54]

In the model parliament, all of the laws enacted by the PLC that relate to women's status in the West Bank and Gaza Strip were discussed, and suggestions and recommendations were introduced.

The MP initiative demonstrated that the Palestinian feminist movement was not only about promoting women to influential positions in the social and political arenas: the demands and issues raised in the parliament also challenged the existing gender regime and even illuminated the attempts made by some women's centers to abolish female subjugation in Palestinian society. The feminist discourse that dominated the parliament challenged the traditional female image loaded with traditional symbolism signifying such concepts as stability, fertility, and continuity. It strove to change the engendered social order and sought to combine the discourse of national identity with one of differences and plurality.

The MP aimed "to pass Palestinian legislation that ensures equality and human rights for Palestinian women, as well as their participation in building a civil society based on justice, equality, respect for human rights and rule of law".[55] Although it had no juridical or legislative status, the MP managed to mobilize different sectors of Palestinian society to discuss issues raised by its members. The convening of the parliament reflected the heavy emphasis the women's movement placed on public lobbying in order to change the social and political reality in Palestinian society. Timing also played a crucial role in women's strategy, for they worked seriously "on modifying the first ever Palestinian legislation".[56]

Participants in the MP were worried by attempts made by the PA president to marginalize the PLC and block efforts by some of its members to initiate a legislative process to draw clear constitutional lines for the emerging Palestinian state. For example, President Arafat was unhappy with the passage by the PLC of the Palestinian Basic Law in 1997, so despite its passage after three readings, he delayed its ratification until 2002. This tension between the two central branches of government served as a warning to the women's movement, which viewed the stalemate in the legislative process as endangering their chances of promoting their own agenda. As a result, the MP became a strong "counter-public" aimed at putting real pressure on the PA leadership.[57]

In preparation for the MP, women's centers – especially the Women's Center for Legal Aid and Counseling – conducted thorough research on all laws applied in Palestinian society. The aim was to provide a documented basis for all women's public initiatives such as the MP or the proposed legislation.[58] The research examined those laws that have implications on the status of women in Palestinian society. The conclusions were presented to the MP in order to provide guidelines to the amendments needed in the legal system. The author of the proposal pointed out the centrality of law to promoting women's rights in society, noting that the law could be "a sharp weapon in the hands of social forces that enable them to turn their policies into binding formulations and practical judgments through which their goals could be achieved". Conversely, however, the law could also be "an effective tool for the oppression and manipulation of authority in order to establish the legitimacy of a non-democratic regime",[59] and could therefore work against women's interests. The women's initiative aimed at raising awareness of a positive interpretation of the law while also preventing the latter ideal from turning into the dominant legal value system.

Following the convening of preparatory discussions, the MP's main sessions were held in March and April 1998, in the West Bank and Gaza Strip, respectively. They included 88 members, in accordance with the actual number of PLC members, with equal representation of women and men. The West Bank session focused on the legal status of Palestinian women and devoted most of its time to a discussion of women's political and civil rights. It dealt with penal legislation and rights related to work, education, and health care. The session in Gaza primarily discussed the Palestinian Family Laws and ways to amend them in the spirit of equality, non-discrimination, and respect for women's human rights.[60] Participants emphasized that the existing laws constituted a barrier to women's participation in the reconstruction of their society and homeland. The press release at the end of both sessions listed the MP's main demands and affirmed the need to amend civil laws for the sake of achieving a just society based on equality and the rule of law. The press release also included efforts by MP participants to achieve an independent Palestinian state and develop a strong civil society. It marked the women's movement's attempt to reject accusations – primarily from the Islamic movement – that the women's movement had anti-nationalist and anti-Islamic goals.

Women's fears regarding the traditional and masculinist implications of the dominant national discourse and its impact on the state-building process were manifested in the serious discussions regarding the Personal Status (or Family) Law. [61] MP participants were aware of the contradictions between the Islamic model of the family and gender relations based on the *shari'a* and the civil law of modern citizenship. The law related to central issues such as age of marriage, dowries, polygamy, child support, divorce, custody, alimony, paternity, inheritance, and custody.[62] Despite the fact that no single unitary Islamic personal status law exists, and significant theological, legal, institutional, cultural, and sociological differences exist within the greater Muslim community, the Personal Status Law has remained almost the only aspect of *shari'a* that has resisted displacement by modern and secular civil law in most Islamic countries.[63] The fact that the Basic Law passed by the PLC in 1997 refers to the *shari'a* as the main basis for legislation in Palestine made the Personal Status Law even more threatening to women's rights. President Arafat stated in 1995, upon the presentation of the women's charter to him, that he "would accept the principles of the women's charter if they did not conflict with *shariʻa* law".[64] This position was articulated in a telegram sent by Arafat and Intissar Al-Wazir, Minister of Social Affairs, to the women's conference held in Jerusalem in August 1994 under the banner of the GUPW.[65]

Despite the unwillingness of most MP participants to confront the *shariʻa*, in the eyes of many women the Personal Status Law is a primary source of oppression for women. But because the Personal Status Law is based on religious codes, any modification to the law is extremely difficult to achieve. Nevertheless, in an effort to promote a liberal understanding of religious law, the MP pointed out the flexibility in the interpretation of the *shariʻa* and cited the pragmatic position that religious scholars have taken in several cases, hinting at the role that the PA – and the PLC in particular – could play in this context.

The MP's participants, aware of the fact that amending the Personal Status Law is a matter of power relations within the PA, split into different camps regarding the appropriate strategy to handle this issue. A number of women advocated a civil family law, to be applied in civil court, based on the principles of gender equality. Others endorsed *shariʻa* and demanded that the matter be left to the religious authorities. A third position, located between the two extremes, advocated a reform of *shariʻa*, claiming that religious law is responsive to change.[66] These different approaches reflected the internal conflict within the women's movement regarding which goals to pursue, and the correct strategy for improving the status of Palestinian women. Most of the MP participants preferred not to confront the PA or the Islamic movement on this particular issue. The conservative positions that the PA had adopted regarding women's rights indicated that the PA would not endorse the women's movement and that, if a confrontation were to erupt between the Islamic movement and the women's movement, it would side with the former.

Feminist Media and the Art of Framing

The women's movement's efforts to change the status of women in Palestinian society were not limited to the legislative process. As a well-organized social movement, women pursued a broader mobilization strategy that included framing public opinion and setting its agenda. Women were aware of the fact that the media plays an important role that goes far beyond merely providing the public with information. They were aware that the Palestinian media did not consider their struggle for equality as an important topic to report. The regular media institutions were not independent enough to adopt, even partially, some of the ideas that the women's movement was propagating, and remained loyal to the traditional nationalist line.[67] Despite some shifts in the media agenda in Palestinian society after Oslo, the media were still reluctant to address several sensitive social problems, such as women's rights.[68] The treatment of social issues remained consistent with the hegemonic political culture according to which issues that expose negative dimensions of Palestinian society to the outside world are usually suppressed or expressed only in vague terms. The media also paid little attention to culturally sensitive issues, such as rape, physical abuse of women and children, and other topics that could instigate familial and tribal unrest. This pattern became more pronounced during the second *Intifada*, when Palestinians returned to the stage of struggle for national liberation.

To overcome the obstacles set before them, women's groups sought out every possible way to attract media attention. Realizing the media's impact on setting the public agenda, they sought out any means by which they could make their voice heard to the public, and also tried to reach high-ranking political figures via the media and other modes of public communication. Their activities in this regard took on a variety of forms and were carried out on several social levels.

One method women's organizations employed was to create and distribute their own publications; brochures, pamphlets, and other printed materials became extremely common on the Palestinian street. By adopting a communication strategy utilized by other women's movements in the world, Palestinian women's organizations sought to reach every individual and communicate their message to every layer of society. They distributed their publications to both public and private institutions. The publications addressed both men and women in an attempt to penetrate public awareness and induce a change in the accepted social norms and values. In this regard, many educational workshops and courses were, and continue to be, held for women, men, and children to promote greater awareness of gender issues.[69]

Women's organizations sought to achieve several goals in their communication policy. The GUPW released a document that detailed its communication strategy:

1   To increase the opportunities for women to participate within the media, express their views and take part in the decision-making processes in the media and other forms of electronic communication;

2   To encourage the introduction of a balanced, non-stereo-typed portrayal of women in the media;

3   To increase the media's attention to the constructive role that Palestinian women have played in the national struggle;

4   To increase the focus placed on social issues that are of concern to all of Palestinian society, but are especially relevant to women because they bear the brunt of the effects of these social issues.[70]

Despite the women's efforts, the Palestinian media – both print and electronic – have maintained a conservative approach regarding gender issues. The image of the Palestinian woman as homemaker is still dominant, even in cases when the media directed its attention to women. The media's treatment of stories and issues related to women is usually superficial, with no serious attention given to discrimination against women in society. Similarly, the media framing of stories related to women reflected the hegemonic patriarchal mentality, as they were almost always written from a patriarchal point of view, even when the authors were women. This pattern reflected the depth to which women had internalized their own oppression. Although some change can certainly be detected in recent years, the generalization that most newspaper stories about Palestinian women deal with pregnancy, motherhood, cooking, and fashion still holds true. Most articles about women's issues are descriptive in nature and lack any feminist valuational judgments. Even commercial advertisements and employment notices are usually formulated in the masculine; only in cases where a secretary is sought is the feminine form used.

In light of these circumstances, and in an attempt to overcome social and cultural barriers, women's organizations created their own publications, with WATC (Women's Affairs Technical Committees) among the pioneering groups. WATC became the first women's coalition to initiate a major publication project – a bi-weekly women's newspaper. The aim was not only to compensate for the traditional media's lack of coverage of women's issues and to express the voice and worldview of the Palestinian women's movement, but also to influence the construction of a Palestinian social reality that is less gender biased. The publication therefore represented an attempt to insert the women's movement into the public agenda and reframe the public's awareness of women's rights and their struggle for equality. The aim was to create a cyclical mechanism – in which women would make their voice heard as part of the public agenda; this in turn would attract enough attention from the Palestinian public, which would again have an impact on setting the public agenda.[71] As a weak social group the women had to find unique and innovative ways to introduce themselves to the public agenda and occupy a central place therein.[72]

If women's organizations were to successfully create a public sympathetic to their positions, they needed to approach the public from a new vantage point. That is, women had to develop and crystallize their preferred depictions in the public sphere.[73] The typical framing of women as housewives and mothers, as "wombs of the nation", depicts them only as passive and subordinate participants in society.[74] In the long term, such media frames have a great impact on the personal views of the audience.

A specialized publication on women's issues to be written in a moderate feminist language was deemed the best vehicle to raise public awareness and reach the largest audience, regardless of gender. The initiative began in May 1996 with an appendix entitled "Women and the Elections" distributed with the daily newspaper *Al-Ayyam*. Although responses to the publication were mixed, the experience helped serve as a basis for turning the publication into a permanent enterprise. The title was changed to the more general and representative name *Sawt al-Nisa'a* (*Women's Voice*), which indicates its feminist worldview. The title also had the effect of attracting the attention of all writers interested in raising public awareness of women's rights and social problems of special significance for women.

From its inception *Women's Voice* introduced itself as a general newspaper, refusing to limit itself to issues traditionally perceived to be the concern of women. The newspaper emphasizes its role as the mouthpiece of a comprehensive social movement that happens to be composed of women. In order to emphasize this orientation, the newspaper calls upon Palestinian men, in a prominently displayed title that appears in every edition, to join the women's struggle for equality. This announcement states "We struggle together for liberation, we shall work together to build the country." Thereby, the newspaper articulates one of the main arguments of the women's movement: that the struggle for equality and social justice is not an issue of importance to women only, but is, rather, the concern of every man and woman interested in building a healthy Palestinian society.

Reframing Gender

A closer look at *Women's Voice* makes it clear that it has been a stage for the coverage of various subjects relevant to women of different ages, professions, and social and economic status. The bi-weekly has adopted a pluralist orientation, reflecting different ideas and positions. It avoids those issues stereotypical of the content found in more popular, mainstream, and commercial women's magazines. It does not contain any photographs or illustrations that could be interpreted as a portrayal of women as sexual objects, nor does it use color photographs to attract attention. A rather unique feature of the newspaper is that its editorial appears on the front page, which demonstrates its centrality in articulating the newspaper's message.

The contents of the newspaper address different issues and subjects, comprising six different subject matters: social (57.5%), cultural (12.5%), legal (10%), economic (9.5%), political, (8.5%) and health (2%). The emphasis put on social issues mirrors the world-view of WATC, conceiving social problems such as violence against women, family honor and the murder of women, rape, marriage at an early age, polygamy, divorce, motherhood and children, violence against children at home and in the school, as the main issues that society in general should deal with.

To clarify the discourse of the newspaper it is necessary to take a closer look at its ideological and normative undercurrents, by examining the editorials of editions 78–105 that appeared between August 12, 1999 and August 15, 2000 – a sample size sufficient to reflect the newspaper's editorial policy and the issues with which it is most concerned. The editorials are a direct indication of the topics that draw the editorial board's attention, and therefore suggest the board's priorities and considerations. The selection of the editorials is related to the fact that they are normative in nature and mirror WATC's worldview. They usually address one central issue or event, and succinctly articulate its framing by the women's movement.

A common feature of the editorials is their universal humanitarian and liberal nature, which characterizes the moderate feminist ideological orientation adopted by the WATC. The liberal values of freedom, equality, social justice, and well-being constitute the main underpinning of the editorial line. Based on this ideological foundation, a comprehensive critique of the patriarchal ideology that dominates not only Palestinian society but also the entire Arab world is formulated. The editorials of *Women's Voice* are directed at Arab readers in general, while criticizing Palestinian culture as a small part of the broader Arab culture. A central claim made in the editorials is that women are the victims of discrimination and deprived of equal social, economic, and political rights because of the dominant patriarchal ideology that differentiates between men and women and creates two separate hierarchical spheres – the public and the private.

The editorials of *Women's Voice* cover developments in the Arab world and follow developments in progressive Arab countries for the purpose of advancing the struggle for women within Palestinian society. This line of thought demonstrates the way in which the newspaper locates itself in the wider Arab cultural circle. The editorials express the view not only that progressive or regressive change in one Arab country could have a positive or negative impact on other Arab societies, but also that Arab culture is the main source of discrimination against women. Therefore, according to the editorial line of the newspaper the struggle of Palestinian women for equality should reach beyond the confines of Palestinian society. The newspaper addresses repressive measures taken against women's equality in Arab countries such as Jordan and Kuwait, in order to demonstrate the similarity of women's status in the various Arab countries.[75] The editorial calls upon Palestinian society to discuss the laws that determine the personal status of men and women, as no development and shift toward modernism can be achieved without putting women on an equal footing with men in *all* spheres of life.

The struggle surrounding the proposed new personal status law in Egypt became an inspiring development that the newspaper addressed. The editorial in Issue 90 notes that the proposed law in Egypt allows women to divorce their husbands based on "incompatibility" without being required to supply other reasons. The editorial praises the proposed law, which is more liberal than that which is currently in effect, and proceeds to explain the sources of rejectionism as voiced by religious movements and institutions which justify their position according to Islamic *shari'a*. According to the editorial:

> Putting forth new ideas . . . has to do with the power structure in society. Reshuffling the relationship between the two sexes on equal footing means power-sharing and participating in decisions that are concerned with change, thinking, inheritance and eliminating the principles of possession and slavery, which many try, in the name of religion, to portray as a normal situation.[76]

Issue 94's editorial discusses Arab culture and claims that the cultural foundations that established the traditional role of women in society are still dominant in large segments of Arab countries today. The slow changes taking place in parts of the Arab world, especially in Morocco and Egypt, are faced with a counter-struggle by traditional segments in those societies. According to the editorial there is a real need to reread history and reinterpret its contents in order to bring about serious change. The editorial claims that one can find an active intellectual movement in Morocco and Egypt that challenges common accepted interpretations of history and culture and is the source of the slightly improved fortunes in the status of women in these societies.[77]

This general orientation of the newspaper is illustrated by an editorial entitled "Silence and Pattern",[78] which criticizes what the author perceives as a common pattern of thinking and conduct in Arabic culture:

> A very influential and interrelated duality has hindered the outcomes of the demand for equal rights for women in history in general and Arabic history in particular. This duality is the "silence" and the "pattern" which have a cause-and-effect relationship between them. Silence results from Arab culture's stagnant stereotyped picture that views women through the concept of shame.[79] Sound is language and language is where culture is usually stored. Therefore, the patterns of stereotyped thinking excluded women from all cultural linguistic fields and considered the silence of woman as the most sublime and beautiful of her characteris-

tics, whereas the chatting of men is considered popular culture . . . In the shadow of silence the pattern grows stronger, therefore the first step toward breaking this pattern is to raise the voice of women high . . . and there is no way to break this pattern but by breaking the barrier of silence . . . There is no "culture of silence" but there is a culture that has led to silence, for culture is articulation, view and awareness. Until a new culture surfaces, there is no way other than having an elite that is able to raise the voice to smash the pattern and create a new era.

Such strong, critical language repeats itself throughout most of the editorials. It passes judgment on a hegemonic culture that deprives women of being an active part of society and subjects them to rigid control by men. The act of silencing referred to in the above citation encompasses both mental and physical dimensions. Accordingly, women are confined to the private sphere, where there is no recognition of their contribution to the welfare of society. The focus on language as the site where culture is stored reflects the editorial's intention to educate the public as to the influence of language. Furthermore, it transforms language into a tool used by women to fight the hegemonic patriarchal culture, which utilizes language for its own purposes.

The second common theme evident in the editorials' discourse is the state's responsibility toward its citizens and the gaps between the expectations of the women's movement and the reality of Palestinian civil society. To this end the editorials utilize the concept of citizenship, understood in this context not only as a collection of rights and duties to which every Palestinian is entitled and obligated, but also as a right to equal participation in shaping the community in which one lives.[80] This reflects the critique of the classical liberal view of citizenship, what has been termed "ruling class strategy".[81] The full participation of women in shaping the future of their community becomes a central demand when the issue of Palestinian citizenship is discussed. Thus, the editorial of Issue 91 asks:

Is citizenship and its related rights going to be treated from the standpoint of full equality for all citizens, men and women? Are the roles that both sides implement in the public and private spheres going to be considered? Is the special case of women, and in particular their contribution on both levels, especially regarding social reproduction, going to be considered?[82]

Not waiting for an answer, the editorial proceeds:

For the sake of a just and equal concept of equality, the one-sided patriarchal criteria should not be adopted. One of the common criteria of
full citizenship is the issue of rights, which include social security and
health insurance and the labor market. It is clear that almost 90 percent
of Palestinian women are not connected to the official labor market, and
therefore the duty of paying taxes does not include them. Any connection between citizenship and the labor market eliminates the women's
claim for basic rights . . . a progressive conception of citizenship focuses
on the individual, man or woman, and looks at them and not on the
family, tribe or other collectives, which limit the freedom of the individual to practice his/her basic rights as the foundation of society.[83]

This formulation of the debate over the concept of citizenship
demonstrates the editorial's liberal views, taking a firm, individualistic stance against attempts by religious and nationalist
organizations to influence citizenship legislation. Citing two drafts
of the Palestinian Basic Law introduced in 1995 and 1997, which
failed to meet the women's movement's expectations, the editorial
rejects communitarian positions, claiming that such legislation
would harm the autonomy of the individual and his/her freedom.[84]
Furthermore, the editorial criticizes the patriarchal discourse of the
proposals, which transforms women into hostages in the hands of
their men, unable to grant citizenship to their children or to non-
Palestinian husbands. The debate surrounding citizenship
demonstrates the editorial's attempts to inform its readers of the
implications of a citizenship law that does not respect individual
rights. The editorial portrays a clear relationship between citizenship, democracy, and development, linking these subjects together
in order to attract the support of a broader spectrum of readers. In
parallel it establishes a connection between tribalism, patriarchal-
ism, citizenship, and underdevelopment drawing the state into this
formula not only in terms of its analysis, but also in terms of the discourse used in this context: the legal discourse used highlights how
issues related to women should not be limited to social matters, such
as poverty, children, education, and development; state law determines citizenship, and women should be partners in determining the
discourse of the law that will shape their lives. Any attempt to build
upon the traditional cultural values in order to construct a citizenship law means directly contributing to a secondary role for women,
who make up half of Palestinian society: this translates into economic submission and poverty. Accordingly, the formulations of the

law constitute social practice and women ought to be part of shaping the law and determining its interpretation.

This line of thought was the focus of an earlier editorial that appeared in Issue 89 in January 2000, where the newspaper brings to the fore another central normative position which draws a connection between development and formal institutionalization, and the creation of modern state organs capable of organizing a modern welfare system. The editorial argues that women in Palestinian society do not suffer only as a result of the salient traditional and patriarchal Arab culture, but also because of the lack of modern welfare institutions and the lack of rule of law – both related to the state.

According to the editorial, one of the main problems that Palestinian women face is:

> the lack of supporting official and unofficial welfare institutions that women could turn to when in need of some help in facing the changing social and economic reality in the age of globalization and information. Women do not need mercy and compassion, which are provided by charity organizations. These organizations go back to the feudal age and the hegemony of the tribe and the clan, which are not satisfactory in the 21st century. In these times there are external factors that influence the economic and social policies of society, and the first to pay the price are women and children.[85]

The editorial concludes by using a mixture of linguistic styles – preaching, instructing, and warning – in order to emphasize what is to be done in order to overcome the lack of welfare support. The space of communicative maneuvering afforded to the women's movement that is illustrated in the above quotation, mirrors the wider social and cultural structures and relations, as well as the ongoing social processes that influence the status of women. Conversely, the three genres utilized in the editorial above reflect the hegemony of the traditional nationalist discourse and the subordinate status of the liberal – democratic worldview. A simple reading of the editorial may create the impression that the various writing styles employed reflect a wide and free communicative proviso. However, closer analysis reveals an obscured connection between linguistic styles and power relations, exemplifying not only the weak status of women, but also the patterns in which identities are constructed and reconstructed by hegemonic discourses. This complex relationship is reiterated in the editorial:

The development of women and achieving their rights could not succeed without building executive and legislative state institutions and organizations of civil society that seek to empower society in all its segments and classes where all of them actively participate in planning and implementing policies. The sought development should be social and not only economic which should be supported by transparent legislation that ensures the welfare of society.[86]

Civil–social development will help reduce one of the most dangerous social phenomena most addressed by *Women's Voice*: violence against women. The beating of women by their spouses, murder of women, and other forms of both physical and psychological violence constitute another central theme found in most of the editorials. Violence is a widespread phenomenon in Palestinian society.[87] The women's movement considers violence to be one of the most dangerous ills Palestinians face. From the perspective of the *Women's Voice* editorials, the sources of violence can be traced to the interrelation between traditional social norms, archaic patriarchal values, and economic exploitation. Whereas the first two sources manifest themselves primarily in the private sphere, economic causes are evident in the public sphere.

The newspaper has dedicated several editorials to the killing of women. In many cases, women were accused of having disgraced the "family honor" and were thus murdered by their own relatives. Violence has increased since the beginning of the *Intifada*, as a result of which mental pressure and social strife has grown and has thus made women an easy target. In most cases battered women are economically dependent and therefore have no power to establish an interdependent relationship with their male partners. Dependent women have no power to negotiate better conditions within the family.

The editorials critically address these phenomena and identify those whom the newspaper holds responsible for the situation. In the editorial of Issue 102 (July 13, 2000), the editor calls on all public institutions to participate in stopping the wave of killings in Palestinian society in which women pay the heaviest price. Here, the discourse places blame on that which it is both challenging to change and asking for help: the law.

The murderous crimes that recently shook our society ring the bell of danger and urge us to move and reactivate the role of the judicial and educational institutions to rectify the social and security chaos . . . There is no doubt that women are the ones who pay the heaviest price because they are the weak side as "popular" culture describes them . . . the violent cases expose the rapid accumulation of the "culture of violence" in our society . . . In order to avoid a situation in which crime becomes habitual in our society there is no alternative but to revitalize the law and separate the judicial and security institutions from narrow social interests and quarrels in order to ensure that their decisions are objective and in the spirit of the law.[88]

The discursive pattern used in this passage exposes the chaos in all the PA institutions, especially the judicial and security apparatuses, and reflects the lack of law and order based on universal humanitarian and liberal criteria. The editorial therefore holds the PA and its institutions ultimately responsible for the killing of women, and makes clear that the police and the court system are also to blame for not dealing more effectively with the rising wave of killings in Palestinian society. It also hints at the relationship between the killing of women and the dominant juridical culture, which does not mete out justice in such cases. In addition to the critical tone, the editorial exposes the dominant political culture in the PA – a political culture fed by chauvinist and patriarchal conceptions. However, the editorial does express some sympathy for these two systems, the juridical and the security, acknowledging that, generally speaking, the crime rate has increased since the creation of the PA, implying that these two systems are also victims of a broader and larger circumstance.

The editorial blames hegemonic Arab culture and the dominant social structure, making clear that it does not accept the clemency the two systems display toward criminals when their victims are women. In many rape cases the perpetrators are not even charged either because the victim's family does not want to go to court, fearing public degradation, or because of tribal interventions in which customary law is applied instead. In the latter case, the incident is usually resolved with the male assailant marrying the raped woman.[89] In either outcome, the woman is not only physically raped but also mentally and spiritually suppressed. Violence within the family is usually considered to be a private affair, and in many cases women prefer to remain silent rather than face the physical and mental torture that accompanies revealing their story.[90]

This editorial policy characterizes editorials that address violations committed against women in the labor market. Such a case is mentioned in the editorial of Issue 84 (November 7, 1999), when 14 young women were burned to death in a small factory in Hebron.[91] According to the police investigation and newspaper reports, the factory operated without a license and employed too many women in one small room with no emergency exits or water supply in case of fire. The editorial, however, does not hold the owner of the firm as the only one responsible for the tragic deaths of the women, calling upon the chamber of commerce, building contractors' union, municipalities, trade unions, and PA institutions to take rightful responsibility for the tragedy, and using a very clear and directive discourse, preaching to the PA on how to behave in order to ensure that such an incident does not recur.

The *Women's Voice* critique of Palestinian society is comprehensive and confrontational in character. It addresses the hegemonic traditional Arab culture, the patriarchal social structure, and the political culture in Palestinian society and the PA. The critique extends to other women's organizations, charitable groups, and hypocritical popular leaders. The newspaper does not limit itself to general social, cultural, and economic issues but has always succeeded in pointing out the specific "addresses" in society to be held accountable for certain misdoings or accidents. The editorial's language uses various discursive patterns in different contexts in order to most accurately express the ideas of the editorial board.

The editorials reveal that there are no rigid boundaries between the discourses used. They overlap and interchange in an attempt to express clear and firm messages. The order of discourse reflected in the editorials mirrors the newspaper's integrative worldview that strives to demonstrate the manner in which different problems that women face are interrelated. According to the newspaper, these problems should be treated as an interconnected whole and addressed by a comprehensive strategy for development. On the other hand, the newspaper's normative discourse means that *Women's Voice* clashes with the dominant social culture accepted by most Palestinians – even by those who are neither conservative nor religious. This order of discourse transforms the newspaper's worldview into an alternative almost completely detached from Palestinian social norms, the consequence of which is to lessen its effectiveness.

The PA Response and the Islamic Imperative

The women's campaign to gain equal citizenship rights generated debates across all levels of Palestinian society. PA officials, as well as opposition groups, were drawn into the debate regarding the status of women in Palestinian society. The Model Parliament became a central public arena in which debate and discussion of critical, social, and political issues took place. The positions adopted by the various political parties toward the MP mirrored the matrix of power in Palestinian society; the PA and its hegemonic party, Fatah, were compelled to adopt firm positions in regard to women's affairs while the Islamic movement was mobilized to assert its influence against the liberal demands of the women's organizations.

The PA's efforts to consolidate its power in the areas under its control led to the formation of new coalitions in Palestinian society. The PA and its Fatah party continued to encourage the nationalist discourse in order to mobilize the Palestinian population for support. Similarly, the PA's transitory nature prevented the PA from adopting policies that could destabilize society. These circumstances conditioned the PA's cautious treatment of the women's movement. Whereas the women's movement represented the pressures exerted on the PA to democratize, the latter was threatened by the rising power of the Islamic movement from both Hamas and Islamic Jihad. Therefore, while the PA endorsed the women's movement so long as this policy helped to contain Hamas, at the same time it frustrated the women's movement's demands in order not to alienate conservative religious sentiments and thereby strengthen the Islamic opposition.[92] Challenged by both internal and external pressures, the PA maintained a cautious position toward the women's movement, while the latter exploited any space *vis-à-vis* the PA in order to lobby for women's rights.

The PA leadership was aware that a majority of the Palestinian public defines itself as conservative. In a public opinion poll conducted by the Jerusalem Media and Communication Center (JMCC) in March 1999, 79.8 percent of the Palestinians surveyed favored a state run according to Islamic law, while only 15.8 percent favored a secular state.[93] According to the same poll, 71 percent of Palestinians favored a national coalition government consisting of all the political and religious parties, including the opposition.

Furthermore, 63.9 percent of Palestinians said they would support the PA more if it implemented Islamic law in Palestinian society. Consequently, any explicit support of the women's movement's demands by the Palestinian Authority, especially regarding issues considered to pose a threat to the Islamic law, would have reflected negatively on the PA and played into the hands of the Islamic opposition. Therefore, the PA adopted an ambivalent stance toward the women's demands.

Conversely, the Islamic movement utilized this conservatism in order to propagate its own programs. In the past, the powerful religious movement had proven its ability to impose Muslim norms on the Palestinian public, as it did during the *Intifada*, when women were required to cover their heads. These efforts included the use of threats and violence and developed into a widespread attack on women. The acquiescence conveyed by Palestinian society's silence, the absence of a firm reaction by the national political parties, and pressure from within the family structure combined to create a situation whereby most women complied with the social demands of Islamic organizations. Hamas used the battle surrounding the head covering for women to redefine gender rules and establish a new political reality on the ground.[94] Understanding the damage to its support base, the PA could not afford to remain silent on the issue. This was especially true because much of the population was becoming dissatisfied with the peace process and upset about reports of rising corruption within PA institutions.[95] In this context, many Palestinians would have felt even more alienated from the PA if it chose to adopt a liberal position in regard to the women's demands, which would have shifted the population's support more in favor of the Islamic organizations.

In fact, the Islamic movement was seeking a showdown with the PA regarding who would determine the prevalent moral order in Palestinian society. After being brutally confronted by PA policies on the political and military levels, the Islamic movement sought out a convenient battleground where it could defeat the PA, and the fields of education and acculturation provided a convenient arena for that very purpose.[96] Consider the Islamic movement's brutal response in opposition to the Model Parliament and those groups which it represented. The wide media coverage of the parliament caught the attention of various religious political figures and made them aware of the serious impact that such a public gathering could have on public opinion. As a result, a dispute erupted between the parliament's participants and influential Islamic public figures. The dispute was based upon the "controversial" nature of the comprehensive legal reform that the parliament initiated, especially in regard to the Personal Status Law.

The liberal atmosphere that was prevalent at the MP prompted many influential religious figures to take action. Sheikh Hamid Bitawi, the head of the West Bank appeals court, issued a sharp denial of the parliament's right to address social issues that have religious implications. A Hamas-affiliated religious figure, Bassam Jarrar, criticized the women's initiative even more harshly, attacking the proposals made by various women's organizations, describing them as "frightening and beyond the imagination of any Palestinian Arab Muslim".[97] He warned the public that the discussions taking place in the parliament had reached a level such that "they might become the law that obliges society, every family and every individual".[98] In his view the proposals presented at the MP regarding the amendment of the Personal Status Law were based upon ignorant ideas and did not reflect a campaign for women's rights, but rather a clash of civilizations. Jarrar published a pamphlet in the daily newspaper *Al-Quds* raising questions in regard to the participation in the Model Parliament of the GUPW, which is controlled by the PA. His attack on the GUPW implied the involvement of the Palestinian Authority in the questionable MP discussions; his goal was to criticize the PA's "hypocritical" posture. Criticism was also raised at a conference held at the Islamic University in Gaza.[99]

Despite the fact that some of the speakers at the conference articulated critical views in regard to the lack of a unified Palestinian Personal Status Law in the areas under PA control, critics still attacked the MP for even raising such an issue. The parliament was accused of trying to deviate from Islamic law and to serve Western interests, with female participants singled out and accused of heresy, and of being servants of Western imperialism against Islam.[100] The new women's centers that were behind the MP were charged with sabotaging the "good Palestinian culture and tradition".[101] An Islamic youth organization distributed a pamphlet in the Al-Aqsa mosque in Jerusalem on the fourth day of Al-Adha – the most important holiday in Islamic culture because it marks the end of the Ramadan fast – which fell close to the dates when the MP was convened. The pamphlet accused women of intervening in religious affairs, such as the Family Law, while MP participants were accused of "degrading Islam" and serving the interests of foreign donor countries. The Islamists' campaign against the MP included a petition signed by religious figures that was sent to the PLC president asking him to ignore the MP participants' proposals regarding the Family Law.

The PA did not take a firm position in regard to the MP, nor toward the Islamic movement's vicious campaign against it. The PA's ambivalent position also characterized that taken by Fatah, which also chose not to adopt a definitive stand in support of the MP against the attacks of Islamic leaders.[102] The few Fatah members who conveyed their support for the MP did so on a personal basis, careful not to portray it as an official position of the party. The Fatah party's secretary in Gaza firmly asserted that "in any walk of life where Quranic judgment was available, modern legislation should not be introduced".[103] The Fatah mouthpiece *Al-Awda* warned the women's movement not to "overdo its demands as the society it worked in was Palestinian and not Swedish, Swiss, or French".[104] Furthermore, a few weeks after the conclusion of the MP project, Arafat formed a committee of four male religious leaders and one female, representing the Hamas-affiliated Islamic Salvation Party, in order to draft an amendment to the Family Law.[105] Despite the fact that the committee has not reached any serious conclusions, its composition is a reflection of Arafat's obligation to accommodate the Islamic movement.

Notwithstanding the different discourses used by the Islamic movement and the PA toward the MP, both explicated an extremely gender-biased interpretation of Islamic principles while seeking to maintain the dominant moral order. Despite the enmity between them, both utilize and manipulate the *shari'a* to impose their worldview upon Palestinian society and win the public's support. The latest version of the Palestinian Basic Law includes provisions added by the PLC's Legal Committee, affirming that "Islam is the official religion of Palestine with respect accorded to the sanctity of all other religions." In addition, the Islamic *shari'a* is considered "a principle source of legislation". Such formulations clash with the status of equal citizenship in public life and become problematic when we consider the language used in the Basic Law to formulate gender equity. The last version of the law did not include the formulation regarding gender equity that had been recommended to the PLC by the women's and legal organizations, who suggested inserting the explicit statement "women and men shall have equal fundamental rights and freedoms without any discrimination." The PLC's final formulation merely states instead that "All Palestinians are equal before the law and the judiciary, without any discrimination between them in respect to rights and obligations, because of race, ethnicity, sex, religion, political opinion or disability." This expression is less than satisfactory to the women's groups for it does not speak specifically about women's rights.[106]

The PA's ambivalent position toward women's rights did not result solely from its attempts to quell Hamas. The PA's structure is conservative, irrespective of the competition with Hamas.[107] The absence of the Islamic movement would *not* have led the PA to adopt a liberal policy toward women's rights. Since the male is the dominant position in the Palestinian family, the system of political patronage in PA institutions resembles that found in the traditional social structure. The institutionalization process in the PA led to a new form of patriarchy where PA institutions have become extensions of the prevailing family structure. This gender regime endorses the primacy of the Palestinian man, and is sustained through law and custom, beginning with replication of the existing gender structure in all other structures. The supremacy of men is reinforced by a patriarchal ideology that finds expression in the mass media, religious, and educational institutions, and in the political organizations.[108] The result of the pairing the two different conceptions – the role of the family and the goals of the national movement – has been to confine the Palestinian woman within the private sphere and marginalize her role in the public sphere.[109]

The socio-political structure of the PA made any potential impact of the women's movement on legislation hard to achieve. The neo-patriarchal social structure also made it hard for women to penetrate public opinion through media output. Notwithstanding these difficulties, the women's struggle for equal rights has become a central theme in Palestinian politics over the last decade.

5

Framing Authenticity

RELIGIOUS DISCOURSE AND THE ISLAMIST MEDIA

In recent years religion has become a driving factor in Palestinian nationalism. Since the end of the 1980s we have witnessed religious movements claiming en masse the right to represent the Palestinian people and attempting to mobilize its energies for the struggle to achieve liberation from Israeli occupation. To achieve this goal, following the establishment of the PA, Hamas and Islamic Jihad – the two largest religious groups – began challenging national movements, centering their political claims on religious discourse.[1] The two movements also introduced new strategies for militant struggle against Israeli occupation, namely suicide bombings. Both movements became the main opposition to the dominant national establishment led by the Fatah movement. The challenge to Fatah has come in several guises. Hamas has never accepted the hegemony of Fatah in Palestinian society, and confronts it across the entire social territory. It presents itself as an alternative movement to the PLO and challenges its worldview; it is now the second largest political movement in the occupied territories.

The PLO's role in the Madrid Peace Conference in October 1991, and later in the Oslo Accords, prompted Hamas to openly challenge the PLO and, subsequently, the PA.[2] Hamas and Islamic Jihad both developed their own ideologies based on Islamic tradition, each claiming to represent the authentic interests of the Palestinians. Both movements claim that the Palestine problem is not solely a national one, but is mainly a religious problem. In accordance with Muslim tradition, the two movements have asserted that the land of Palestine is holy and therefore no part of it can be relinquished to anyone. Therefore, the PLO's decision to enter into negotiations with Israel and sign a peace accord with it violates religious belief and recognizes Israel's legitimate right to exist.[3] In the view of the Islamic movements, the peace process undermines the Palestinians' rights to the land of Palestine. Therefore, the two movements have called into question the PA's legitimacy and sought to establish their ideology as a viable alternative to the PA.

Notwithstanding its opposition efforts, Hamas has sought to influence Palestinian politics from without, as opposed to within, the official political system, and has taken care to distance itself from the legitimation of the peace negotiations between Israel and the PA. Like other social movements, Hamas sought to utilize for its own ends the plethora of opportunities created with the establishment of the PA. The movement sought to become a dominant part of the emerging Palestinian public sphere by introducing an alternative political and cultural discourse to that of the PA. It sought to frame public opinion and set its agenda in a way that would delegitimate the PA. One of the tools utilized for that purpose has been the media.

This chapter will explore the framing policies Hamas uses by examining its order of discourse as reflected in the movement's newspaper, *Al-Risalah* ("The Message"), which began publishing from Gaza in January 1997. The history and organizational structure of Hamas have been extensively documented in many other books; the objective here is to reinforce the understanding of the pluralist structure of the Palestinian public sphere that emerged with the establishment of the PA in 1994. The discourse of Hamas is ideologically, politically, and functionally designed to undermine the foundations of the PA and its media regime; its newspaper and its editorial framing mirror the fundamental challenge the movement poses to the PA on the one hand, and the efforts made by the movement to bypass the media regime of the PA in order to portray its political agenda, on the other.

The Political Positioning of Islamic Movements

Hamas is a political organization with deep social roots and a broad organizational infrastructure. The involvement of Hamas in the activities of the first *Intifada* and its military actions against the Israeli army and inside Israel legitimated it as a national movement.

The weakening position of the national leftist factions turned Hamas into the central opposition movement and the only viable alternative to Fatah. Public support for Hamas in the occupied territories has been steady, with opinion polls showing that the movement has the support of 12–15 percent of the Palestinian public.[4]

Hamas has utilized all political and discursive means in order to convince the Palestinian public that negotiations will not solve the Palestinian problem. Hamas leaders attacked the defects of the PA and of its policies as the result of the peace talks between the national elite and Israel. When the Oslo Accords were made public, Hamas sought to mobilize Palestinians against it. It utilized political means only, considering armed confrontation with the PA a "red line" that should not be crossed. Despite its hostile rhetoric toward the PA, the Hamas leadership expressed a warm welcome to the returning police forces of the PA and even demonstrated a willingness to contribute to the reconstruction process under the auspices of the PA, without committing themselves to the Oslo Accords.[5] These tactics toward the PLO/PA were expressed by one of the movement's prominent leaders, Mahmud Zahhar: "We know that the PLO's practice will inevitably lead to its downfall. There is no need therefore to bring this about through confrontation. It is enough to wait."[6]

The declared policy of Hamas toward the PA has been based on dialogue and "calculated participation".[7] Besides proving its ability to seize diplomatic opportunities and manipulate them for its interests, Hamas has propagated and practiced a violent, military strategy against Israel, insisting on its policy of "retaliation" in order to fight the Israeli occupation. As a result, it positioned itself in direct opposition to the PA as the authority that has a monopoly over the means of violence in Palestinian society. Ziad Abu Amr summed up the emerging relationship between Hamas and the PA thus:

> At the heart of relations between the PNA and the opposition lies essential contradiction: The authority is bound by the DoP [Declaration of Principles] to provide security and not to endanger the Israeli presence, while the opposition insists on its legitimate right to combat the remaining forms of occupation and resist the continued existence of Israeli settlements.[8]

This contradictory relationship between the two major political players on the Palestinian scene mirrored the impasse between them.

The PA now found itself in a dilemma. It could not afford to overlook the armed resistance against Israel favored by Hamas, especially its growing aggression against Israeli civilians. Nor did the PA want to enter into direct confrontation with Hamas – something that could drift into a civil war and lead to the delegitimation of the PA among the Palestinian public. The PA was not in a position to make any progress in the peace negotiations that would convince Palestinians the diplomatic option was going to bear fruit.[9] The deterioration in relations between the PA and Israel was fully seized upon by Hamas for its political interests.

Hamas found itself in a similar dilemma, however. It could either pursue its military activities, risking a clash with the PA and possible civil war, or it could freeze such activities, which would undermine its credibility in pursuing a resistance-based alternative to the peace talks. Hamas rejected peace negotiations as an acceptable strategy, warning against offering concessions to Israel as long as the occupation continued. Therefore, the strategy of resistance was the only viable option to justify its claim for representing the generic interests of the Palestinian people. Halting resistance or accepting a compromise on this issue would have turned Hamas into a pragmatic organization similar to Fatah and the PA – an image that Hamas leaders were already criticizing and delegitimating. The Hamas leadership framed the conflict with Israel in religious terms. Accepting a compromise on matters of principle would not have corresponded with the movements declared ideological–religious platform.[10]

In attempting to skip over their dilemmas and resolve differences, the two parties sought dialogue and negotiations.[11] On several occasions the leaders of both parties met in order to iron out various differences.[12] The last round of meetings took place in Cairo under the auspices of the Egyptian President, Husni Mubarak, between November 2002 and February 2003.[13] These negotiations were suspected by Hamas as an attempt to co-opt the opposition and undermine its capability to harm the political course followed by the dominant national elite.[14] Hamas refused to accept the peace negotiations with Israel as a legitimate reason to stop its resistance of Israeli occupation policies in areas that are not under Palestinian control.

The structural reality of the West Bank and Gaza Strip, especially the continuation of Israeli occupation of most of the Palestinian territories and the expansion of Jewish settlements, intensified the contradictions between Hamas and the PA. Israeli security and economic policies led to a growing frustration among increasing numbers of the Palestinian public. Israel's policies unwittingly supplied Hamas with the political legitimacy to continue its military resistance and suicide bombings in Israeli cities. The support Hamas enjoyed in the Palestinian public was heavily based on its resistance strategy. Nevertheless, Hamas sought to legitimate its strategy and to propagate its worldview among the Palestinian public, using all means available to justify its policies against Israel and its critical position toward PA policies.

Defining the New Communicative Space of Hamas

The two main communication methods utilized by Hamas in order to promote themselves to the Palestinian public prior to the establishment of the PA, were through secretly distributing leaflets and via preaching in the mosques.[15] These traditional communication institutions were safe under occupation and did not expose the movement to the Israeli army. Since then, Hamas has grown as a social movement, and has developed an extensive organizational network that operates on virtually every level of Palestinian society, through which it provides a variety of much-needed social, economic, and medical services to the wider Palestinian public. This network has enabled Hamas to maintain daily contact with a large number of people who became accustomed to the services provided to them.[16] Indeed, Hamas has been able to expand its services to virtually all strata of Palestinian society,[17] with its social network becoming the central communication mechanism. Charity services, deemed legitimate for religious reasons, were also manipulated for political purposes.

Hamas sought to communicate its worldview through the new means that became available with the establishment of the PA. The weekly *Al-Watan*, which expressed an Islamic worldview close to Hamas, was formally established on April 28, 1995. The newspaper was comprehensive in its journalistic orientation and addressed various social, economic, and religious issues, but its main focus was political. It described the peace process in highly critical tones, and depicted Israel in a negative manner. Nor did the newspaper refrain from criticizing the PA and its policies in regard to the peace process. *Al-Watan* presented the peace process as a defeatist strategy and criticized the PA's "conformist" position. In the newspaper's view, the peace process served Israeli interests, with the PA reduced to an administrative arm of the Israeli government designed to clamp down on the Palestinian people. Most of the political articles and editorials that appeared in *Al-Watan* addressed the negative consequences of the Oslo Accords and the Interim Agreement. The newspaper's editorial line presented the worldview of Hamas as an alternative to the PA ethos. Most political articles and views were aimed at convincing the reader that the PA's peace strategy simply does not work.

The paper's direct (and indirect) criticism of the PA was not limited to foreign policy. On the contrary, a large amount of space in the weekly's political and social affairs sections addressed internal PA affairs such as health, social policy, security, and human rights. Journalists for *Al-Watan* reported different events and measures taken by PA officials that were intended to reflect the PA's authoritarian character. In many cases the discourse used was indirect and sarcastic, with names and the inappropriate behaviors of PA officials hidden under various metaphors in order to avoid direct clashes with them.

In May 1995 – barely a month after *Al-Watan* began publishing – the PA ordered the newspaper closed for a period of two-and-a-half months. While no straightforward reason was provided to the editors, the General Secretary to the PA President declared that it was due to the publishing of a report claiming that the name of Arafat's daughter, "Zahwa", was to appear in a commercial advertisement.[18] After negotiation, the newspaper was reopened, but only for a short period of time. On August 5, 1995 the *Al-Watan* editor found a police order on the door of the paper's offices closing the newspaper until further notice. Again no clear reason was given, but informed sources told the editor that the closure was in response to an article published that personally criticized Yasser Arafat. Negotiations between the PA and the editor led to its reopening, albeit for another short period of time.

The newspaper was completely closed on December 25 of the same year, having appeared for a period of only eight months, with two closures occurring during that period. The experience of *Al-Watan* served as a good lesson for many journalists and editors in

Gaza and the West Bank. With the PA still in its inaugural year, the lack of a decisive institutional and legal order troubled the PA leadership and led to many human rights violations, especially in the field of freedom of expression.

Despite its short lifespan, the newspaper succeeded in making its mark and created a legacy which was continued with the new Hamas-affiliated weekly *Al-Risalah*, which was first issued on January 1, 1997. The reason for the two-year hiatus was twofold. First, 1996 was marked by extreme tension between Hamas and the PA. Some 59 Israeli civilians were killed in several terrorist attacks carried out by Hamas activists on Israeli civilian buses in Jerusalem and Tel Aviv. The tension between the PA and Hamas caused by the attacks calmed down only after negotiations were held between them in Khartoum and Cairo. Second, the Islamic Salvation Party (Khalas), which is affiliated with Hamas but has adopted a more pragmatic, conciliatory position *vis-à-vis* the PA, was behind the new newspaper. Khalas, which was established as a political party in the run-up to the Palestinian elections in February 1996, stated in its platform that *Al-Risalah* "speaks in the name of the party and represents its worldview opposing the political and social policy of the PA".[19] Despite the organizational difference, Khalas is an integral part of Hamas and has never managed to establish itself as a separate political player.

The editor of *Al-Risalah*, Dr Ghazi Hamad, had previously served as editor of *Al-Watan*. As a result, one finds little substantial difference between content and style of the two publications. Nevertheless, *Al-Risalah* does seem to be more cautious and less provocative in its formulations. It is a comprehensive Palestinian, as well as Islamic, weekly. While mainly concerned with Palestinian politics from an Islamic standpoint, the weekly also deals with other issues, such as economics and sports. *Al-Risalah*'s main stylistic orientation is analytical: topics of concern are examined in-depth, and allotted the space needed for such coverage. The newspaper heavily investigates almost every topic it addresses, covering at length topics like the negotiations with Israel, the peace process in general, services provided to the public by the PA, developments on the internal Palestinian political stage, and relevant interviews. While most of the newspaper's articles have an obvious Islamic leaning, they are not overloaded with religious preaching. The Islamic worldview that generally characterizes the publication does not always make it clear that *Al-Risalah* is affiliated specifically with Hamas or even Khalas.

The newspaper utilizes a political discourse that is based on secular concepts such as human rights, political pluralism, freedom of speech, social justice, and the transfer of rule via elections. This discourse is a means to facilitate the creation of a space for the party within the new Palestinian political reality,[20] and reflects the language of the younger generation of Hamas leaders, who recognize the need for a pragmatic political strategy in order to protect the movement's achievements.[21] The newspaper brings this discourse to the fore as a constitutive tool that attempts to present the party's emerging new identity as well as to facilitate setting the Palestinian public agenda according to a new framing strategy.

Since its creation, *Al-Risalah* has been closed, and its editor detained, on several occasions. The first closure was on September 8, 1997 after it had published an article written by Al-Najah National University Professor Abdel-Sattar Qasim, who criticized Egyptian financial support of the PA, which he claimed was used to promote the image of Mubarak among Palestinians.[22] The newspaper was closed "until further notice" – an expression commonly used by the Palestinian police authorities. The editor of the newspaper appealed to the High Court, but long before the court issued its decision (May 15, 1998) the newspaper was reopened on December 4, 1997 after high-ranking politicians intervened and facilitated a compromise between the editor of the newspaper and the police authorities.

On March 2, 1999 Dr Hamad was detained along with all of the members of the Khalas Party's political bureau for allegedly inciting public disorder in the Gaza Strip city of Rafah following the State Security Court conviction of three people for killing a police officer in the city.[23] Hamad, who in addition to being *Al-Risalah*'s editor is also a member of the political bureau and the party speaker, was warned not to reproduce in the newspaper a leaflet that Khalas had distributed, condemning the brutal behavior of the police force and the PA for enacting the will of Israel. Although the other party leaders were released after a short interrogation, Hamad was imprisoned for five days and accused of direct involvement in inciting violence in Rafah.

On April 27, 1999 Hamad was again summoned to police headquarters and informed that the newspaper would be closed until further notice. Again, no specific reason was given, and the police officer who issued the order claimed that he did not know the reason.[24] However, on this occasion *Al-Risalah* escaped closure thanks to the intervention of the head of the President's office, Tayeb Abdel-Rahim. Less than one month later, on May 22, three of the newspaper's senior editors were detained and accused of publishing inciting material against the PA. On this occasion the detainees included the weekly's chief editor, Salah Bardawil. According to *Al-Risalah* itself, the article that was published in May 1999 led to the detention of the editors because it dealt with administrative corruption in the PA security forces.[25] According to the newspaper, "With these policies the PA seeks to impose clear boundaries and borders as well as red lines that will make the Palestinian journalist subject to self-censorship which will prevent the need for a real one."[26] It should also be added that, aside from the closing of the newspaper, journalists employed by *Al-Risalah* were subject to detention and harassment by PA security forces, a phenomenon which for reasons of space could not be fully covered in this context.[27]

Islamic Press: Identity and the Discourse of Authenticity

Al-Risalah learned very quickly to play according to the rules of the game set by the PA and to bypass the regulations set by it when necessary in order to express its views. The newspaper aimed at expressing the worldview of Hamas and therefore depicted a social reality in accordance with the movement's philosophy. The various media framing devices utilized by *Al-Risalah,* and its order of discourse, will now be discussed. This will be achieved through a closer look at its underlying normative, ideological, and value principles as they are portrayed through speech acts and forms, framing patterns, and different agenda-setting mechanisms. The analysis will focus on the editions issued in March, May, and September of 1999 and 2000. These three months of each year were selected because they include many Palestinian occasions of national importance, such as Land Day in March, and Al-Nakba in May.

A general observation that one gets from reviewing *Al-Risalah* over a long period of time is that it is less a party platform than an organ for a wide spectrum of Islamic believers facing their own unique problems and difficulties. In this sense *Al-Risalah* mirrors the growing emphasis placed by Hamas and Khalas on social issues within Palestinian society.[28] *Al-Risalah* addresses a wide variety of political, social, economic, and cultural problems, in a professional, journalistic fashion.

The peace process as a trap

While the PA's legitimacy as an entity is not directly questioned, despite the fact that the Islamist movement's official position is unsympathetic to the PA, which it views as a "baby" of the Oslo process, its foreign policies are criticized on several levels. The PA's peace policy is lambasted for not being effective, practical, or rational. The peaceful settlement of the Palestinian problem sought by the PA is depicted as a moral and political defeat for the Palestinians, who have recognized Israel's right to exist on Palestinian land without getting any tangible reward in return. As a result of developments on the ground, the newspaper focuses on the stagnation in the peace process and demonstrates how the Israeli government continues to build settlements in the territories, demolish Palestinian homes, and confiscate Palestinian land.

Several articles from *Al-Risalah* illustrate this point. One article dealt with the May 1999 Israeli elections, explaining how a central pillar in then Prime Minister Benjamin Netanyahu's election campaign against Ehud Barak was Netanyahu's support of the West Bank and Gaza Strip settlements and his government's decision to transfer $80 million to those areas.[29] Furthermore, in the same issue the newspaper reported on the reality on the ground five years after signing the Interim Agreement and provided readers with numerical evidence as to increases in the numbers of settlers, the number of trees uprooted by the Israeli army, the number of Palestinian homes demolished, the number of Palestinians killed, and the number of Palestinians detained in Israeli jails.[30] To support his position, the writer of the article quotes several national figures involved in the peace process. This form of documented article appears in every edition of the newspaper. By pinpointing the Israeli policies on the ground, the newspaper seeks to delegitimize the entire peace process and calls upon the PA to change its policy, for according to *Al-Risalah*, negotiations will neither lead to the establishment of the long-awaited Palestinian state nor improve the miserable reality in which most Palestinians live. This same line of thought is adopted by the editor one week later when he claims that "The waiting strategy and 'deep breath policy' adopted by the PA since it signed – fell into – the Oslo agreement was a good opportunity for the Zionist enemy to practice its ugly policy of confiscation, demolition, bulldozering and revoking identity cards . . . It is now clear that these policies intensified under the cover of the peace process."[31] In a similar fashion the September 2, 1999 issue provides extensive details of the Israeli government's settlement policies by focusing on several main examples, such as the construction of 1,600 housing units in the Abu Gnaim mountains in East Jerusalem, 1,300 units in a new settlement called Tel Zion near Ramallah, 500 units in Ma'aleh Adumim between Jerusalem and Jericho, and the expansion of the Gaza Strip settlement of Neve Dekalim located west of the Khan Yunis refugee camp.[32]

On May 6, 1999, two days after the transitional period was to end according to the Oslo Accords, the newspaper asked if the agreement was already dead or still valid. The newspaper also reported on the meetings of the PLO's Central Council, which was to decide how to proceed if the time limit allotted for the transitional period ended without significant progress in implementing the Interim Agreement or with the redeployment of the Israeli army. Building on the views of several lawyers and political scientists, *Al-Risalah* emphasized the deadlock that the peace talks had reached, leaving the Palestinians facing an uncertain future. In this manner, the Palestinians find themselves caught in the trap that Israel set for them and have no choice but to renegotiate, from a position of relative weakness, the conditions for a new transitional period. This assessment of future developments signifies the newspaper's critical line and is intended to demonstrate the inherent structural weakness of the Palestinian position in the negotiations.[33] The editorial of May 6, 1999, headlined "Awaiting . . . a State!!!", declares:

> When one of us speaks of principles and ideals the world is turned on its head and the speaker is usually told that we live in a world of politics. The essence of politics is to deal with that which is possible, far removed from principles and ideals. Those aware of the science of politics invest a great amount of energy to explain the Machiavellian and pragmatic mode of thinking and their importance to those studying politics. This makes the Palestinian man feel unpleasant when he speaks of principles

and rights or even about United Nations resolutions. So everything is subject to discussion and from this mode of thinking have emerged such modern expressions, as 'There aren't any holy days.'[34] Such a saying became one of the 'virtues' [sarcastically] after it was said by the Zionist leader Rabin and Netanyahu after him.

This editorial was written during a period of serious debate among Palestinians regarding how to proceed with the peace process with the transitional period set by the Oslo Accords already expired. A central question that arises in the mind of the reader approaching this editorial content is, How do you "await a state"? You await a bus, train or an airplane, or even a friend. But what is the meaning of awaiting a state? Is it to be given to you? Do you expect it? One would expect that such questions would prepare the reader for transparent answers regarding the issue of the state, but instead the editor chooses to set the background for the philosophical debate over this question.

The editorial's first paragraph exemplifies the sarcastic and satiric language used by the author in order to designate the borderlines between "we" – in this case the Islamist movement – and "they" – the Palestinian leadership. The latter group understands politics and speaks the language of pragmatism, whereas the former is accused of not being acquainted with the science of politics because it speaks the language of "principles" and "ideals". The contrast between these two modes of thinking and their related conduct, which is presented later in the editorial, constitutes two different identities and worldviews. The pragmatics claim to possess the knowledge needed to determine the future of the Palestinians and ridicule those who speak in the name of principles and ideals. But in the next paragraph, the editor turns this picture upside down:

> But it seems that this approach is subject to change and modification by the Palestinian leadership which retreated from the idea that there are no principles and reached an understanding according to which the only principle in the world is the United States. The most satisfying and convincing thing would be that the [American] leadership pays attention to the Palestinian question, giving it a look, a smile, or a written or verbal guarantee. From here on the Palestinian state became a hostage of the American will . . . If she gives [us] even a hint then maybe the Palestinian dream will become real, and if not then we should put our hands on our cheeks and await her just as Samuel Beckett awaited Godot . . . It is worth

asking if it is possible that the state could be given as a gift wrapped in an envelope from the White House or from the Israeli Knesset . . . Is it possible that the enemy be the juridical guarantor for a Palestinian state?

The editorial not only inverts the traditional concept of those who know politics and those who do not, but also transforms the image of the fool by demonstrating the extent of the Palestinian leadership's naïveté. Here, it is argued, the Palestinian leadership should be scorned: it does not understand that politics does not operate based on submitting your will to the charity of others or by seeking to persuade them. Using the image of Samuel Beckett's waiting conveys several significant messages. First, it reflects the editor's wide knowledge of Western, especially English, literary sources, which is an indicator of his education. Second, it portrays the editor as someone who does not only speak in the language of religion and force, but can communicate with the American and Israeli mind in its own language because he knows their culture. Third, he challenges the Palestinian leaders who he assumes do not even know who Samuel Beckett is. Fourth, by using the metaphor of Beckett, the editor portrays not only the Palestinian leadership's tragic character, but also its obscure nature, an obscurity that characterizes the leadership's handling of international affairs, and in local matters – evident in the treatment of its own people and the distrust it has shown toward them. Intermingled in the metaphor of Becket is Thomas Hardy's novel, *Jude the Obscure*. One of the most famous sentences of the novel was perhaps in the mind of the editor, when Jude is described thus: "You are Joseph the dreamer of dreams, dear Jude, and a tragic Don Quixote. And sometimes you are St. Stephen, who while they were stoning him, could see Heaven opened. O my poor friend and comrade, you'll suffer yet." This may be how the editor sees the Palestinian leadership, complete with its tragic and unrealistic behavior.

The editor then moves to address the alternative stance, as represented by the Hamas. Here he shifts from sarcasm to a more authoritative tone, using declarative sentences indicative of assured self-knowledge and experience:

We need to embark upon the battle of establishing our state on our land. This battle could be long and cruel and demands strong people – physically and mentally – in order to achieve victory, meaning to free man from cruelty, submission and discrimination. This is the first condition

> to liberating the land, for the nation that lifts up its men has the right to
> exist whereas the nation that kills its men has no right to live.
>
> This battle can only begin with the strong side relinquishing its
> attempts to impose by force its positions on the minds and thoughts of
> others . . . Then should come another more important step, namely to
> involve everyone in making the fateful decisions of the Palestinian people
> in a brotherly dialogue founded on national interest and a strong polit-
> ical will.

The declarative sentences create a sense of alarm in the readers'
minds, emphasizing the importance of what is being said. In this
context the contrast between the foolish leadership of the PA and
the holy leadership of the Islamic movement is clear. Furthermore,
the correct way to achieve statehood is not by awaiting someone to
"give" it. The editor echoes historical experiences without even
mentioning any specific cases – states are achieved by force and this
is the strategy of the Islamic movement. Internally, dialogue is the
key concept, for brothers should settle their differences through
speaking to each other and not discriminating against one another.
For the editor, mutual respect is an ideal and the foundation stone
upon which a nation exists; without this respect, the nation has no
right to ask it of others. The editor uses here the discourse of *ta'nib*
– which in Arabic refers to a kind of scolding tone – with the aim of
reminding the audience that only through cooperation and understanding between Palestinians will their rights be returned. The
editor's worldview is clearly reflected in the wish to work together,
even with those who have excluded him and his movement.

The editor concludes with a sophisticated formulation that
reflects both his wit and ability to effectively frame language:

> In this form of conduct which stems from our pure will, we will be able
> to make the state and impose it on the world . . . *Those who like it are
> welcome and those who do not like it, can keep saying no.* No power in the
> world can invade the walls of our will and firm unity and our state will
> become a reality instead of being a dream to be expected from the
> enemies!! [emphasis added]

The sentence marked in italics above is often used by Yasser
Arafat. This form of intertextuality has its own impact, for most, if
not all, Palestinians automatically associate this sentence with
Arafat. The editor echoes Arafat in order to expose him to the judgment of the people by reminding the reader that the Palestinian

president is responsible for the current situation of the Palestinians. Furthermore, reiterating words spoken by the leader of those whom the editorial criticizes conveys several important messages. First, the editor seeks to demonstrate closeness to, and sympathy with, Arafat. Second, the editor reminds Arafat of his words and promises, such as that he will never give up, and that he views the Palestinian people as capable of paying a heavy price to create a state. The editor therefore employs an active voice aimed at mobilizing people for collective action, and bypasses Arafat by using the words of the Palestinian president himself.

With the signing of the Wye River Agreement, *Al-Risalah* repeats its criticisms of the PA negotiation policy, arguing that Israel will again delay the implementation of the new agreement so as to force the Palestinians to enter into new negotiations over the same points that were already negotiated and agreed upon in previous agreements.[35] The paper claims that Wye has freed Israel from the Interim Agreement framework. This means that the Jewish state can now take unilateral measures against the Palestinians without fearing the threat of the PA unilaterally declaring a Palestinian state.[36] According to the article, the Israeli government has managed to reshuffle the papers in terms of the timetable, which is another step by Israel to escape the full and strict implementation of agreements to give Palestinians the right to have their own state. *Al-Risalah* states its opposition to the strategy of negotiations, as it seeks to prove Israel's lack of commitment to a real and lasting peace in the region.

The newspaper also goes into the details of the peace process negotiations and raises serious questions regarding the reasons behind the failure of the Palestinians to achieve their goals. The composition of the negotiating team comes in for especially heavy criticism. Specialists and officials directly and indirectly involved in the negotiations are interviewed in an attempt to provide the reader with thorough information regarding the content of the negotiations and the efficacy of the Palestinian negotiating team. Based on the positions presented by several specialists, the newspaper makes clear that the main problem with the negotiations does not lie with the personalities of those who take part in them, but rather with the political authority that wields all the power to decide on the crucial matters in the negotiations – namely Yasser Arafat. He alone directs the negotiations; all the other figures involved in the negotiations are reduced to mere puppet roles. As the pre-eminent negotiator and sole decision-maker, Arafat is exposed and vulnerable to Israeli pressure. The newspaper compares the tactics of the Palestinian team with its Israeli counterpart demonstrating the clear separation of responsibilities on the Israeli side. *Al-Risalah* points out that for the Israelis the political authority over negotiations is the government, which takes into consideration the positions of the Israeli military and the political system, especially the Knesset, as well as public opinion.[37] In contrast, in several places the newspaper discusses the Palestinian situation and reveals the lack of a coherent negotiating strategy, well-defined "red lines", and sufficient sensitivity to the importance of collective decision-making mechanisms on such crucial matters.[38]

The Legitimacy of Violent Resistance to Occupation

Al-Risalah is critical of the PA's peace strategy and seeks to promote armed struggle as a legitimate means to resist the Israeli occupation. However, it is not always apparent whether resistance is meant to *replace* negotiations altogether or to provide a means to enforce agreements. This apparent indecisiveness over policy preference reveals the cautious position taken by the newspaper, fearful of a direct confrontation with the PA.

The main point of departure in dealing with the concept of resistance is the reality of the Israeli occupation and its violent nature, which most articles that address this issue take for granted. *Al-Risalah* submits the idea of resistance and its effectiveness to serious debate in order to demonstrate that Palestinians have not decided to fight for the sake of killing alone. The lack of progress in the peace process constitutes a scenario that legitimizes the use of force in response to the occupying forces. The newspaper also seeks to explain the roots of the strong Palestinian urge to take up arms and fight. The unfortunate state of deprivation in which most Palestinians are born and grow up, as well as Israel's continued use of aggressive measures intended to break the national Palestinian will to achieve statehood and a normal existence, have led many of the younger Palestinian generation to view military resistance as the only method that can possibly change their miserable existence.

In several cases the newspaper discusses the rationale for using force to resist Israeli occupation,[39] assessing both local and international political circumstances that have historically conditioned the activities of similar national movements which used military resistance.[40] Many case studies are explored in order to lend credence to the idea of a guerrilla war, or other similar forms of resistance to foreign occupation. One of the most commonly cited is the experience of Hizbullah, which according to *Al-Risalah* was the motivating factor behind Israel's withdrawal from south Lebanon. The newspaper openly praises Hizbullah's success, as it was based on an ideology of fighting without regard for the political and international circumstances. In this context the publication seeks to show that resistance can take on different forms based on the specific circumstances. In an editorial published May 25, 2000 entitled "A Message . . . From South Lebanon", the editor argues:

> The timing of the Israeli army exit from Lebanese territory, its surroundings and waters – in this degrading and humiliating manner – expresses an important and strong message to Arab leaders and negotiators: Israeli power is an imagined power . . . It is a power made of paper as one Israeli military observer portrayed it when describing the pullout from Lebanon. It is a power that cannot remain still in the face of popular will and resistance. The path that Hizbullah adopted is good for the Arab nation to continue its march to regain the rest of its lands and to encircle the physical expressions of occupation until they give up and flee our Arab land.
>
> The dramatic change that south Lebanon witnessed this week reflects the centrality of resistance and jihad in making history, defeating occupation and achieving the desired victory no matter the differences in the balance of power on the ground as long as the people and the nation have a strong will.[41]

The passive form used to describe how south Lebanon witnessed the dramatic change contrasts with the active, present voice of the resistance in making history. The editorial emphasizes the fact that reality does not just change: there must be an agent of change – in this case it is the resistance. The newspaper remains aware of the political reality in the West Bank and Gaza Strip, where the peace process has made resistance to Israel more complicated. Therefore, the newspaper criticizes the security cooperation between Israel and the PA, which is viewed as an obstacle to any attempt to resist. Resistance is viewed as a basic right as long as the occupation continues:

The victory achieved in the pullout of the Israeli army in a degrading and humiliating fashion and the disintegration of the collaborating South Lebanese Army, whose members either gave up or fled, all of this forms a lightning bolt of hope in the sky of the Arab citizen, who as a result of the tragedies of the Arab defeats and the pursuit of Israel, has almost forgotten his splendid heroes, past and history. The scene in southern Lebanon reflects the fake myth portrayed by the Israeli army about itself in recent decades, which we accepted to be true and even exaggerated . . . The victory in Lebanon renews hope and portends the future which is awaited by this nation in facing the Jewish presence in the region and pushing it beyond the borders of the Arab land to the diaspora where it came from and renewing unity and continuity between the Arab and Islamic nations.[42]

The editor writes of the violent destruction of Israel and returning Jews to their "original" countries. To convince the reader, the editor establishes a correlation between the Jewish presence in the region and the lack of unity of the Arab and Islamic nations. Since the editor assumes that most Arabs would like to reunite, they must choose the road of resistance he is propagating. The visual and contextual priming of certain topics over others is another mechanism used in this context, in order to lend support to the system of knowledge presented by the editor. As such, a clear hierarchy exists between resistance and politics; the former is associated with, among other things, hope, unity, and the liberation of land, while the latter is connected to humiliation, degradation, and internal differences. By simultaneously presenting negative images of the negotiators' conduct and positive images of the resistance, as depicted by Hizbullah's success in Lebanon, the editor establishes a definitive agenda of resistance, placed within a theoretical framework that creates a highly stylized and politicized worldview.

The newspaper constantly seeks to stress the importance of military resistance and to legitimize support for this position, without ever disclosing whether this option is conceived as a mere tactic to be abandoned at some later stage, or represents a strategy toward which all Palestinian efforts should be directed. The newspaper also seeks to demonstrate that resistance is much more effective when based on national unity, for in its view most Palestinians are prepared to make the personal sacrifices that resistance demands for the sake of independence.[43] This conviction is behind Hamas' continuation of suicide bombings in Israeli cities even after the

Israeli military operations in Palestinian cities in early 2002 and despite the heavy costs these operations demanded in Palestinian lives and material resources.

Administrative Efficiency and the Rule of Law as Guarantees to Statehood

Virtually every edition of *Al-Risalah* includes three to six articles or reports addressing social, economic, and moral issues. The newspaper uses a variety of methods, formulations, genres, and orders of discourse to convey its critical worldview *vis-à-vis* the PA. There are reports, articles, interviews, and editorials that seek to construct a negative picture of the PA and all of its institutions. Some information is repeated several times in different formulations in order to infiltrate the public consciousness and formulate a critical frame of mind. The administration[44] and the court system[45] are two of the PA institutions the newspaper regularly attacks, but *Al-Risalah* makes references to all other aspects of the PA apparatus.

The behavior and functioning of the PA is criticized for failing to meet even the minimum standards of performance that are expected from it. The critique is usually directed at the leadership, which is held responsible for the deteriorating economic conditions and standard of living among the Palestinian population. In an article that appeared on September 30, 1999 the newspaper provides information on development in Palestine by citing the 1998–9 Human Development Report produced at Bir-Zeit University.[46] The report is quoted as saying that economic development over that period was modest and limited because of the closure policy imposed by Israel. The newspaper also reveals that 44 percent of Palestinians say that their standard of living has not improved since the establishment of the PA, while a further 41 percent say that their living standard had actually declined. A mere 14 percent said that their living standard improved. Furthermore, the newspaper reports that 73 percent of Palestinians think that the gap between the rich and poor has widened since the creation of the PA. The article adds that administrative problems within the PA, where official appointments are rarely made on a meritocratic basis, constitute the main problem that blocks development and prevents the indicated hardships from getting the professional treatment they require.

Al-Risalah provides further information that confirms the falling living standards and the rising unemployment rate inside the PA, which corresponds with assessments supplied by independent academic sources.[47] The newspaper also discusses the rising living costs, which only worsens the situation, and interviews economists who try to provide explanations as to the causes.[48] In addition to external factors related to changes in the global economy, the newspaper also points out that the economic situation is connected to internal Palestinian causes related to monetary and fiscal policies. This includes the economic monopolies by which the PA and influential figures have control over, usually imported, central commodities, which enables them to play with the prices.[49] A special point the newspaper makes is the connection between the monopolies, rising prices, and political corruption.[50]

Infrastructure in the PA-Controlled Areas

Al-Risalah provides, in one of its editions, a report on changes in the Palestinian infrastructure, which it claims provide a reliable indication of the "development, modernity and standards of living in a country and an example of the effectiveness of its economy and its ability to meet the challenge of technological and architectural developments".[51] Examining the economics of the PA's infrastructure, the report contends that "the infrastructure in the PA areas has not developed in the last five years."[52] The newspaper points out, for instance, that the most serious problems are in the fields of electricity, water, housing, education, health, sewage, streets, the port in Gaza, and the airport. Given this information, the newspaper quotes the Director-General of the Ministry of Local Government, who claims that in comparison with the limited measures of the Palestinian Authority under the given circumstances, the achievements have met expectations. The newspaper concludes the report by arguing: "As we have indicated, the average of achievements is low as compared to needs. If the special three and five year development plans for the infrastructure are applied on the ground and the donor countries meet their commitments, they will certainly contribute to the development of the different sectors of the infrastructure."[53] The aim is to prove that doubts exist as to whether the PA ministries will implement the existing plans. The report is written in an inquisitive, probing manner that raises doubts about the PA's real intentions in regard to the announced development plans.

The Deteriorating Social Conditions in Palestinian Society

The newspaper emphasized the PA's poor handling of social problems. An example is the teachers' strike in protest of low wages, the deteriorating education system, and delays in receiving their salaries from the PA. In contrast to the relatively modest and descriptive coverage the issue in the daily newspapers, *Al-Risalah* devoted considerable space to the strike, carefully following its developments,[54] examining its roots while trying to convey the hardships Palestinian teachers face on a low monthly salary of about 1,000 Israeli shekels (about $200). The problem is especially harsh because teachers are forbidden from simultaneously holding any other job. The newspaper covered the various demonstrations and rallies as well as the PA's treatment of the strikers, emphasizing the fact that teachers received no salary for the days they were on strike after they returned to work. For the sake of presenting a balanced picture, the newspaper includes responses of PA officials who clarify attempts made by the ministry to meet the teachers' demands.[55] Nevertheless, the newspaper remains loyal to its critical line by allotting more space to the teachers' voice and by conveying the public support for the teachers as expressed by letters of support and sympathetic rallies organized by various civil organizations.[56]

Human Rights Violations

Political prisoners and the implications for national unity and social stability are regularly discussed in *Al-Risalah*. In an article entitled "Political Imprisonment: Whose Interest?" the newspaper points out the worrying phenomenon of the rising number of opposition members arrested by the PA. In this article, as with other reports on this topic, the arrests are attributed to the PA's commitments in its agreements with Israel. The newspaper seeks to demonstrate that the detainment of political activists is not an internal Palestinian need, for they do not pose a genuine threat to the public order in Palestinian society. Behind every imprisonment of a Palestinian political activist – mainly from the Islamist movement – stands Israel, whose demands tear at the fabric of Arab, or Palestinian, unity. According to the newspaper, Israeli pressure on the PA to imprison a rising number of people demonstrates the "negative dialectics" of the current peace process. Thus the PA has become, in essence, Israel's security contractor and behaves in a manner based on the demands of the latter which actively seeks "to divide the Palestinian people who have proven the value and power of unity during the years of occupation".[57] The newspaper also addresses the utility of political imprisonment and seeks to demonstrate that the practice is viewed negatively by most Palestinians, fails to achieve any Palestinian goal, and has negative implications on the PA's moral positioning *vis-à-vis* Israel.[58] A central question *Al-Risalah* poses in this regard is how the PA can demand that Israel free its Palestinian political prisoners when hundreds of them sit in *Palestinian* jails without any clear charges or convictions for their alleged crimes.[59]

In order to present political imprisonment as a counter-productive practice, the weekly provides information on the positions taken by various human rights organizations, both generally and in the specific Palestinian case. Befitting the newspaper's fully documented treatment of such serious issues, *Al-Risalah* examines political imprisonment in great detail, to demonstrate the chaotic manner in which the PA enforces the rule of law, addressing the PA's fusion of the judicial and policing functions, and the lack of law and order in regard to the detention process.[60] *Al-Risalah* accuses the PA executive apparatus and its hegemony over all other branches of government of being the primary reason behind human rights violations that repeat themselves constantly, despite promises made by senior officials to solve the problem.

Extensive space is devoted in the newspaper to the central dilemma faced by the approximately 11,000 members of the Palestinian police force between commitment to the rule of law and following orders that do not always meet legal standards.[61] This topic is raised to provide a main gateway to two main issues of crucial importance for the newspaper and its mother movement. The first issue is the absence of law and order within the PA, and in particular the lack of providing a fair trial, which results in the imprisonment of many innocent Palestinians who are not given a fair chance to defend themselves. The newspaper emphasizes the negative social implications of this phenomenon and its high social, economic, and cultural costs. The second issue is to demonstrate to ordinary people in the PA that this phenomenon results from the agreements with Israel. To this end, *Al-Risalah* supplies tragic stories and reports on the subject, such as the imprisonment of Al-

Najah University professor Abdel-Sattar Qasim[62] and the aggressive reaction and excessive use of force by security personnel during the February 2000 visit of French Prime Minister Lionel Jospin to Bir-Zeit University.[63]

The Fusion between Social, Political and Moral Order

The newspaper's emphasis on the abysmal state of the Palestinian national entity and its poor relationship with the existing moral order reveals the strained relationship between the social, moral, and political imperatives. Corruption within the PA is addressed not only from an administrative point of view, but from a moral perspective as well, according to which the economic and financial situation in Palestinian society is criticized for failing to respect the communitarian spirit of Islamic religion. These issues are not usually raised as separate topics, but are rather inserted indirectly in different forms and formulations within the newspaper. This editorial policy reflects the view that Islam is not only a religion, but a social, economic, political, and cultural theory as well, and that no clear separation can be made between religion and other spheres of life just as there is no division between public and private. *Al-Risalah* therefore introduces an integrative and organic communitarian worldview in which the world cannot always be ordered according to categories that have their roots in Western political thought.

Conclusion

There is a lack of data available on Palestinian patterns of media consumption and exposure. Estimating readership of weeklies, especially Islamist weeklies such as *Al-Risalah* and *Al-Esteqlal* is even more difficult. Only one public opinion survey related to the newspapers of the opposition in PA areas exists. In its poll number 29 in August 1998, JMCC asked a sample of people if they knew of any newspaper related to the opposition. Whereas 25.2% of the respondents replied positively, 58.6% answered with "no". Among those who knew about the newspapers of the opposition, 37.7% named *Al-Risalah* as the newspaper they knew and 14.3% named *Al-Esteqlal*. More people knew about these newspapers in Gaza than in the West Bank (55.8% from Gaza versus 15.6% in the West Bank knew about

Al-Risalah; 18.2% knew *Al-Esteqlal* in Gaza, whereas only 9.6% knew about it in the West Bank). While these numbers are an indication that the circulation of the Islamist newspapers is low, it should be kept in mind that in a society where cash is very scarce and 15.5% of the people confess that they read a paper that others have bought, the number of people exposed to newspaper influence might be higher than the above numbers indicate. In a mobilized society, such as Palestinian society, opinion leaders – regular readers of newspapers – play a major role in setting public agenda by spreading newspaper reports via public gatherings, meetings, and in prayer places. Therefore, we find that newsmakers often use the media to reach their public; the impact of newspapers is therefore higher than some surveys indicate, especially because of the traditional social structure, where people come together and meet very often, and even more so truer when we are discussing a society that has a high rate of unemployment and is besieged in its villages and towns. The seriousness with which the PA is treated in the newspapers indicates that the newspapers have at least some influence on public agenda.

Having said that, it is almost impossible to determine the impact of the Islamist media on the public based on the available data. But this does not prevent us from drawing some conclusions regarding the Islamist media in terms of agenda setting and strategies of media framings of the two Islamist movements.[64]

Al-Risalah represents Islamic concepts, ideas, and beliefs as it seeks to penetrate the public agenda with what it conceives to be a more authentic discourse for a Muslim society and thereby constitutes a new collective public consciousness. But *Al-Risalah* does not limit itself to Islamic issues, nor is it full of religious preaching. On the contrary, one is surprised to find that the newspaper resembles the "secular" dailies, with special but separate pages for religious affairs. The newspaper's layout, which is divided according to different sections – political, social, economic, religious, cultural, and sports – allows readers to easily find the subjects in their regular assigned place. *Al-Risalah's* articles, and the general focus of the paper, analyze political issues, tending to favor the national Islamic worldview. The layout is clearly pluralistic, with the inclusion of diverse and even conflicting opinions, when this serves the message of the newspaper. The newspaper reflects a religious worldview in its conception of the conflict with Israel as well in the public order it desires for Palestinian society.

The newspaper plays the role of the "fourth estate" *vis-à-vis* the PA and perceives Palestinian reality from a democratic and even liberal point of view. It utilizes a democratic discourse as a means to promote Hamas' interests in creating an alternative to the main political platform of the dominant elite. The newspaper differentiates between the PA as an entity and the PA's policies, which are subjected to heavy criticism. Any attempts by the PA to limit the freedom of expression result in an attack on issues and topics that are embarrassing to its leadership. Nepotism, corruption, waste of public resources, and violations of basic human rights are widely addressed. The editorials are concise, and utilize the linguistic capabilities available to religious scholars in order to convey a clear message to the reader. In this context, mobilization by way of effective agenda setting and framing is a central goal. The newspaper plays the role of the mouthpiece of a political movement, despite the fact that its discourse is usually formulated in universal and general language. It creates public spaces in which different voices are articulated, with a special emphasis on the religious discourse. The newspaper, in this sense, is a central player in the Palestinian public sphere that had been emerging in the occupied territories until the outbreak of the second *Intifada*.

Contrary to its democratic domestic conceptions, the Hamas-affiliated weekly conveys a militant worldview on foreign affairs. It proclaims armed resistance to be the only viable strategy for the Palestinians to achieve their national goals. Despite the religious influences, its discourse in this regard is based mainly on the historical experiences of national struggles in different areas of the world. Unsurprisingly, the newspaper is highly critical of Israel. *Al-Risalah* tends to accept Israel's existence and frames the conflict as one of borders, despite the fact that it sometimes speaks about a conflict of existence. This ambiguous position is subject to ever-shifting political circumstances. When progress is achieved in the peace talks, *Al-Risalah* generally respects the discourse of the PA regarding a possible political settlement. But during times of clashes between Palestinians and the Israeli army, *Al-Risalah* uses other formulations in order to express its disgust with what it calls the "Zionist entity" and resorts to depicting the conflict in religious terminology. The outbreak of the second *Intifada* was anticipated, and even provoked, in the pages of the weekly: *Al-Risalah's* analysis of Palestinian reality after Oslo emphasized that its editors did not agree with the peace strategy of the PA and would like nothing more than for its implementation to be a total failure. The newspaper therefore greatly contributed to deligitimating the peace process and the promoting the pursuit of a militant strategy.

Conclusion

OCCUPATION, STATE FORMATION AND DEMOCRATIC PROSPECTS

In the Introduction to this study, it was argued that Palestinian politics cannot be fully understood if it is viewed as a linear process dominated by a single homogeneous entity or group. Palestinian society, it was presumed, has always been a pluralistic society, one where internal splits played major roles in determining its course of development. Differences between the dominant political elite and the diverse opposition movements in civil society are crucial to understanding Palestinian politics. The strategies adopted by the different political players pluralize the emerging public sphere in Palestine.

There has been a process of institutionalization in the PA that has led to the establishment of a state structure, and the composition of a particular type of political regime. The brief Palestinian experience has demonstrated that, in postcolonial settings, the process of state-building is never disconnected from the colonial past, or from the connection with the colonial power. The Palestinian institutional structures chosen after Oslo were not merely a result of free Palestinian choice; they were conditioned by the peace agreements between the PLO and Israel as much, and perhaps more, than they were determined by internal Palestinian political dynamics. The peace process has not only conditioned the *type* of political regime, but has also imposed certain political patterns stemming from the task given to the PA during the transitional phase. The PA's security forces, for instance, were expanded in order to meet demands made by Israel. Furthermore, the inflated bureaucratic apparatus of the PA resulted from the lack of economic opportunities in the Palestinian territories. Israeli closure policies have cut off the Israeli labor market for Palestinian unskilled workers – an act that puts the PA leadership in a difficult social dilemma. The Palestinian economy cannot possibly sustain the entire Palestinian labor force. The choice that faced the dominant elite of the PA was either a massively high unemployment rate, with all its social and political implications, or absorbing part of the labor force into the administrative PA apparatus and the security forces.

The latter option was eventually chosen, since it not only fulfilled the conditions arising from the peace process, but also because it met the immediate political interests of the PA elite, which, returning from exile, needed the support of the local population of the West Bank and Gaza Strip. Therefore, the dominant national elite began recruiting cadres of the local Fatah party and others into the PA structures. This process has opened the opportunity of patronage and cliental-political recruitment policies, and has resulted in the transplantation of the social structure into the administrative apparatus of the PA. It has conditioned the dynamics of Palestinian politics in the PA and emptied formal institutions of legitimate role. Processes of decision-making took place outside the institutions founded for that very purpose. This set of dynamics facilitated the hegemony of the PA's founding father, Yasser Arafat, and opened the way for the personalization of Palestinian politics.

Political scientist Ali Jarbawi, from Bir-Zeit University, has openly criticized the political process in the PA:

> Our country suffers from the widespread existence of the "personalism" sickness, which is widespread in the countries of our Arab homeland and in many other countries that for reasons of convenience are called the Third World . . . (Personalism) relates everything to persons and personalities. The regimes are personal . . . their reference, goals and pleasures are a person who becomes the axis, the symbol, the ruler and the sovereign. Around him everything occurs and he is the redemption, the explanation and the reference. Therefore, if you have a comment, critique or a position on a certain issue or subject, it is very quickly shifted from the public to the private sphere. It gets personalized and is transformed into a personal issue received with full sensitivity and defensively, leading to the dissolution of the subject matter discussed under the shell of personal revenge.[1]

Jarbawi's analysis may not provide an explanation to *all* aspects of Palestinian politics, but it *does* highlight some of the main characteristics of the emerging political culture in the PA. "Personalism", it is clear, is a growing phenomena.

The Palestinian national elite has felt extreme anxiety in regard to its authority, and therefore its forms and patterns of rule have assumed an authoritarian character. The elite of the Palestinian returnees, alongside the elitist segments of the local society in the West Bank and Gaza Strip (especially the influential large families), have been engaged in constructing a state structure that meets their particular needs rather than the demands of a modern state system designed to suit its citizenry. The PA's administrative structure and the inflation in its functions, positions, and institutions that have no specific remit, is symptomatic of the political and administrative culture of these elites. Although the functional inflation in the PA's administration is justified by the argument that it serves national interests by preventing high rates of unemployment, it seems that the needs of the elites – especially the returnees – to imprint their authority deep into Palestinian society has been the major factor in terms of the patterns of employment and institutionalization. In this sense, the experience of the PA has fallen into the same trap as other postcolonial states.

A special role is played by the "founding father" of the emerging Palestinian state. Yasser Arafat has proved to be autocratic in his manner of rule, and has sought to institutionalize his power by bypassing or manipulating formal state structures and legal procedures. Arafat plays a major role in the building of a bureaucracy centered around him by intervening in most aspects of development and employment without setting comprehensive and universally binding outlines. Freedom of expression has not been respected as a principle that ensures the freedoms of citizens and protects social stability and political reliability. The media, even those that support the national elite, have been living under the constant arbitrary danger of closure by the authorities.

Personalism, or the patrimonialism of politics, alone cannot provide an explanation for the complexity of the Palestinian process of national reconstruction that has occurred in the last decade. In spite of the authoritarian tendencies and the autocratic patterns of rule, there remains an active civil sector within Palestinian society. This sector is not homogeneous; it is pluralist, and different social groups within it struggle for diverse values and norms. The civil sector, its social movements and NGOs, is able to advocate its worldviews: it seeks to promote modes of political conduct that meet democratic standards. The NGOs, the women's movement, and the Islamic movement, all struggle for more democratic space and strive to influence policy-making. Most of these forces demand the liberalization of the emerging authority and the institutionalization of transparent and accountable legal and political procedures. Although this sector has not coordinated its activities, it has managed to establish its voice as an integral and legitimate part of the Palestinian public sphere. The sheer number of publications, gatherings, and other means of communication testifies to the viability of the civil discourse in Palestinian society. Any understanding of Palestinian politics cannot escape the existence of Palestinian counter-public spheres that seek to negotiate the political minefield and facilitate their impact on the emerging political culture.

Despite the socio-political cleavages in Palestinian society, especially the national–Islamist one, there is clear evidence pointing to emerging patterns of negotiations between the different civil sectors and the central authorities of the PA. National as well as Islamic civil organizations, such as parties and civil networks, have managed to establish open communicative channels, seeking to reach understandings in order to avoid confrontations that might cause further harm to Palestinian society. Although these negotiations have not managed to overcome the obstacles created by the emerging state structure, or the differences resulting from the peace process, they have demonstrated the plural dimension of Palestinian reality. The high level of political participation by Palestinian citizens in the formal as well as informal political game testifies to the potentiality of the institution of plural politics in Palestine.

The Palestinians must free themselves from the grip of Israeli occupation and establish an independent state before they will be able to freely determine their institutional choices and political culture. The experience of the last decade has established deep doubts as to the possibility of reaching a peaceful solution to the Palestine question. The rise of the national right in Israel, and its unwillingness to reach a compromise based on giving back *all* the occupied territories, has placed almost insurmountable, difficulties along the road to a peaceful solution.

The eruption of the Al-Aqsa *Intifada* in September 2000 prompted a serious change in the relationship between Israel and the Palestinian Authority. Despite the fact that there had been prior clashes between the Israeli army and Palestinian police and civilians, developments since then have signaled a breakdown in most communicative networks, both open and covert, that the two sides had built over the last several years. This dramatic change has prompted a restructuring of Palestinian society. The clashes between the Israeli army and the Palestinian civil community – sometimes supported by armed individuals from the security forces – has imposed a new state of emergency on all sectors of Palestinian society. Confrontations between the opposition and the PA have taken on a new form. Social movements as well as the media have restructured their priorities so as to invest most of their energies toward supporting the collective efforts for independence.

The changes brought about by the Al-Aqsa *Intifada* have had a major impact on Palestinian politics, and will continue to do so for some time. While it is difficult to evaluate its future implications, the second *Intifada* has brought home to the Palestinians, once again, that they have not achieved their independence, despite the establishment of a national authority on parts of their homeland. It has also made clear that Palestinian politics and the experience of self-rule over the last several years was not completely disconnected from the regional political reality. A central player in this reality has been Israel. The Israelis, through the form of agreements, the delays in their implementation, and their settlement and military policies, have influenced every realm of Palestinian public and private life.

The national political elite in the PA failed to understand that only through institutionalizing its authority in formal and legal procedures based on accountability and transparency could it guarantee the support of wide swathes of Palestinian society. As long as the dominant elite manipulates traditional institutions, using methods such as patronage and clientalism, it cannot stabilize its power in a situation where it has a strong civil sector and active social movements that actively challenge its power. The centralization of power in the PA and the concomitant lack of accountability have led to alienation among an increasing number of people who have either turned their backs on the political process completely, or transfered their support to the Islamic movement.

The representative bodies of the PA, especially the Palestinian Legislative Council, need to be empowered in order to meet the minimum norms of democratic rule. The executive authority has to be reduced and held accountable to the PLC. The reform in the PA's administrative structure, introduced in mid-2002, did not prove helpful in democratizing the Palestinian political system. The weak postion of the Palestinian Prime Minister *vis-à-vis* the President has proved to be a weak link in the chain of democratizing Palestinain politics, especially with regard to freeing it from the centralized control of Arafat something that will certainly change after his death. Nevertheless, the weakness of the prime minister and the marginal role of the PLC have not elimated the chances of democracy in Palestine; but it has made it easy to delegitimate the executive authority of the PA, especially when it comes to Arafat and the confrontation with Israel.

The Islamic movements Hamas and Islamic Jihad have refused to be a part of the peace process or the negotiation strategy. They chose "calculated participation" in Palestinian political life, placing their organizational interests above those of the PA. By emphasizing the military struggle as the only way to achieve Palestinian independence, the Islamic movement has put itself in direct confrontation not only with Israel, the most powerful and influential side in the equation, but also with the PA. As a result, the PA's national leadership has viewed Hamas as a threat not only to its chances to achieve independence but also to its own power base among Palestinians. The Islamic worldview of Hamas has threatened large parts of the civil sector, which has continually shown allegiance to the national elite for its (relatively) more liberal views, despite the fact that its patience is being tested by the PA's intransigence.

Such a complex reality will not disappear as a result of the second *Intifada*. If the peace process *is* resumed at one stage or another, it seems that all the diverse political players will have to be part of the Palestinian political scene if it is to reach a settlement agreed upon by all, in order to avoid a repeat of the post-Oslo fragmentation of Palestinian society. The relationship between each group, and the willingness of each to compromise and establish negotiation as the only means of dialogue between them, will determine the character of the future Palestinian state and its political regime. The politics of exclusion that characterized the PA's short history until the outbreak of the second *Intifada* will have to be replaced by incorporative politics if internal Palestinian stalemate is to be avoided: success, or otherwise, will not only impact on the immediate environment – Israel, Palestine, Jordan – but will act as the catalyst to potentially destabilize the entire Middle East region.

Notes

Introduction

1 Jamil Hilal, *The Palestinian Political System after Oslo: An Analytical Study* (Ramallah: Muwatin, 1998) (Arabic); Jamil Hilal, *The Formation of the Palestinian Elite: From the Emergence of the National Movement to the Establishment of the National Authority* (Ramallah and Amman: Muwatin and Al-Urdun Al-Jadid, 2002) (Arabic); Khalil Shikaki, "Palestinians Divided", *Foreign Affairs* (January–February 2002): 89–105; Yezid Sayigh, *Armed Struggle and the Search for Statehood: The Palestinian National Movement, 1949–1993* (Oxford: Clarendon Press, 1997); As'ad Ghanem, *The Palestinian Regime: A Partial Democracy* (Brighton & Portland: Sussex Academic Press, 2001); Hillel Frisch, *Countdown to Statehood: Palestinian State Formation in the West Bank and Gaza* (New York: State University of New York Press, 1998); Glenn E. Robinson, *Building a Palestinian State: The Incomplete Revolution* (Bloomington: Indiana University Press, 1997); Barry Rubin, *The Transformation of Palestinian Politics: From Revolution to State Building* (Cambridge, MA: Harvard University Press, 1999).
2 Many Israeli critics of the PA, especially from the national right who opposed progress of the peace process and the establishment of a Palestinian state, propagated this impression.
3 Ghanem, *The Palestinian Regime*.
4 On social movements and the concept of structural opportunities see: Sidney Tarrow, *Power in Movement: Social Movements and Contentious Politics,* 2nd edn (Cambridge: Cambridge University Press, 1998).
5 For more on "state-in-society" theory see: Joel S. Migdal, "The State in Society: An Approach to Struggles for Domination", in Joel S. Migdal, Atul Kohli, and Vivienne Shue, eds., *State Power and Social Forces* (Cambridge: Cambridge University Press, 1996), pp. 7–34.
6 Ibid., pp. 7–34.
7 George Steinmetz, ed., *State/Culture: State Formation After the Cultural Turn* (Ithaca: Cornell University Press, 1999), p. 9.

8 Charles Tilly, *Coercion, Capital, and European States, AD 990–1990* (Cambridge, MA: Blackwell, 1990).
9 Max Weber, *Political Writings*, edited by Peter Lassman and Ronald Speirs (Cambridge: Cambridge University Press, 1994).
10 Brendan O'Leary, Ian Lustick and Thomas Callaghy, eds., *Right-Sizing the State: The Politics of Moving Borders* (Oxford: Oxford University Press, 2001).
11 Pierre Bourdieu, "Rethinking the State: Genesis and Structure of the Bureaucratic Field", in Steinmetz, *State/Culture*, pp. 53–75.
12 Ernesto Laclau and Chantal Mouffe, *Hegemony and Socialist Strategy: Towards a Radical Democratic Politics* (London: Verso, 1985).
13 Brian McNair, *An Introduction to Political Communication* (London: Routledge, 1995); Doris Garber, ed., *Media Power in Politics* (Washington, DC: CQ Press, 2000).
14 Gianfranco Poggi, *The Development of the Modern State: A Sociological Introduction* (Stanford, CA: Stanford University Press, 1978).
15 Anthony Giddens, *The Nation-State and Violence* (Oxford: Polity Press, 1985), p. 46.
16 Charles Tilly, ed., *The Formation of National States in Western Europe* (Princeton: Princeton University Press, 1975).
17 Gianfranco Poggi, *The State: Its Nature, Development and Prospects* (Stanford: Stanford University Press, 1990), p. 21.
18 John Keane, ed., *Civil Society and the State* (London: Verso Press, 1988), p. 16.
19 Nazih Ayubi, *Over-stating the Arab State: Politics and Society in the Middle East* (London: I. B. Tauris Publishers, 1995), p. 3.
20 Robert H. Jackson and Carl G. Rosenberg, "Why Africa's Weak States Persist", *World Politics*, vol. 35, no. 1 (October 1982): 1–24.
21 Michael Hudson, *The Arab World: The Search for Legitimacy* (New Haven, CT: Yale University Press, 1977), pp. 1–30.
22 Hamza Alavi, "The State in Post-Colonial Societies: Pakistan and Bangladesh", *New Left Review*, no. 74 (1972): 59–81.
23 Richard Augustus Norton, "The Future of Civil Society in the Middle East", *Middle East Journal*, vol. 47, no. 2 (Spring 1991): 205–16.
24 Ayubi, *Over-stating the Arab State*, p. 14.
25 For a thorough study of this conflict see Burhan Ghalion, *Le Malaise Arabe: L'Etat Contre la Nation* (Paris: La Decouverte, 1991).
26 Roger Brubaker, *Nationalism Reframed: Nationhood and the National Question in the New Europe* (Cambridge: Cambridge University Press, 1996); Zygmunt Bauman, *Postmodern Ethics* (Cambridge: Blackwell, 1994), pp. 135–8.
27 Samuel N. Eisenstadt, Luis Roniger and Adam Seligman, eds., *Centre Formation, Protest Movements and Class Structure in Europe and the United States* (New York: New York University Press, 1987).
28 Nancy Fraser, "Rethinking the Public Sphere: A Contribution to the Critique of Actually Existing Democracy", in Bruce Robbins, ed., *The Phantom Public Sphere* (Minneapolis: University of Minnesota Press, 1993), pp. 1–32.
29 Jüergen Habermas, *Die Nachholende Revolution: Kleine politische Schriften VII* (Frankfurt: Suhrkamp, 1991), p. 196.
30 Charles Taylor, *Philosophical Arguments* (Cambridge, MA: Harvard University Press, 1995), p. 259.
31 Sidney Tarrow, *Power in Movement*; Doug McAdam, John McCarthy, and

Mayer Zald, eds., *Comparative Perspectives on Social Movements: Political Opportunities, Mobilization Structures, and Cultural Framing* (New York: Cambridge University Press, 1996); Nicholas Garnham, "The Media and the Public Sphere", in Craig Calhoun, ed., *Habermas and the Public Sphere* (Cambridge, MA: The MIT Press, 1993), pp. 359–76.

32   Jürgen Habermas, *The Structural Transformation of the Public Sphere* (Cambridge: Polity Press, 1992), p. 27.

33   Calhoun, *Habermas and the Public Sphere.*

34   Max Pensky, "Universalism and the Situated Critic", in Stephen K. White, ed., *The Cambridge Companion to Habermas* (Cambridge: Cambridge University Press, 1995), pp. 67–94.

35   Seyla Benhabib, "Models of the Public Space: Hannah Arendt, the Liberal Tradition, and Jüergen Habermas", in Calhoun, *Habermas and the Public Sphere,* pp. 73–98.

36   Nancy Fraser, "Rethinking the Public Sphere: A Contribution to the Critique of Actually Existing Democracy", in Calhoun, *Habermas and the Public Sphere,* pp. 109–42.

37   Jean L. Cohen and Andrew Arato, *Civil Society and Political Theory* (Cambridge, MA & London: MIT Press, 1995), p. 216.

38   Monroe E. Price, *Television, the Public Sphere, and National Identity* (Oxford: Clarendon Press, 1995), p. 24.

39   Charles Taylor, "Modes of Civil Society", *Public Culture*, vol. 3, no. 1 (Fall 1990): 95–118.

40   Michel Foucault, *The Archeology of Knowledge,* trans. A.M. Sheridan Smith (New York, Pantheon Books, 1992), p. 216; Edward Said, *The World, The Text and The Critic* (London: Vintage, 1991), pp. 47–8.

41   Teun A. Van Dijk, ed., *Discourse as Social Interaction* (London: Sage Publications, 1998).

42   Roger Fowler, "Power", in Teun A. Van Dijk, ed., *Handbook of Discourse Analysis*, vol. IV (London: Academic Press, 1985), p. 61.

43   Van Dijk, *Handbook*, p. 41.

44   Norman Fairclough, "Critical Discourse Analysis and the Marketization of Public Discourse: The Universities", *Discourse and Society*, vol. 4, no. 2 (1993): 133–68.

45   Gunther Kress, "Ideological Structures in Discourse", in Teun A. Van Dijk, ed., *Handbook.* pp. 27–8.

I   Institutionalizing the Political System and the Politics of Control

1   "West Bank and Gaza Economic Policy Framework Progress Report", *Journal of Palestine Studies*, vol. 30, no. 1 (Autumn 2000): 178.

2   Ibid., pp. 144–62.

3   The transitive period is conceived as "the interval between one political regime and another", see: Guillermo O'Donnell, Philippe C. Schmitter, and Laurence Whitehead, eds., *Transition From Authoritarian Rule: Tentative Conclusions About Uncertain Transitions* (Baltimore: Johns Hopkins University Press, 1986), p. 4.

4   Glenn Robinson, *Building a Palestinian State: The Incomplete Revolution* (Bloomington: Indiana University Press, 1997), p. 177.

5   Rema Hammami, "Palestinian NGOs since Oslo: From NGO Politics to Social Movements?" *Middle East Report*, no. 214 (Spring 200): 188–202.
6   Yossi Shain and Juan Linz, *Between States* (Cambridge: Cambridge University Press, 1995), p. 4.
7   Terry-Lynn Karl, "Dilemmas of Democratization in Latin America", *Comparative Politics*, vol. 23, no. 1 (1990): 1–21.
8   James. G. March and Johan. P. Olson, "The New Institutionalism: Organizational Factors in Political Life", *American Political Science Review*, no. 78 (September 1984): 734–49.
9   John Zvesper, "The Separation of Powers in American Politics: Why We Fail to Accentuate the Positive", *Government and Opposition*, vol. 34, no. 1 (Winter 1999): 3–23.
10 Article XVIII of the *Israeli–Palestinian Interim Agreement on the West Bank and Gaza Strip* defines the head of the PA as Ra'ees, which means president. The name Ra'ees was chosen as a compromise between Israel and the PLO. It satisfied the latter's expectations for a title of a president, which was Arafat's official title since the declaration of the Palestinian state in November 1988.
11 Ibid., Chapter I, Article III.
12 Ibid., Article XVIII, sub-article 4.
13 See interview with Azmi Shua'ybi, "A Window on the Working of the PA: An Inside View", *Journal of Palestine Studies*, vol. 30, no. 1 (Autumn 2000): 88–97.
14 *Interim Agreement*, Article V.
15 *Interim Agreement*, Article XVIII.
16 The president has issued several decrees that subdue the regular legislative process. An important decree was issued on February 7, 1995 and established the State Security Court. Among the important decrees was the one issued on January 10, 2000 which established "A Higher Council for Development" charged with "promoting investment in Palestine and ensuring good revenue performance and sound revenue administration, as well as strengthening the public finance system". See: <www.pna.net/events/decree.htm>.
17 *Palestine Policy*, vol. 2, no. 5 (Winter 1995): 83–186 (Arabic).
18 *Ha'aretz*, February 14, 2003 and March 10, 2003.
19 The importance of promulgation was indicated by St. Thomas Aquinas *Summa Theologica* Ia, Iiae, Q 90, Art. 4.
20 *Parliamentary Horizons*, a documentary newsletter published by Muwatin, The Palestinian Institute for the Study of Democracy, vol. 3, no. 3 (June 1999): 6.
21 *PLC Report*, PLC: Information Department, vol. 3, no. 1 (2000): 1.
22 Aziz Kaid, *On the Overlapping Responsibilities in the Institutions of the Palestinian Authority* (Ramallah: Palestinian Independent Commission for Citizen's Rights, 1999), p. 35.
23 *Peoples' Rights*, no. 5, July 1997, p. 18.
24 Kaid, *Overlapping*.
25 Kaid indicates the numbers of the orders given by the president and their exact dates. For more details see, ibid., p. 13.
26 *Parliamentary Horizons*, vol. 3, no. 8 (November 1999): 2.
27 *Middle East International*, April 10, 1998, p. 19.
28 See the report prepared by the PA in cooperation with the IMF and presented to the Ad Hoc Liaison Committee that met in Lisbon in June 2000. *Journal of Palestine Studies*, vol. 30, no. 1 (Autumn 2000): 144–6.
29 Shua'ybi, *An Inside View*.

30 Rick Hooper, "The International Politics of Assistance to Palestinians in the West Bank and Gaza Strip, 1993–1997", in Sara Roy, ed., *The Economics of Middle East Peace: A Reassessment* (Stanford, CT: JAI Press, 1999), pp. 59–95.

31 Sara Roy, "De-development Revisited: Palestinian Economy and Society since Oslo" *Journal of Palestine Studies*, vol. 28, no. 3 (Spring 1999): 64–82.

32 Adel Samara, "Globalization, The Palestinian Economy, and the "Peace Process", *Journal of Palestine Studies*, vol. 29, no. 2 (Spring 1999): 20–34.

33 Ibid., p. 146.

34 For information on the donors' role and financial aid for development see, "Aid for Trade: Putting Donors to Work", *Palestine Economic Pulse*, vol. 1, no. 5. (September–October 1996), in: <www.palecon.org/ pulsedir/september/ pulssep2.html>.

35 Ziad Abu Amr, "The Palestinian Legislative Council: A Critical Assessment" *Journal of Palestine Studies*, vol. 26, no. 4 (Summer 1997): 90–7.

36 Abu-Amr, *The Palestinian Legislative Council.*

37 Saleh Ra'fat, "The Palestinian Legislative Council", in *Palestine Policy*, vol. v, no. 17 (Winter 1998): 90 (Arabic).

38 Ra'fat, *The Palestinian Legislative Council,* p. 91.

39 Public opinion poll no. 24, September–October 1996, CPRS, Nablus, The West Bank.

40 Public opinion poll no. 46, January 2000, CPRS, Nablus, The West Bank.

41 Public opinion polls no. 42–6, July 1999–January 2000, CPRS, Nablus, The West Bank.

42 The Plan was published by WAFA, the Palestinian News Agency and a copy of it was published by Al-Jazeera. See: <www.aljazeera.net/info/ Special%20Report/Differe.../100_days_plan_of_the_Palestinian.htm>.

43 On the crises in the PA after Ahmed Qurei presented his resignation to Arafat see, *Al-Ayyam*, July 13–27, 2004.

44 Rex Brynen, "The Neopatrimonial Dimensions of Palestinian Politics", *Journal of Palestine Studies*, vol. 25, no. 1 (Winter 1998): 23–36.

45 As'ad Ghanem, "Founding Elections in Transitional Period: The First Palestinian General Elections", *The Middle East Journal*, vol. 50, no. 4 (Autumn 1996): 513–28.

46 Robinson, *Building a Palestinian State*, pp. 178–81.

47 Sara Roy, "The Seeds of Chaos, and of Night: The Gaza Strip after the Agreement", *Journal of Palestine Studies*, vol. 23, no. 3 (Spring 1994): 86.

48 Robinson, *Building a Palestinian State, pp.* 175–200.

49 Salim Tamari, "The Local and the National in Palestinian Identity" in Kamal Abdel-Malek and David C. Jacobson, *Israeli and Palestinian Identities in History and Literature* (New York: St. Martin's Press, 1999), pp. 3–8.

50 Jamil Hilal, *The Palestinian Political System After Oslo: An Analytical Study* (Beirut: Institute of Palestine Studies, 1998), pp. 138. (Arabic)

51 Khalil Shikaki, "The Peace Process, National Reconstruction, and the Transition to Democracy in Palestine", *Journal of Palestine Studies*, vol. 25, 98 (1996): 5–20.

52 Saed Ahmad Sidqah, *Al-Quds*, October 12, 1995.

53 *Report of PLC Special Committee* based on the Report of the Public Oversight Committee (Ramallah: PLC, 1997).
54 The mediation with the kidnappers was conducted by brigadier Rashid Abu Shubbak, director of the preventive security apparatus in Gaza strip, Ahmad Hillis Secretary of Fatah's mainstream and Abdallah Abu Samhadaneh, governor of central Gaza. For details see: <http://www.palestine-pmc.com/details.asp?cat=1&id=1377>.
55 <www.palestinechronicle.com/ story>.
56 Ibid.
57 *Palestine the Revolution*, no. 987, June 5, 1994 (Arabic).
58 See the composition of the government: *Journal of Palestine Studies*, vol. 24, no. 1 (Autumn 1994): 133.
59 *Journal of Palestine Studies*, vol. 28 (Autumn 1996): 209 (Arabic).
60 Amal Jamal, "The Palestinian Media: An Obedient Servant or a Vanguard of Democracy?", *Journal of Palestine Studies*, vol. 29, no. 3 (2000): 45–59.
61 *Palestine Policy*, vol. 5, no. 20 (Fall 1998): 121 (Arabic).
62 *Journal of Palestine Studies*, vol. 28, no. 1 (Autumn 1998): 145.
63 According to the Basic Law passed by the PLC but not ratified by the president, there should be 18 ministers in any government.
64 Shua'ybi, *An Inside View*, pp. 89.
65 Hilal, *Palestinian Political System*, pp. 188–202.
66 Report of the Council on Foreign Relations: *Strengthening Palestinian Public Institutions*. <www.cfr.org/public/pubs/palinstfull.html>, pp. 32–4.
67 See the report and the reactions of different people on this issue in *Palestine Policy*, vol. 5, no. 20 (Fall 1998): 116–30 (Arabic).
68 BBC News, September 11, 2002; Al-Jazeera, September 11, 2002.
69 BBC News, September 11, 2002.
70 BBC News, September 11, 2002.
71 Dauod Suliman Dauod, Al-Jazeera, April 12, 2002.
72 Yassir Za'atreh, Al-Jazeera, October 15, 2002.
73 *Al-Quds*, March 11, 2003; *Al-Ayyam*, March 11, 2003.
74 <www.newsday.com>.
75 *Ha'aretz*, April 8, 2003.
76 *Ha'aretz*, April 8 ,2003.
77 *Al-Quds*, April 29, 2003.
78 Abu Mazen's speech appears in JMCC's website: <www.jmcc.org>.
79 *Al-Quds*, May 24, 1994; *Journal of Palestine Studies*, vol. 24, no.1 (Autumn 1994): 133.
80 Kamal S. Zuabi, *The Administrative Law and its Applications in the Hashimite Kingdom of Jordan* (Amman: Jordanian University Press, 1993).
81 Personal interview with Maaruf Zaharan, Qaliqilia's governor, Qaliqilia, April 13, 2004.
82 Amal Jamal, "State-Building, Institutionalization and Democracy: The Palestinian Experience", *Mediterranean Politics*, vol. 6, no. 3 (Autumn 2001): 1–30.
83 Personal interviews with rank and file people in the districts.
84 See the frequent advertisements of gratitude for the president in the Palestinian daily newspapers.

85 *Al-Quds*, April 29, 2003.
86 Ghassan Al-Shakaa, for instance, was the appointed head of the municipality in Nablus and at the same time a member of the PLC.
87 Nathan Brown, "Constituting Palestine: The Efforts To Write a Basic Law for the Palestinian Authority", *The Middle East Journal*, vol. 54, no. 1 (2000): 25–43; Asma Khader, *The Law and the Future of Palestinian Women* (Jerusalem: Women Center for Legal Aid and Counseling, 1998); Gregory Mahler, *Constitutionalism and Palestinian Constitutional Development* (Jerusalem: PASSIA, 1996), p. 35.
88 See the debates on the draft Palestinian constitution in: Nathan Brown, *Palestinian Politics after the Oslo Accords: Resuming Arab Palestine* (Berkeley: University of California Press, 2003).
89 Mohammed Abu Harthiyeh, "The Duties of the Security Forces," in: Ziad Arif, Adnan Amr, Mohammed Abu Harthiyeh and Amin Makki Madani, *The Rules of the Police in Palestine* (Ramallah: PICCR, 1998), pp. 53–64. (Arabic)
90 The case of Dr. Abdel-Satar Qasim, a history professor from Al-Nagah University in Nablus, is a good example. Qasim was one of the twenty signatories on a petition published in November 1999 that accused the PA of corruption. He was arrested by the Preventive Security Forces (PSF) on February 18, 2000. The PA High Court twice ordered the PSF – on April 3, 2000 and July 11, 2000 – to release Qasim, but its decision was not respected. See: <www.lawsociety.org>.
91 *People's Rights*, vol. 1, no. 9 (November 1997): 24.
92 *Monitor*, vol. 3, no. 1 (January 1999): 22.
93 See an interview with the fired Chief Justice in *Al-Risalah*, January 15, 1998.
94 *Al-Quds*, May 6, 1998, p. 2.
95 *People's Rights*, vol. 1, no. 12 (February 1998): 10.
96 See an interview with the ousted Chief Justice in *People's Rights*, vol. 1, no. 12 (February 1998): 11–13.
97 Public opinion polls show that the public evaluation of the judicial authority and court system declined from 50 percent in 1997 to 40 percent today. CPRS, Nablus, the West Bank.
98 Hillel Frisch, "Modern Absolutist or Neopatriarchal State Building? Customary Law, Extended Families, and the Palestinian Authority", *International Journal of Middle Eastern Studies*, 29 (1997): 341–58.
99 Public opinion polls show that 63–71 percent of the population think that the PA institutions are corrupt. See: polls 29–45, September 1997–December 1999, CPRS, Nablus, The West Bank.
100 On the importance of party design and its impact on regime type see: H. Gilliomee & C. Simkins, eds., *The Awkward Embrace: One Party Domination and Democracy* (Switzerland: Harwood Academic Publishers, 2000).
101 The rate of voter participation in the elections reached 75.86 percent. Details of the elections can be found in the Central Election Commission, *Palestinian Authority Elections* 1996. (Gaza: Palestinian National Authority, 1996).
102 For more details on the candidates See: Ghanem, "Founding Elections" and Hilal, *Palestinian Political System*.

103 Hannah Arendt has suggested differentiating between these two concepts. Whereas majority decision is a legitimate technical procedure in democracy, majority rule is a form of authoritarianism where the majority utilizes its power to supress the minority. Hannah Arendt, *On Revolution* (New York: Viking Press, 1963), pp. 163–4.

104 Baruch Kimmerling, *Politicide: Ariel Sharon's wars against the Palestinians* (New York: Verso, 2003).

2 Deconstructing Autocracy: NGOs and the Politics of Contention

1 Al-Taher Labib, "The Relationship Between The Democratic Project and the Arab Civil Society", *Al-Mustqbal Al-Arabi* (The Arab Future), no. 158 (April 1992): 103.

2 Salim Tamari, "The Local and the National in Palestinian Identity", in Kamal Abdel-Malek and David C. Jackobson, eds., *Israeli and Palestinian Identities in History and Literature* (New York: St. Martins Press, 1999), pp. 3–8.

3 See the *Directory* prepared by the UN Office of the Special Coordinator in the Occupied Territories, 1999/2000/2001. These directories include all NGOs that operate in the West Bank and Gaza Strip, their dates of inception and their special field of action.

4 See the "Position of the Non-Governmental Organizations of the Occupied Territories in the Light of the Palestinian–Israeli Declaration of Principle (1993)", <www.pngo.net/position.htm>.

5 Yehoshua Porath, *The Emergence of the Palestinian-Arab National Movement, 1918–1929* (London: Frank Cass 1974); Yehoshua Porath, *The Palestinian Arab National Movement: From Riots to Rebellion, Volume Two, 1929–1939* (London; Totowa, NJ: Frank Cass, 1977); Ann Mosely Lesch, *Arab Politics in Palestine, 1917–1939 : The Frustration of a Nationalist Movement* (Ithaca, NY: Cornell University Press, 1979).

6 Bayan Nuwayhis Al-Hut, *The Leadership and the Institutions in Palestine, 1917–1948* (Beirut: Institute for Palestine Studies, 1981) (Arabic).

7 Laurie A. Brand, *The Palestinians in the Arab world : Institution Building and the Search for State* (New York: Columbia University Press, 1988).

8 Rosemary Sayigh, *Palestinians: From Peasants to Revolutionaries – A People's History* (London: Zed Press, 1979), pp. 177–225.

9 Helga Baumgarten, *Befreiung in den Staat: Die palestinensiche Nationalbewegung seit 1948* (Frankfurt an Main: Suhrkamp, 1991), pp 63–80.

10 Emile Sahliyeh, *In Search of Leadership: West Bank Politics* (Washington, DC: Brookings Institution, 1988), p 24.

11 Michael M. Cernea, *Non-governmental Organizations and Local Development*, World Bank, Discussion Papers, no. 40 (1988).

12 Ali Jarbawi, "Palestinian National Identity and the Relations between the Returnees and the people of the Homeland", in Mahdi Abdul-Hadi, ed., *Dialogue on Palestinian State-Building and Identity* (Jerusalem: PASSIA, 1999), pp. 56–66.

13 Jamil Hilal, *The Palestinian Political System After Oslo: An Analytical Study* (Beirut: Institute of Palestine Studies, 1998). (Arabic)

14 Review Chapter 5 on Islamic media. For more details on the relationship

between Hamas and the PA see: Shaul Mishal and Avraham Sela, *The Palestinian Hamas* (New York: Columbia University Press, 2000).

15 Review the newspaper of Khalas party which is affiliated with Hamas, *Al-Risalah*, in particular see issues 188–190, January 2001.

16 More on this issue see: Helena Lindholm Schultz, *The Reconstruction of Palestinian Nationalism* (Manchester: Manchester University Press, 1999). See in particular Chapter 5, pp. 119–43.

17 This list is taken from Mohammed Dajani, "Government and Civil Society: Relationships and Roles", in Abdul-Hadi, *Dialogue on Palestinian State-Building*, pp. 81–5.

18 Denis J. Sullivan, "NGOs in Palestine: Agents of Development and Foundation of Civil Society", *Journal of Palestine Studies*. vol. 25, no. 3 (Spring 1996): 93–100.

19 See the Palestinian Non-Governmental Organizations Network's *Annual Report*, 1997, pp. 27–9.

20 See Dajani, "Government and Civil Society", p. 85.

21 See the Palestinian Non-Governmental Organizations Network, *Annual Report*, 1997, p. 9.

22 Mustafa Barghouthi, "Palestinian NGOs and their Contribution to Policy Making", in Abdul Hadi, *Dialogue on Palestinian State-Building*, pp. 73–80.

23 Augustus Richard Norton, ed., *Civil Society in the Middle East* (Leiden: Brill, 1995).

24 *Al-Hadaf*, October 14, 1997, p. 19; *MERIP Report*, no. 205. October–December, 1997.

25 Bala'wi was appointed as a minister of interior in the government of Abu Ala'.

26 *Palestine Report*, vol. 2, no. January 10, 1997.

27 See the campaign led by the Minister of Justice against the NGOs, *Al-Esteqlal*, June 18, 1999, p. 11. Until March 2003 nobody was charged directly regarding such corruption. In early 2003 the director of the legal NGO LAW was charged with betraying the trust of the funders of the NGO and was jailed as a result.

28 Personal interview with Khalida Ratrut, Septemper 19, 2001.

29 See details in the publication of Palestinian Non-Governmental Organizations Network, *Al-A'mal Al-Ahli*, no. 22, September 25, 2000, pp. 1 &7.

30 Dr Riyad Za'noun, Palestinian Minister of Health in a coordination workshop between the health NGO sector and the Palestinian Ministry of Health in December 1996. Ibid., p. 2.

31 See a memo published by PNGO in the Palestinian press, May 21, 1998.

32 For the recommendation see the document of the Commission issued on May 26, 1999.

33 Personal interviews with civil activists, Ramallah, July 2001.

34 See *Al-A'mal Al-Ahli*, no. 28, June 27, 2001.

35 See the PNGOs *Annual report*, 2000, p. 16 (Arabic version).

36 Glenn Robinson, *Building a Palestinian State: The Incomplete Revolution* (Bloomington: Indiana University Press, 1997).

37 There are hundreds of publications released every year by the different organizations which seek to reach the wide public by all means.

38 See the newsletters of PICCR as well as the presidential decree on the website of the Ministry of Information: <www.pna.org/mininfo/general/>.
39 See The Palestinian Independent Commission for Citizens Rights, *Annual Report*, 2000.
40 See *Political Imprisonment*, Report Series (3), PICCR, Novemer 2000.
41 Ibid., p. 2.
42 More on this publication see: *The Periodical: A Periodical on the Human Rights of Palestinians* (Ramallah: PICCR, 2000).
43 See the PNGO *Annual Report*, 1998, p. 8.
44 PNGO *Working Plan*. October 1997, p. 10.
45 *Al-A'mal Al-Ahli*, no. 16, April 26, 2000, p. 1.
46 Ibid., p. 11.
47 PNGO, *Annual Report*, 1999, p. 7.
48 *Al-A'mal Al-Ahli*, Septemper 25, 2000, pp. 1 and 7.
49 See *Al-Esteqlal* newspaper, June 18, 1999, p. 11.
50 See *Al-A'mal Al-Ahli* on the week of the community work, Septemper 25, 2000, pp. 1–2.
51 See George Giacaman's article in *Al-A'mal Al-Ahli*, Septemper 25, 2000, p. 5.

3 The Constitutive National Press: Mechanisms of the Palestinian Media Regime

1 Ami Ayalon, *The Press in the Middle East: A History* (New York: Oxford University Press, 1995).
2 Rashid Khalidi, *Palestinian Identity: The Construction of Modern National Consciousness* (New York: Columbia University Press, 1997).
3 Ibid.
4 The Voice of Palestine began broadcasting in 1965 from Cairo. In 1966 the Voice of Palestine-Jordan went on the air. Since then many Arab countries have paid tribute to the Palestinian question by enabling a Palestinian radio broadcast. These radio stations were poorly equipped and controlled by the host state. As part of a comprehensive media campaign the PLO tried in 1972 to unite all its radio services under the name The Voice of Palestine, but it never succeeded.
5 Dov Shinar, *Palestinian Voices: Communication and Nation Building in the West Bank* (Boulder, CO: Rienner, 1987).
6 Dov Shinar and Danny Rubinstein, *Palestinian Press in the West Bank: The Political Dimension* (Jerusalem: The Jerusalem Post, 1987).
7 Ruba Al-Hussari, Ali Khalili and Bassam Al-Salhi, *The Palestinian Press Between Now and Future Developments* (Ramallah: Muwatin, 1993) (Arabic).
8 Shinar and Rubinstein, *Palestinian Press in the West Bank*.
9 Miron Benvenisti, *Israeli Censorship of Arab Publications* (Jerusalem: The West Bank Data Base Project, 1983).
10 An archive of CPRS polls is available online at <http://www.cprs-palestine.org/polls/index.html>. The polls show the support that the Oslo process won among Palestinians in the West Bank and Gaza Strip.
11 *Al-Nahar*'s editor, Othman Hallaq, met with Arafat thirty-six days after the

closure and received a permit to publish, but the paper never regained its circulation and had to close permanently.

12   Imad Musa, "The Palestinian Media System", unpublished MA Thesis, University of Missouri-Columbia (1995), p. 66.

13   *The Journalist*, a publication of the Journalists Training Center at Bir-Zeit University, April 1997 (Arabic).

14   Jerusalem Media and Communication Center (JMCC), public opinion poll no. 12, January 12, 1996.

15   JMCC public opinion polls no. 29 & 33, August 1998 and October 1999 respectively.

16   Mickey was assassinated in Gaza in January 2001. Rumors said that he had exploited his position for personal benefit and had diverted sums of money to personal accounts in Europe. See *Al-Risalah*, January 25, 2001.

17   See interview with Abu Dhair in *Al-Risalah*, March 9, 2000, p. 12.

18   <www.pcbs.org/english/culture/media_00/media00/tab_5_b.htm>; or for a brief press release on the survey see: <www.minfo.gov.ps/statements/est_2109.htm>.

19   Since then there has not been any survey that examined this topic, despite the fact that the numbers of people connected to the Internet could have grown.

20   Jerusalem Media and Communication Center, public opinion polls number 33, October 1999. See: <www.jmcc.org/publicpoll/results/1998/no.29b.htm>.

21   Jerusalem Media and Communication Center, public opinion polls number 33, October 1999. See: <www.jmcc.org/publicpoll/results/1999/no.33b.htm>.

22   <www.pcpsr.org/survey/polls/2001/p2a.html>.

23   Khalil Shikaki, "The Peace Process, National Reconstruction and the Transition to Democracy in Palestine", *Journal of Palestine Studies,* vol. 25, no. 2 (1996): 5–20.

24   Usher Graham, *Palestine In Crisis* (London: Pluto Press, 1995).

25   Ziad Abu-Amr, "Report from Palestine", *Journal of Palestine Studies,* vol. 24, no. 2 (1995): 40–7.

26   Ministry of Information Web site at: <http://www.pna.org/mininfo>.

27   See the homepage of the Ministry of Information, <www.pna.org/mininfo/general/princ.htm>.

28   See interview with Yasser Abed Rabbo in *Palestine-Israel Journal*, vol. 5, no. 3/4 (1998): 13–20.

29   See the study on the new states of Eastern Europe: Jean K. Chalaby, "The Media and the Formation of the Public Sphere in the new Independent States", *Innovation: The European Journal of Social Science*, vol. 11, no. 1 (March 1998): 73–85.

30   Interview with Mutawakil Taha, the director of the Palestinian Ministry of Information. *Al-Sahafi* (1997). (Arabic)

31   Leora Frankel-Shlosberg, "The Palestinian News Game", *Columbia Journalism Review*, vol. 35, no. 1 (May/June 1996): 16–18.

32   See Palestinian Press Law, Ministry of Information.

33   <www.pcbs.org./english/culture/media_00/media00/tab_17.htm>.

34   For original copy of the order, see files of Internews. East Jerusalem.

35   *Al-Risalah*. February 26, 1998.

36 *Al-Quds*. February 10, 1998.
37 *Al-Risalah*. February 26, 1998.
38 Sami Muhsin, *Freedom of Press under the Palestinian Authority* (Jerusalem: The Palestinian Society for the Protection of Human Rights and the Environment, 1996). (Arabic)
39 Muhamad Qwasmi, "Political Reasons Behind *Al-Nahar's* Closure", *Al-Sahafi* (1997).
40 JMCC public opinion polls no. 29 & 33, August 1998 and October 1999 respectively.
41 Hillel Frisch, and Menachem Hofnung, "State Formation and International Aid: The Emergence of the Palestinian Authority", *World Development*, vol. 25, no. 8 (1999): 1251–2.
42 William A. Rugh, *The Arab Press* (Syracuse: Syracuse University Press, 1979), p. 5.
43 Donald Pick, "Dictatorship vs. Developing Democracy: The Case of the Palestinian Press". <www.arches.uga.edu/~dpick/palpress.html>.
44 Ibid.
45 Ibid.
46 See Appendix number 4 in the "*Report of the Budgetary and Financial Affairs Committee*" regarding the budget proposal law of the year 2000. February 26, 2000.
47 According to the speaker of the International Finance Corporation only 13 percent of the paper's income came from its own sources. The paper's press produces the educational books for the PA educational system and 73 percent of the revenues go to *Al-Ayyam*. See Middle East Media and Research Institute, "World Bank set to Bankroll Papers that Call US 'Satan'", November 20, 1998.
48 Said Ghazali, "The Best Journalist is the Best Loyalist", Arabic Media Internet Network, <www.amin.org>.
49 Interview with the General Director of the paper and the son of the owner, Marwan Abu Zuluf. Jerusalem, April 6, 2000.
50 Michael Scammell, "Censorship and Its History – A Personal View", in Kevin Boyle, ed., *Article 19 World Report 1988: Information, Freedom, and Censorship* (New York: Times Books, 1988), p. 10.
51 Ilan Peleg, ed., *Patterns of Censorship around the World* (Boulder, CO: Westview Press, 1993), p. 4.
52 See Palestinian Press Law, Ministry of Information.
53 Deborah Holmes, *Governing the Press: Media Freedom in the U.S. and Great Britain* (Boulder, CO: Westview Press, 1986).
54 John A. Lent, "The Mass Media in Asia", in Patrick H. O'Neil, ed., *Communicating Democracy: The Media and Political Transitions* (Boulder, CO: Lynne Rienner Publishers, 1988), pp. 147–70; Dale F. Eickelman and Jon W. Anderson, eds., *New Media in the Muslim World: The Emerging Public Sphere* (Bloomington: Indiana University Press, 1999).
55 On the detention of the editors of *Al-Risalah* see: *Palestine Report*, Jerusalem Media and Communication Center, vol. 6, no. 50, June 14, 2000.
56 For more details see *Palestine Report* published by Jerusalem Media and Communication Centre, 20 December, 1996.

57 Michael Gurevitch and Jay G. Blumler, "Linkages between the Mass Media and Politics: A Model for the Analysis of Political Communications Systems", in James Curran, Michael Gurevitch and Janet Woollacott, eds., *Mass Communication and Society* (London: Edward Arnold, 1977), pp. 133–68.
58 On the theory of priming see: Shanto Iyengar and Donald R. Kinder, *News That Matters* (Chicago: University of Chicago Press, 1987).
59 On this issue see Barbie Zelizer, "Journalists as Interpretive Communities", in Dan Berkowitz, ed., *Social Meaning of News* (London: Sage, 1997), pp. 401–19.
60 See *Al-Ayyam* and *Al-Hayat Al-Jadida* on September 28, 29, 30, 1999.
61 Walid Batrawi, "Palestinian Media: Pre-Intifada to the Present", *Bir-Zeit News Report* (1997).
62 Personal interview with Radwan Abu Ayyash in Ramallah, February 8, 2000.
63 This is a very widespread phenomenon in the Arab World.
64 Personal interview with editors and managers in PBC. Ramallah, February 8, 2000.
65 Reporters Sans Frontiers. December 1995.
66 Amayreh Khalid, *Middle East International*, no. 542 (January 24, 1997): 18–19.
67 Batrawi, *Palestinian Media*, p. 7.
68 Ghazali, *The Best Journalist is the Best Loyalist*, p. 2.
69 Ibid.
70 A special report of the Palestinian Independent Commission for Citizens Rights, *No to the Justice of the Street*, August 2001 (Arabic).
71 The Interim Agreement, 1994.
72 For more information see: Daud Suleiman, *The PA in One Year, 1994–1995* (Amman: Dar Al-Bashir, 1996), pp. 74–109.
73 More on the court see the special report of the Palestinian Independent Commission for Citizens Rights, *No to the Justice of the Street*.
74 Ghazali, *The Best Journalist is the Best Loyalist*, p. 2.
75 See paragraph 37 resolution 6 in the Palestinian Press Law.

4 The Deconstruction of Gender Regime: The Women's Movement and the Predicament of Equal Citizenship

1 Nira Yuval-Davis and Anthias Floya, eds., *Woman-Nation State* (Basingstoke: Macmillan, 1989).
2 Rabab Abdulhadi, "The Palestinian Women's Autonomous Movement: Emergence, Dynamics, and Challenges," *Gender and Society*, vol. 12, no. 2 (December 1998): 649–73.
3 Nahla Abdo, "Nationalism and Feminism: Palestinian Women and the Intifada – No Going Back?" in Valentine M. Moghadam, *Gender and National Identity: Women and Politics in Muslim Societies* (London: Zed Books, 1994).
4 Nancy Fraser, *Justice Interruptus* (New York: Routledge, 1997).
5 Chris Weedon, *Feminist Practice and Post-structuralist Theory* (Oxford: Basil Blackwell, 1987).
6 Rober William Connell, *Gender and Power: Society, the Person and Sexual Politics* (Stanford: Stanford University Press, 1987), p. 130.

7 Deniz Kandiyoti, "Identity and its Discontents: Women and the Nation", *Millennium*, vol. 20, no. 3 (1991): 429–43.
8 Elizabeth Weed, *Coming to Terms: Feminism, Theory, Politics* (London: Routledge, 1989), p. xix.
9 Connell, *Gender and Power*, pp. 107–42.
10 Patricia Hill-Collins, *Black Feminist Thought: Knowledge, Consciousness and the Politics of Empowerment* (Boston: Unwin Hyman, 1990).
11 Weedon, *Feminist Practice*.
12 Ibid., p. 37.
13 Nancy Fraser, *Justice Interruptus*.
14 Ibid., p. 153.
15 Hisham Sharabi, *Neopatriarchy: A Theory of Distorted Change in Arab Society* (New York and Oxford: Oxford University Press, 1988).
16 Nadera Kevorkian-Shalhoub, "Wife Abuse: A Method of Social Control", *Israeli Social Sciences Research*, no. 12 (1997): 59–72.
17 Chandra Talpade Mohanty, "Under Western Eyes: Feminist Scholarship and Colonial Discourse", in Chandra Talpade Mohanty, Ann Russo and Lourdes Torres, eds., *Third World Women and the Politics of Feminism* (Bloomington: Indiana University Press, 1991), pp. 51–80.
18 Nadera Kevorkian-Shalhoub, "Tolerating Battering: Invisible Methods of Social Control", *International Review of Victimology*, no. 5 (1997): 1–21.
19 Amal Kawar, *Daughters of Palestine: Leading Women of the Palestinian National Movement* (Albany, New York: State University of New York Press 1996); Islah Jad, "From Salons to the Popular Committees: Palestinian Women, 1919–1989", in Jamal Nassar and Roger Heacock, eds., *Intifada: Palestine at the Crossroads* (New York: Praeger Press, 1990), pp. 125–42; Julie Peteet, *Gender in Crisis: Women and the Palestinian Resistance Movement* (New York: Columbia University Press, 1991).
20 Judith Butler, *Gender Trouble: Feminism and the Subversion of Identity* (New York: Routledge, 1990), p. 8.
21 Lisa McLaughlin, "Beyond 'Separate Spheres': Feminism and the Cultural Studies/Political Economy Debate" *Journal of Communication Inquiry*, vol. 23, no. 4 (October 1999): 327–54.
22 Suha Sabbagh, "The Declaration of Principles on Palestinian Women's Rights: An Analysis", in Suha Sabbagh, ed., *Arab Women: Between Defiance and Restraint* (New York: Olive Branch Press, 1996), pp. 115–20.
23 Maha Abu-Dayyeh Shamas, *Towards Equality: Examination of the Status of Palestinian Women in Existing Law* (Jerusalem: Women's Center for Legal Aid and Counseling, 1995), p. 3.
24 *Women and Men in Palestine: Directions and Statistics*. Palestinian Central Bureau of Statistics, 1998, p. 170.
25 *Decision Making Positions for Women in Six Palestinian Ministries*. Women's Studies Center – The Research Unit. Jerusalem, 1999, p. 9.
26 Ibid., p. 24.
27 Ibid., p. 9.
28 Women's Affairs Technical Committee's website: <www.pal-watc.org/background.html>.

29   A copy of the declaration is found in: Maria Holt, *Women in Contemporary Palestine: Between Old Conflicts and New Realities* (Jerusalem: PASSIA, 1996), pp. 99–102.

30   Nathan J. Brown, "Constituting Palestine: The Effort to Write a Basic Law for the Palestinian Authority", *Middle East Journal*, vol. 54, no. 1 (Winter 2000): 25–43.

31   See the charter in: Holt, *Women in Contemporary Palestine.*

32   Islah Jad, Penny Johnson and Rita Giacaman, "Transit Citizens: Gender and Citizenship under the Palestinian Authority," in Suad Joseph, ed., *Gender and Citizenship in the Middle East* (Syracuse, New York: Syracuse University Press, 2001), p. 234.

33   Personal interviews with women's rights activists in the West Bank and Gaza Strip.

34   Glenn E. Robinson, *Building a Palestinian State: The Incomplete Revolution* (Bloomington: Indiana University Press, 1997).

35   Flah Al-Safadi and I'atidal Qunita, "Political Parties Are Schizophrenic Regarding Women Issues", *Women's Voice*, no. 97, May 4, 2000 (A biweekly publication of WATC) (Arabic).

36   For a deeper understanding of the rationale behind this stream of thought see: Zuhaira Kamal, "The Role of NGOs in Meeting the Basic Needs of Citizens before and after the PA: A Critical Viewpoint", paper presented in a workshop of UNESCO, February 14–17, 2000; Zuhaira Kamal, "The Experience of the Women's Movement: Between the Popular and the Governmental", paper presented to the women's movement conference: *The Predicament of Democratization: Future Strategies*, January 17–18, 1999.

37   Rema Hammami, *Palestinian Women: A Status Report-Labor and Economy* (Bir-Zzeit University: Women''s Studies Program, 1997).

38   Eileen Kuttab, "Manpower Development and Gender", *Women's Voice*, no. 82 (October 7, 1999), p. 9 (Arabic).

39   Ibid., p. 9.

40   Ibid., p. 9.

41   Rema Hammami and Penny Johnson, "Equality with Difference: Gender and Citizenship in Traditional Palestine", *Social Politics* (Fall 1999): 314–43.

42   Ibid., p. 319.

43   Suheir Azzouni, "Lobbying for Citizenship Rights: The Palestinian Case", WATC publications, 1999.

44   Sherena Berger-Gluck, "Palestine: Shifting Sands: The Feminist-Nationalist Connection in the Palestinian Movement", in Lois A. West, ed., *Feminist Nationalism* (London: Routledge, 1997), pp. 101–29.

45   This was one of the main demands of WATC, especially prior to the national elections for the PLC. See Suhheir Azzouni, "Palestinian Women and Equal Status in Society", <www.pal-watc.org/women.html>.

46   Deniz Kandiyoti, "Islam and Patriarchy: A Comparative Perspective", in Nikki Keddie and Beth Baron, eds., *Women in Middle Eastern History: Shifting Boundaries in Sex and Gender* (New Haven: Yale University Press, 1991), p. 31.

47   Sylvia Walby, *Theorizing Patriarchy* (Oxford: Blackwell, 1990), p. 24.

48   Deniz Kandiyoti, "Introduction", in Deniz Kandiyoti, ed., *Women, Islam and the State* (Philadelphia: Temple University Press, 1991), pp. 1–21.

49   Women's Affairs Technical Committee's websight. <www.pal-watc.org/background.html>. See the editorial of vol. 4, no. 1 (Autumn 1998).

50 An indication of such a learning process could be seen through the women from other Arab countries invited for workshops and lectures in women centers. See *Palestinian Women's Network*, vol. 2, no. 5 (Summer/Autumn 1997). On the marginalization of the women's movement in Algeria see Marnia Lazreg, *The Eloquence of Silence: Algerian Women in Question* (New York: Routledge, 1994).

51 Asmah Khader, *The Law and the Future of Palestinian Women* (Jerusalem: Women's Center for Legal Aid and Counseling, 1998).

52 One has to indicate that the Jews are ruled by Jewish law which is the official religion of the state. As a result we find that the religious communities of Arab origin are discriminated against as compared to the Jewish religious establishment.

53 Jad, Johnson and Giacaman, "Transit Citizens".

54 A document entitled: *The Model Parliament: Women and Legislation* (Jerusalem: Women's Center for Legal Aid and Counseling. 1998).

55 Azzouni, *Lobbying for Citizenship Rights*.

56 Ibid.

57 Hammami and Johnson, *Equality with Difference*, p. 22.

58 Lynn Welchman, *Islamic Family Law: Text and Practice in Palestine* (Jerusalem: Women's Center for Legal Aid and Counselling, 1999); Asma Khader, *The Law and the Future of Palestinian Women* (Jerusalem: Women's Center for Legal Aid and Counseling, 1998) (Arabic).

59 Khader, *The Law*, p. 19.

60 Nahda Y. Shahada, *Gender and Politics in Palestine: Discourse Analysis of the Palestinian Authority and Islamists*, unpublished MA Thesis, Institute of Social Studies, The Netherlands, 1999, p. 41.

61 Ziad Othman, "The Palestinian Model Parliament –Women and Legislation: Between Renewal and Reframing", *Palestine Policy*, vol. 5, no. 19 (Summer 1998): 57–85.

62 Nahla Abdo, "Muslim Family Law: Articulating Gender, Class and the State", *International Review of Comparative Public Policy*, no. 9 (1997): 169–94.

63 Abdullhadi Ahmed Al-Na'im, "Foreword", in Lynn Welchman, *Islamic Family Law* (Jerusalem: WACLAC, 1999), pp. 11–14.

64 Gluck, *Palestine: Shifting Sands*, p. 112.

65 Azzouni, *Lobbying for Citizenship Rights*, p. 3.

66 Zuhhaira Kamal, "Introduction", in Asma Khader, *The Law and the Future of Palestinian Women*, pp. 9–13; Hamammi and Johnson, *Equality with Difference*, p. 241.

67 Joseph Massad, "Conceiving the Masculine: Gender and Palestinian Nationalism", *Middle East Journal*, vol. 49, no. 3 (Summer 1995): 467–83.

68 Amal Jamal, "Palestinian Media: Public Servant or a Vanguard of Democracy", *Journal of Palestine Studies*, vol. 29, no. 3 (2000): 45–59.

69 Sama Awida-Liftawi, *Workshop on Integrating Gender in Leadership and Planning* (Ramallah: Women's Affairs Committee, 1995).

70 See the Work Plan, National Strategy Project for Palestinian Women,

prepared by the General Union of Palestinian Women, 2000. A circulated document.

71 See the meaning and importance of agenda setting in: James W. Dearing and Everett M. Rogers, *Agenda-Setting* (London: Sage Publications, 1996).

72 Gadi Wolfsfeld claims that weak groups need to behave or articulate themselves in a deviant way in order to attract the attention of the media. See his book: Gadi Wolfsfeld, *Media and Political Conflict* (Cambridge: Cambridge University Press, 1997).

73 William A. Gamson & Andre Modigliani, "The Changing Culture of Affirmative Action", in: Richard G. Braungart & Margaret Braungart, eds., *Research in Political Sociology*, no. 3 (New Haven, CT: Yale University Press, 1987), pp. 53–76.

74 Liesbet Van Zoonen, *Feminist Media Studies* (London: Sage, 1994).

75 See Issue 78, August 12,1999 and Issue 92, February 24, 2000.

76 See Issue 90, January 27, 2000.

77 See Issue 94, March 23, 2000.

78 See Issue 105, August 24, 2000.

79 "Shame" is a concept prominent in Arab culture that imposes specific norms of behavior on Arab women. Arab women are also perceived as a source of shame, disgrace or dishonor.

80 For a theoretical elaboration of this point of view see the introduction of Bryan Turner in his edited volume, *Citizenship and Social Theory* (London: Sage, 1993).

81 For more on this critique see, Michael Mann, "Ruling Class Strategies and Citizenship", *Sociology,* vol. 21, no. 3 (August 1987): 339–54; see also Jad, Johnson and Giacaman, "Transit Citizens".

82 See Issue 91, February 10, 2000.

83 See Issue 91, February 10, 2000.

84 On the individualistic–communitarian debate see: Shlomo Avineri and Avner de-Shalit, *Communitarianism and Individualism* (Oxford: Oxford University Press, 1992).

85 See Issue 89, January 2000.

86 See Issue 89, January 2000.

87 Kevorkian-Shalhoub, "Tolerating Battering", pp. 1–21.

88 See Issue 102, July 13, 2000.

89 See a critique of such social habits and norms in the novels and stories of the Palestinian novelist Sahar Khalifa, especially in *We Are Not Your Slaves Anymore* and *The Inheritance* (Arabic).

90 For a tragic account of such a case see: Fawaz Turki, *Exiles Return: The Making of a Palestinian American* (New York: Free Press, 1994).

91 See Issue 84, November 7, 1999.

92 Jad, Johnson, and Giacaman, "Transit Citizens", p. 218.

93 Jerusalem Media and Communication Center (JMCC). Jerusalem, March 1999.

94 Moghadam, *Gender and National Identity;* Shahada, *Gender and Politics.*

95 For a detailed view of the public opinion towards the PA see: *Public Opinion Polls*, no. 25–48, December 1996–April 2000, Center for Palestine Research and Studies, Nablus, Palestine.

96 Sara Roy, "The Transformation of Islamic NGOs in Palestine", *Middle East Report*, vol. 30, no. 1 (Spring 2000): 24–6.
97 *Al-Quds*, March 26, 1998.
98 *Al-Quds*, March 26,1998.
99 Ibid.
100 *Al-Quds*, March 27, 1998.
101 Ibid..
102 Azzouni, *Lobbying for Citizenship Rights*, p. 10.
103 Shahada, *Gender and Politics*, p. 66.
104 Ibid., p. 3.
105 Azzouni, *Lobbying for Citizenship Rights,* p. 10.
106 Jad, Johnson and Giacaman, "Transit Citizens", p. 224.
107 Bernard Sabella, "Political Trends and the New Elites in Palestine", in Mahdi Abdul Hadi, ed., *Dialogue on Palestinian State-Building and Identity* (Jerusalem: PASSIA, 1999), pp. 35–42.
108 For a good comparason see: Arato Yesim, *The Patriarchal Paradox: Women Politicians in Turkey* (Cranbury, NJ: Associated University Press, 1989).
109 Lisa Taraki, *Palestinian Society: Contemporary Realities and Trends* (Bir-Zeit: Women's Studies Center, 1997), p. 17.

5 Framing Authenticity: Religious Discourse and the Islamist Media

1 Meir Hatina, *Palestinian Radicalism: The Islamic Jihad Movement* (Tel Aviv: Moshe Dayan Center, 1994) (Hebrew).
2 Ziad Abu Amr, *Islamic Fundamentalism in the West Bank and Gaza* (Bloomington: Indiana University Press, 1994).
3 These radical positions have been changed slightly. For more details see: Shaul Mishal and Avraham Sela, *The Palestinian Hamas* (New York: Columbia University Press, 2000).
4 See the polls of JMCC: <www.jmcc.org>.
5 Khaled Hurub, *Hamas: Political Thought and Practice* (Washington, DC: Institute for Palestine Studies, 2000), p. 103; on the willingness of Hamas to take part in the PA administration see the Interview with Mahmud Zahhar, "Hamas: Waiting for Secular Nationalism to Self-Destruct", *Journal of Palestine Studies*, vol. 24, no. 3 (Spring 1995): 81–8.
6 Ibid., p. 83.
7 Mishal and Sela, *The Palestinian Hamas.*
8 Hamas has published a new document explaining its policies towards the PA and the peace process in mid-August 2004. The movement explained that it plans to participate in running the Gaza Strip with the PA in case of an Israeli one-sided withdrawal without negotiations from this area. This has marked a change in the movement policies, resulting maybe from its weakening position as a result of the assassination of its founder, Sheikh Ahmad Yassin and its elected leader, Abdel Aziz Rantisi by Israel. *Ha'aretz*, August 15, 2004.
9 Ziad Abu Amr, "Report from Palestine", *Journal of Palestine Studies*, vol. 24, no. 2 (Winter 1995): 40–7.
10 George Giacaman and Dag Jorund Lonning, *After Oslo: New Realities, Old Problems* (London Pluto, 1998).

11 On Hamas' framing policies and the methods of image construction see: Ahmed Bin Yusef, *The Islamic Resistance Movement (Hamas): An Ephemeral Event or Permanent Alternative?* (Chicago: The International Center for Studies and Research, 1990) (Arabic).

12 On the dialogue between the PA and Hamas see: Hurub, *Hamas*; Mishal and Sela, *The Palestinian Hamas*.

13 Most of the meetings took place in Cairo under the auspecies of the Egyptian government. Egypt's security personnel, such as Omar Sulayman, were deeply involved in these negotiations in an effort to reduce the damage that the PA-Hamas differences caused to the Palestinian image and to the chances to resume peace talks in the future.

14 These negotiations were covered by many news agencies, see: <www.aljazeera.com; www.haaretz.co.il>.

15 Hurub, *Hamas*, p. 107.

16 For more details on the role of the mosques and collages in raising a new generation of Moslem political activists see: Beverly Milton-Edwards, *Islamic Politics in Palestine* (London: I. B. Tauris, 1999).

17 Hurub, *Hamas*.

18 On the social network of Hamas, see Abu Amr, *Report from Palestine*.

19 See the report of the Palestinian Human Rights Monitoring Group, *Media in Palestine: Between the PNAs Hammer and the Anvil of Self-Censorship*, November 1999.

20 See the homepage of the Khalas party: <www.khalas.org/define>.

21 Mishal and Sela, *The Palestinian Hamas*, p. 145.

22 Jamal Mansur, *Palestinian Democratic Transformation: An Islamic Perspective* (Nablus: Center for Palestine Research and Studies, 1999) (Mansur was among the eight Palestinians killed in an Israeli missile attack on a building in downtown Nablus in August 2001.)

23 *Al-Risalah*, March 23, 2000, p. 5.

24 *Al-Risalah*, March 11, 1999, p. 3.

25 Such a type of answer is authenticated by the Palestinian Minister of Information, Yasser Abed Rabbo in an interview in *Palestine–Israel Journal*, vol. v, no. 3/4 , 1998, pp. 13–28.

26 *Al-Risalah*, March 23, 2000, p. 5.

27 *Al-Risalah*, March 23, 2000, p. 5.

28 See the Annual Reports of The Palestinian Independent Commission for Citizens Rights, 1997, 1998, 1999, 2000.

29 Sara Roy, "The Transformation of Islamic NGOs in Palestine", *Middle East Report*, vol. 30, no. 1 (Spring 2000): 24–6.

30 *Al-Risalah*, May 6, 1999, p. 3.

31 *Al-Risalah*, May 6, 1999, p. 4.

32 *Al-Risalah*, May 13, 1999, p. 5.

33 *Al-Risalah*, September 2, 1999, p. 3.

34 See *Al-Risalah*, May 6, 1999, p. 4.

35 This expression was used by Israeli leaders in particular when referring to deadlines set by in the agreements between Israel and the Palestinians for

particular steps to be implemented, such as withdrawal of Israeli forces from certain areas in the territories.

36 See *Al-Risalah*, September 9, 1999, p. 2.
37 *Al-Risalah*, September 9, 1999, p. 2.
38 *Al-Risalah*, September 16, 1999, p. 4.
39 See *Al-Risalah*, September 16, 1999, p. 4; September 30, 1999, p. 13; May 25, 2000, p. 5.
40 *Al-Risalah*, September 9, 1999, p. 13.
41 *Al-Risalah*, May 11, 2000, p. 21.
42 Here the author is referring to such manifestations of the occupation as settlements, army roadblocks and army bases.
43 *Al-Risalah*, September 9, 1999, p. 13; March 23, 2000, p. 10; March 30, 2000, p. 10; May 11, 2000, p. 21.
44 *Al-Risalah*, March 23, 2000, p. 10; March 30, 2000, p. 10; May 11, 2000, p. 21.
45 See editions, March 4, 1999, p. 16; March 11, 1999, p. 3; March 25, 1999, p. 12; May 13, 1999, p. 5; September 23,1999, p. 4; September 30, 1999, p. 4; March 2, 2000, p. 2.
46 See editions, March 4, 1999, p. 16; March 11, 1999, p. 10; March 18, 1999, p. 4 and 5.
47 *Al-Risalah*, September 30, 1999, p. 13.
48 See Adel Samara, "Globalization, The Palestinian Economy, and the 'Peace Process'", *Journal of Palestine Studies*, vol. 29, no. 2 (Winter 2000): 20–34; Sara Roy, "The Seeds of Chaos, and of Night'": The Gaza Strip after the Agreement', *Journal of Palestine Studies*, vol. 23, no. 3 (Spring 1994): 86; Sara Roy, "Development Revisited: Palestinian Economy and Society Since Oslo", *Journal of Palestine Studies*, vol. 28, no. 3 (Spring 1999): 64–82.
49 See *Al-Risalah*, March 9, 2000, p. 3.
50 *Al-Risalah*, May 18, 2000, p. 11.
51 *Al-Risalah*, July 13, 2000, p. 19.
52 *Al-Risalah*, September 9, 1999, p. 7.
53 *Al-Risalah*, September 9, 1999, p. 7.
54 Ibid., p. 7.
55 *Al-Risalah*, March 15, 2000, p. 3.
56 *Al-Risalah*, May 4, 2000, p. 3.
57 Many civil organizations such as the PNGO identified with the teachers and criticized the way they are treated by the PA. See the memorandum issued by PNGO in the Palestinian press, February 23, 2000.
58 *Al-Risalah*, March 4, 1999, p. 17.
59 On political imprisonment see the special report prepared by The Palestinian Independent Commission for Citizens Rights, *Political Imprisonment by the PA in the Year 2000*, November 2000.
60 I am speaking specifically about political prisoners and not those imprisoned for their military (i.e. "terrorist") activities.
61 *Al-Risalah*, March 11, 1999, p. 10, and March 18, 1999, p. 4.
62 *Al-Risalah*, March 25, 1999, p. 12.
63 *Al-Risalah*, May 11, 2000, p. 17.

64   See *Al-Risalah*, March 2, 2000, p. 2; March 15, 2000, p. 3; May 25, 2000, p. 3; July 13, 2000, p. 3; July 27, 2000, p. 6; September 14, 2000, p. 9.

Conclusion

1   See *Al-Ayyam*, November 27, 1999, p. 3.

Bibliography

Books

Abu Amr, Ziad, *Islamic Fundamentalism in the West Bank and Gaza* (Bloomington: Indiana University Press, 1994).

Al-Hussari, Ruba, Khalili, Ali and Al-Salhi, Bassam, *The Palestinian Press Between Now and Future Developments* (Ramallah: Muwatin, 1993) (Arabic).

Al-Hut-Nuwayhid, Bayan, *The Leadership and the Institutions in Palestine, 1917–1948* (Beirut: Institute for Palestine Studies, 1981) (Arabic).

Aquinas, St. Thomas, *Summa Theologica* Ia, Iiae, Q 90, Art. 4.

Arato, Yesim, *The Patriarchal Paradox: Women Politicians in Turkey* (Cranbury, NJ: Associated University Press, 1989).

Arendt, Hannah, *On Revolution* (New York: Viking Press, 1963).

Avineri, Shlomo and De-Shalit, Avner, *Communitarianism and Individualism* (Oxford: Oxford University Press, 1992).

Awida-Liftawi, Sama, *Workshop on Integrating Gender in Leadership and Planning* (Ramallah: Women's Affairs Committee, 1995).

Ayalon, Ami, *The Press in the Middle East: A History* (New York: Oxford University Press, 1995).

Ayubi, Nazih, *Over-stating the Arab State: Politics and Society in the Middle East* (London: I. B. Tauris Publishers, 1995).

Bauman, Zygmunt, *Postmodern Ethics* (Cambridge: Blackwell, 1994).

Baumgarten, Helga, *Befreiung in den Staat: Die Palestinensiche nationalbewegung seit 1948* (Frankfurt an Main: Suhrkamp, 1991).

Benvenisti, Miron, *Israeli Censorship of Arab Publications* (Jerusalem: The West Bank Data Base Project, 1983).

Bin Yusef, Ahmed, *The Islamic Resistance Movement (Hamas): An Ephemeral Event or Permanent Alternative?* (Chicago: The International Center for Studies and Research, 1990) (Arabic).

Brand, A. Laurie, *The Palestinians in the Arab world: Institution Building and the Search for State* (New York: Columbia University Press, 1988).

Brown, Nathan, *Palestinian Politics after the Oslo Accords: Resuming Arab Palestine* (Berkeley: University of California Press, 2003).

Brubaker, Roger, *Nationalism Reframed: Nationhood and the National Question in the New Europe* (Cambridge: Cambridge University Press, 1996).

Butler, Judith, *Gender Trouble: Feminism and the Subversion of Identity* (New York: Routledge, 1990).

Cohen, L. Jean and Arato, Andrew, *Civil Society and Political Theory* (Cambridge, MA & London: MIT Press, 1995).

Connell-Robert, William, *Gender and Power: Society, the Person and Sexual Politics* (Stanford: Stanford University Press, 1987).

Dearing, W. James and Rogers, M. Everett, *Agenda-Setting* (London: Sage Publications, 1996).

Eickelman, F. Dale and Anderson, W. Jon, eds., *New Media in the Muslim World: The Emerging Public Sphere* (Bloomington: Indiana University Press, 1999).

Eisenstadt, N. Samuel, Luis, Roniger and Adam, Seligman, eds., *Centre Formation, Protest Movements and Class Structure in Europe and the United States* (New York: New York University Press, 1987).

Foucault, Michel, *The Archeology of Knowledge,* trans. A. M. Sheridan Smith (New York: Pantheon Books, 1992).

Fraser, Nancy, *Justice Interruptus* (New York: Routledge, 1997).

Frisch, Hillel, *Countdown to Statehood: Palestinian State Formation in the West Bank and Gaza* (New York: State University of New York Press, 1998).

Garber, Doris, ed., *Media Power in Politics* (Washington, DC: CQ Press, 2000).

Ghalion, Burhan, *Le Malaise Arabe: L'Etat Contre la Nation* (Paris: La Decouverte, 1991).

Ghanem, As'ad, *The Palestinian Regime: A Partial Democracy* (Brighton & Portland: Sussex Academic Press, 2001).

Giacaman, George and Lonning-Dag, Jorund, *After Oslo: New Realities, Old Problems* (London Pluto, 1998).

Giddens, Anthony, *The Nation-State and Violence* (Oxford: Polity Press, 1985).

Gilliomee, Herman and Simkins, Charles, eds., *The Awkward Embrace: One Party Domination and Democracy* (Switzerland: Harwood Academic Publishers, 2000).

Graham, Usher, *Palestine in Crisis* (London: Pluto Press, 1995).

Habermas, Jürgen, *Die Nachholende Revolution: Klein politische Schriften* VII (Frankfurt: Suhrkamp, 1991).

Habermas, Jürgen, *The Structural Transformation of the Public Sphere* (Cambridge: Polity Press, 1992).

Hammami, Rema, *Palestinian Women: A Status Report – Labor and Economy* (Birzeit University: Women"s Studies Program, 1997).

Hatina, Meir, *Palestinian Radicalism: The Islamic Jihad Movement* (Tel Aviv: Moshe Dayan Center, 1994) (Hebrew).

Hilal, Jamil, *The Palestinian Political System after Oslo: An Analytical Study* (Ramallah: Muwatin, 1998) (Arabic).

Hilal, Jamil, *The Formation of the Palestinian Elite: From the Emergence of the National Movement to the Establishment of the National Authority* (Ramallah and Amman: Muwatin and al-Urdun al-Jadid, 2002) (Arabic).

Hill-Collins, Patricia, *Black Feminist Thought: Knowledge, Consciousness and the Politics of Empowerment* (Boston: Unwin-Hyman, 1990).

Holmes, Deborah, *Governing the Press: Media Freedom in the U.S. and Great Britain* (Boulder: Westview Press, 1986).

Holt, Maria, *Women in Contemporary Palestine: Between Old Conflicts and New Realities* (Jerusalem: PASSIA, 1996).

Hurub, Khaled, *Hamas: Political Thought and Practice* (Washington, DC: Institute for Palestine Studies, 2000).

Iyengar, Shanto and Kinder, R. Donald, *News That Matter* (Chicago: University of Chicago Press, 1987).

Kaid, Aziz, *On the Overlapping Responsibilities in the Institutions of the Palestinian Authority* (Ramallah: Palestinian Independent Commission for Citizen's Rights, 1999).

Kawar, Amal, *Daughters of Palestine: Leading Women of the Palestinian National Movement* (Albany, New York: State University of New York Press 1996).

Keane, John, ed., *Civil Society and the State* (London: Verso Press, 1988).

Khader, Asma, *The Law and the Future of Palestinian Women* (Jerusalem: Women Center for Legal Aid and Counseling, 1998).

Khalidi, Rashid, *Palestinian Identity: The Construction of modern National Consciousness* (New York: Columbia University Press, 1997).

Khalifa, Sahar, *Lam Nau'od Jawari Lakum* (We Are Not Your Slaves Anymore (Beirut: Dar Al-Adab, 1988); *Al-Mirath* (The Inheritance) (Beirut: Dar Al-Adab, 1997).

Kimmerling, Baruch, *Politicide: Ariel Sharon's wars against the Palestinians* (New York: Verso, 2003).

Laclau, Ernesto and Mouffe, Chantal, *Hegemony and Socialist Strategy: Towards a Radical Democratic Politics* (London: Verso, 1985).

Lazreg, Marnia, *The Eloquence of Silence: Algerian Women in Question* (New York: Routledge, 1994).

Mahler, Gregory, *Constitutionalism and Palestinian Constitutional Development* (Jerusalem: PASSIA, 1996).

Mansur, Jamal, *Palestinian Democratic Transformation: An Islamic Perspective* (Nablus: Center for Palestine Research and Studies, 1999).

McAdam, Doug, McCarthy, John, and Zald, Mayer, eds, *Comparative Perspectives on Social Movements: Political Opportunities, Mobilization Structures, and Cultural Framing* (New York: Cambridge University Press, 1996).

McNair, Brian, *An Introduction to Political Communication* (London: Routledge, 1995).

Michael, Hudson, *The Arab World: The Search for Legitimacy* (New Haven, CT: Yale University Press, 1977).

Milton-Edwards, Beverly, *Islamic Politics in Palestine* (London: I. B. Tauris, 1999).

Mishal, Shaul and Sela, Avraham, *The Palestinian Hamas* (New York: Columbia University Press, 2000).

Mosely-Lesch, Ann, *Arab Politics in Palestine, 1917–1939 : The Frustration of a Nationalist Movement* (Ithaca, N.Y. : Cornell University Press, 1979).

Muhsin, Sami, *Freedom of Press under the Palestinian Authority* (Jerusalem: The Palestinian Society for the Protection of Human Rights and the Environment, 1996). (Arabic)

Norton-Augustus, Richard, ed., *Civil Society in the Middle East* (Leiden: Brill, 1995).

O'Donnell, Guillermo, Schmitter, C. Philippe, and Whitehead, Laurence, eds.,

Transition From Authoritarian Rule: Tentative Conclusions About Uncertain Transitions (Baltimore: Johns Hopkins University Press, 1986).

O'Leary, Brendan, Lustick, Ian and Callaghy, Thomas, eds., *Right-Sizing the State: The Politics of Moving Boarders* (Oxford: Oxford University Press, 2001).

Peleg, Ilan, ed., *Patterns of Censorship around the World* (Boulder: Westview Press, 1993).

Peteet, Julie, *Gender in Crisis: Women and the Palestinian Resistance Movement* (New York: Columbia University Press, 1991).

Poggi, Gianfranco, *The Development of the Modern State: A Sociological Introduction* (Stanford, CA: Stanford University Press, 1978).

Poggi, Gianfranco, *The State: Its Nature, Development and Prospects* (Stanford: Stanford University Press, 1990).

Porath, Yehoshua, *The Emergence of the Palestinian-Arab National Movement, 1918–1929* (London: Frank Cass, 1974).

Porath, Yehoshua, *The Palestinian Arab National Movement: from riots to rebellion Volume two, 1929–1939* (London; Totowa, NJ: Frank Cass, 1977).

Price, E. Monroe, *Television, the Public Sphere, and National Identity* (Oxford: Clarendon Press, 1995).

Robinson, E. Glenn, *Building a Palestinian State: The Incomplete Revolution* (Bloomington: Indiana University Press, 1997).

Rubin, Barry, *The Transformation of Palestinian Politics: From Revolution to State Building* (Cambridge, MA: Harvard University Press, 1999).

Rugh, A. William, *The Arab Press* (Syracuse: Syracuse University Press, 1979).

Sahliyeh, Emile, *In Search of Leadership: West Bank Politics* (Washington, DC: Brookings Institution, 1988).

Said, Edward, *The World, The Text and The Critic* (London: Vintage, 1991).

Sayigh, Rosemary, *Palestinians: From Peasants to Revolutionaries: A People's History* (London: Zed Press, 1979).

Sayigh, Yezid, *Armed Struggle and the Search for Statehood: The Palestinian National Movement, 1949–1993* (Oxford: Clarendon Press, 1997).

Schultz-Lindholm, Helena, *The Reconstruction of Palestinian Nationalism* (Manchester: Manchester University Press, 1999).

Shain, Yossi and Linz, Juan, *Between States* (Cambridge: Cambridge University Press, 1995).

Shamas-Abu-Dayyeh, Maha, *Towards Equality: Examination of the Status of Palestinian Women in Existing Law* (Jerusalem: Women's Center for Legal Aid and Counseling, 1995).

Sharabi, Hisham, *Neopatriarchy: A Theory of Distorted Change in Arab Society* (New York and Oxford: Oxford University Press, 1988).

Shinar, Dov, *Palestinian Voices: Communication and Nation Building in the West Bank* (Boulder, CO: Rienner, 1987).

Shinar, Dov and Rubinstein, Danny, *Palestinian Press in the West Bank: The Political Dimension* (Jerusalem: The Jerusalem Post, 1987).

Steinmetz, George, ed., *State/Culture: State Formation After the Cultural Turn* (Ithaca: Cornell University Press, 1999).

Suleiman, Daud, *The PA in One Year, 1994–1995* (Amman: Dar Al-Bashir, 1996).

Taraki, Lisa, *Palestinian Society: Contemporary Realities and Trends* (Birzeit: Women's Studies Center, 1997).

Tarrow, Sidney, *Power in Movement: Social Movements and Contentious Politics,* 2nd edn (Cambridge: Cambridge University Press, 1998).

Taylor, Charles, *Philosophical Arguments* (Cambridge, MA: Harvard University Press, 1995).

Tilly, Charles, ed., *The Formation of National States in Western Europe* (Princeton: Princeton University Press, 1975).

Tilly, Charles, *Coercion, Capital, and European States, AD 990–1990* (Cambridge, MA: Blackwell, 1990).

Turki, Fawaz, *Exiles Return: The Making of a Palestinian American* (New York: Free Press, 1994).

Turner, Bryan, *Citizenship and Social Theory* (London: Sage, 1993).

Van-Dijk, A. Teun, ed., *Discourse as Social Interaction* (London: Sage Publications, 1998).

Van-Zoonen, Liesbet, *Feminist Media Studies* (London: Sage, 1994).

Walby, Sylvia, *Theorizing Patriarchy* (Oxford: Blackwell, 1990)

Weber, Max, *Political Writings,* edited by Peter Lassman and Ronald Speirs (Cambridge: Cambridge University Press, 1994).

Weed, Elizabeth, *Coming to Terms: Feminism, Theory, Politics* (London: Routledge, 1989).

Weedon, Chris, *Feminist Practice and Post-structuralist Theory* (Oxford: Basil Blackwell, 1987).

Welchman, Lynn, *Islamic Family Law: Text and Practice in Palestine* (Jerusalem: Women's Center for Legal Aid and Counselling, 1999)

Wolfsfeld, Gadi, *Media and Political Conflict* (Cambridge: Cambridge University Press, 1997).

Yuval-Davis, Nira and Floya, Anthias, eds., *Woman–Nation–State* (Basingstoke, Hants: Macmillan, 1989).

Zuabi, S. Kamal, *The Administrative Law and its Applications in the Hashimite Kingdom of Jordan* (Amman: Jordanian University Press, 1993).

Articles

Abdulhadi, Rabab, "The Palestinian Women's Autonomous Movement: Emergence, Dynamics, and Challenges," *Gender and Society* vol. 12, no. 2 (December 1998): 649–673.

Abdo, Nahla, "Nationalism and Feminism: Palestinian Women and the Intifada – No Going Back?" in Moghadam, M. Valentine, *Gender and National Identity: Women and Politics in Muslim Societies* (London: Zed Books, 1994), pp. 148–170.

Abdo, Nahla, "Muslim Family Law: Articulating Gender, Class and the State", *International Review of Comparative Public Policy, no.* 9 (1997): 169–194.

Abu-Amr, Ziad, "Report from Palestine", *Journal of Palestine Studies*, vol. 24, no. 2 (Winter 1995): 40–47.

Abu-Amr, Ziad, "The Palestinian Legislative Council: A Critical Assessment" *Journal of Palestine Studies*, 26, no. 4 (Summer 1997): 90–97.

Abu-Harthiyeh, Mohammed, "The Duties of the Security Forces," in: Ziad, Arif,

Amr, Adnan, Abu-Harthiyeh, Mohammed and Makki-Madani, Amin, *The Rules of the Police in Palestine* (Ramallah: PICCR, 1998), pp. 53–64. (Arabic).

Al-Safadi, Flah and Qunita, I'atidal, "Political Parties Are Schizophrenic Regarding Women Issues", *Women's Voice*, no. 97, May 4, 2000 (A biweekly publication of WATC) (Arabic).

Al-Taher, Labib, "The Relationship Between The Democratic Project and the Arab Civil Society", *Al-Mustqbal Al-Arabi* (The Arab Future), no. 158 (April 1992): 103.

Amayreh, Khalid, *Middle East International*, no. 542 (January 24, 1997): 18–19.

An-Na'im-Abdullhadi, Ahmed, "Forward", in Welchman, Lynn, *Islamic Family Law* (Jerusalem: WACLAC, 1999), pp. 11–14.

Azzouni, Suheir, "Lobbying for Citizenship Rights: The Palestinian Case", WATC publications, 1999.

Azzouni, Suheir, "Palestinian Women and equal Status in Society", <www.pal-watc.org/women.html>.

Barghouthi, Mustafa, "Palestinian NGOs and their Contribution to Policy making", in Abdul Hadi, *Dialogue on Palestinian State-Building*, pp. 73–80.

Batrawi, Walid, "Palestinian Media: Pre-Intifada to the Present", *Bir Zeit News Report* (1997).

Benhabib, Seyla, "Models of the Public Space: Hannah Arendt, the Liberal Tradition, and Jürgen Habermas," in Calhoun, *Habermas and the Public Sphere*, pp. 73–98.

Berger-Gluck, Sherena, "Palestine: Shifting Sands: The Feminist-Nationalist Connection in the Palestinian Movement", in Lois A. West, ed., *Feminist Nationalism* (London: Routledge, 1997), pp. 101–129.

Bourdieu, Pierre, "Rethinking the State: Genesis and Structure of the Bureaucratic Field", in Steinmetz, *State/Culture*, pp. 53–75.

Brown, Nathan, "Constituting Palestine: The Efforts To Write a Basic Law for the Palestinian Authority", *The Middle East Journal*, vol. 54, no. 1 (2000): 25–43.

Brynen, Rex, "The Neopatrimonial Dimensions of Palestinian Politics", *Journal of Palestine Studies*, vol. 25, no. 1 (Winter 1998): 23–36.

Chalaby, K. Jean, "The Media and the Formation of the Public Sphere in the new Independent States", *Innovation: The European Journal of Social Science*, vol. 11, Iss. 1 (March 1998): 73–85.

Dajani, Mohammed, "Government and Civil Society: Relationships and Roles", in Abdul-Hadi, *Dialogue on Palestinian State-Building*, pp. 81–85.

Fairclough, Norman, "Critical Discourse Analysis and the Maketization of Public Discourse: The Universities", *Discourse and Society*, vol. 4, no. 2 (1993): 133-168.

Fowler, Roger, "Power," in Van-Dijk, A. Teun, ed., *Handbook of Discourse Analysis*, vol. IV, (London: Academic Press, 1985), pp. 61-82.

Frankel-Shlosberg, Leora, "The Palestinian News Game", *Columbia Journalism Review*, vol. 35, no. 1 (May/June 1996): 16–18.

Fraser, Nancy, "Rethinking the Public Sphere: A Contribution to the Critique of Actually Existing Democracy", in Bruce, Robbins, ed., *The Phantom Public Sphere* (Minneapolis: University of Minnesota Press, 1993), pp. 1–32.

Fraser, Nancy, "Rethinking the Public Sphere: A Contribution to the Critique of

Actually Existing Democracy," in Calhoun, *Habermas and the Public Sphere,* pp. 109–142.

Frisch, Hilel, "Modern Absolutist or Neopatriarchal State Building? Customary Law, Extended Families, and the Palestinian Authority", *International Journal of Middle Eastern Studies*, 29 (1997): 341–358.

Frisch, Hillel and Menachem, Hofnung, "State Formation and International Aid: The Emergence of the Palestinian Authority", *World Development*, vol. 25, no. 8 (1999): 1251–1252.

Gamson, A. William and Modigliani, Andre, "The Changing Culture of Affirmative Action", in: Richard, G. Braungart & Margaret, Braungart, eds., *Research in Political Sociology*, no. 3 (New Haven, CT: Yale University Press, 1987), pp. 53–76.

Garnham, Nicholas, "The Media and the Public Sphere," in Craig, Calhoun, ed., *Habermas and the Public Sphere* (Cambridge, MA: The MIT Press, 1993), pp. 359–376.

Ghanem, As'ad, "Founding Elections in Transitional Period: The First Palestinian General Elections", *The Middle East Journal*, vol. 50, no. 4 (Autumn 1996): 513–528.

Ghazali, Said, "The Best Journalist is the Best Loyalist", Arabic Media <www.amin.orgInternet Network>.

Gurevitch, Michael and Blumler, G. Jay, "Linkages between the Mass Media and Politics: A Model for the Analysis of Political Communications Systems", in Curran, James, Gurevitch, Michael and Woollacott, Janet, eds., *Mass Communication and Society* (London: Edward Arnold, 1977), pp. 133–168.

Hammami, Rema and Johnson, Penny, "Equality with Difference: Gender and Citizenship in Traditional Palestine," *Social Politics* (Fall 1999): 314–343.

Hammami, Rema, "Palestinian NGOs since Oslo: From NGO politics to Social Movements?" *Middle East Report*, no. 214 (Spring 2000): 188–202.

Hamza, Alavi, "The State in Post-Colonial Societies: Pakistan and Bangladesh", *New Left Review*, no. 74 (1972): 59–81.

Hooper, Rick, "The International Politics of Assistance to Palestinians in the West Bank and Gaza Strip, 1993–1997", in Roy, Sara, ed., *The Economics of Middle East Peace: A Reassessment* (Stanford, CT: JAI Press, 1999), pp. 59–95.

Jackson, H. Robert and Rosenberg, G. Carl, "Why Africa's Weak States Persist", *World Politics*, vol. 35, no. 1 (October 1982): 1–24.

Jad, Islah, "From Salons to the Popular Committees: Palestinian Women, 1919–1989", in Nassar, Jamal and Heacock, Roger, eds., *Intifada: Palestine at the Crossroads* (New York: Praeger Press, 1990), pp. 125–142.

Jad, Islah, Johnson, Penny and Giacaman, Rita, "Transit Citizens: Gender and Citizenship under the Palestinian Authority," in Joseph Suad, ed., *Gender and Citizenship in the Middle East* (Syracuse, New York: Syracus University Press, 2001), pp. 137–157.

Jamal, Amal, "The Palestinian Media: An Obedient Servant or a Vanguard of Democracy?", *Journal of Palestine Studies*, vol. 29, no. 3 (2000): 45–59.

Jamal, Amal, "State-Building, Institutionalization and Democracy: The Palestinian Experience", *Mediterranean Politics*, vol. 6, no. 3 (Autumn 2001): 1–30.

Jarbawi, Ali, "Palestinian National Identity and the Relations between the Returnees and the people of the Homeland", in Abdul-Hadi, Mahdi, ed., *Dialogue on Palestinian State-Building and Identity* (Jerusalem: PASSIA, 1999), pp. 56–66.

Kamal, Zuhhaira, "Introduction", in Khader, Asma, *The Law and the Future of Palestinian Women*, pp. 9–13

Kamal, Zuhhaira, "The Experience of the Women's Movement: Between the Popular and the Governmental", paper presented to the women's movement conference: *The Predicament of Democratization: Future Strategies*, January 17–18, 1999.

Kamal, Zuhhaira, "The Role of NGOs in Meeting the Basic Needs of Citizens before and after the PA: A Critical Viewpoint", paper presented in a workshop of UNESCO, February 14–17, 2000.

Kandiyoti, Deniz, "Identity and its Discontents: Women and the Nation", *Millennium*. vol. 20, no. 3 (1991): 429–443.

Kandiyoti, Deniz, "Islam and Patriarchy: A comparative Perspective", in Keddie, Nikki and Baron, Beth, eds., *Women in Middle Eastern History: Shifting Boundaries in Sex and Gender* (New Haven: Yale University Press, c1991), Pp. 23–42.

Kandiyoti, Deniz, "Introduction," in Kandiyoti, Deniz, ed., *Women, Islam and the State* (Philadelphia: Temple University Press, 1991),pp. 1–21.

Kevorkian-Shalhoub, Nadera, "Wife Abuse: A Method of Social Control", *Israeli Social Sciences Research*, no. 12 (1997): 59–72.

Kevorkian-Shalhoub, Nadera, "Tolerating Battering: Invisible Methods of Social Control", *International Review of Victimology*, no. 5 (1997): 1–21.

Kress, Gunther, "Ideological Structures in Discourse," in Van-Dijk, A. Teun, ed., *Handbook of Discourse Analysis*, vol. IV (London: Academic Press, 1985), p. 27–28.

Kuttab, Eileen, "Manpower Development and Gender", *Women's Voice*, no. 82 (October 7, 1999), p. 9 (Arabic).

Lent, A. John, "The Mass Media in Asia", in O'Neil, H. Patrick, ed., *Communicating Democracy: The Media and Political Transitions* (Boulder, CO: Lynne Rienner Publishers, 1988), pp. 147–170.

Mann, Michael, "Ruling Class strategies and Citizenship", *Sociology*, vol. 21 no. 3 (August 1987): 339–354.

March, G. James and Olson, P. Johan., "The New Institutionalism: Organizational Factors in Political Life", *American Political Science Review*, no. 78 (September 1984): 734–749.

Massad, Joseph, "Conceiving the Masculine: Gender and Palestinian Nationalism", *Middle East Journal*, vol. 49, no. 3 (Summer 1995): 467–483.

McLaughlin, Lisa, "Beyond 'Separate Spheres': Feminism and the Cultural Studies/Political Economy debate" *Journal of Communication Inquiry*, vol. 23, no. 4 (October 1999): 327–354.

Migdal, S. Joel, "The State in Society: An Approach to Struggles for Domination", in Migdal, S. Joel, Kohli, Atul and Shue, Vivienne, eds., *State Power and Social Forces* (Cambridge: Cambridge University Press, 1996), pp. 7–34.

Mohanty-Chandra, Talpade, "Under Western Eyes: Feminist Scholarship and

Colonial Discourse", in Mohanty-Chandra, Talpade, Russo, Ann and Torres, Lourdes, eds., *Third World Women and the Politics of Feminism* (Bloomington: Indiana University Press, 1991), pp. 51–80.

Norton-Augustus, Richard, "The Future of Civil Society in the Middle East", *Middle East Journal,* vol. 47, no. 2 (Spring 1991): 205–16.

Othman, Ziad, "The Palestinian Model Parliament –Women and Legislation: Between Renewal and Reframing", *Palestine Policy*, vol. 5, no. 19 (Summer 1998): 57–85.

Pensky, Max, "Universalism and the Situated Critic", in White, K. Stephen, ed., *The Cambridge Companion to Habermas* (Cambridge: Cambridge University Press, 1995), pp. 67–94.

Pick, Donald, "Dictatorship vs. Developing Democracy: The Case of the Palestinian Press". <www.arches.uga.edu/~dpick/palpress.html>.

Roy, Sara, "The Seeds of Chaos, and of Night: The Gaza Strip after the Agreement", *Journal of Palestine Studies*, vol. 23, no. 3 (Spring 1994): 85–98.

Roy, Sara, "De-development Revisited: Palestinian Economy and Society since Oslo" *Journal of Palestine Studies*, vol. 28, no. 3 (Spring 1999): 64–82.

Roy, Sara, "The Transformation of Islamic NGOs in Palestine", *Middle East Report*, vol. 30, no. 1 (Spring 2000): 24–26.

Sabbagh, Suha, "The Declaration of Principles on Palestinian Women's Rights: An Analysis", in Sabbagh, Suha, ed., *Arab Women: Between Defiance and Restraint* (New York: Olive Branch Press, 1996), pp. 115–120.

Sabella, Bernard, "Political Trends and the New Elites in Palestine", in Abdul-Hadi, Mahdi, ed., *Dialogue on Palestinian State-Building and Identity* (Jerusalem: PASSIA, 1999), pp. 35–42.

Saleh, Ra'fat, "The Palestinian Legislative Council", in *Palestine Policy*, vol 5, no. 17 (Winter 1998): 94–99. (Arabic).

Samara, Adel, "Globalization, The Palestinian Economy, and the "Peace Process", *Journal of Palestine Studies*, vol. 29, no. 2 (Spring 1999): 20–34.

Shikaki, Khalil, "The Peace Process, National Reconstruction, and the Transition to Democracy in Palestine", *Journal of Palestine Studies*, vol. 25 (1996): 5–20.

Shikaki, Khalil, "Palestinians Divided", *Foreign Affairs* (January–February 2002): 89–105

Shua'ybi, Azmi, "A Window on the Workings of the PA: An Inside View", *Journal of Palestine Studies*, vol. 30, no. 1 (Autumn 2000), pp.88–97.

Scammell, Michael, "Censorship and Its History – A Personal View" in Boyle, Kevin, ed., *Article 19 World Report 1988: Information, Freedom, and Censorship* (New York: Times Books, 1988), pp. 1–18.

Sullivan, J. Denis, "NGOs in Palestine: Agents of Development and Foundation of Civil Society", *Journal of Palestine Studies.* 25, no. 3 (Spring 1996): 93–100.

Tamari, Salim, "The Local and the National in Palestinian Identity" in Abdel-Malek, Kamal and Jacobson, C. David, *Israeli and Palestinian Identities in History and Literature* (New York: St. Martin's Press, 1999), pp. 3–8.

Taylor, Charles, "Modes of Civil Society", *Public Culture*, vol. 3, no. 1 (Fall 1990): 95–118.

Terry-Lynn, Karl, "Dilemmas of Democratization in Latin America", *Comparative Politics*, vol. 23, no. 1 (1990): 1–21.

Zelizer, Barbie, "Journalists as Interpretive Communities", in Berkowitz, Dan, ed., *Social Meaning of News* (London: Sage, 1997), pp. 401–419.
Zvesper, John, "The Separation of Powers in American Politics: Why We Fail to Accentuate the Positive", *Government and Opposition*, vol. 34, no. 1 (Winter 1999): 3–23.

MA Thesis and Ph.D.

Musa, Imad, "The Palestinian Media System" (unpublished MA Thesis), (University of Missouri–Columbia, 1995).
Sh'ahada, Y. Nahda, *Gender and Politics in Palestine: Discourse Analysis of the Palestinian Authority and Islamists*, unpublished M. A. Thesis, Institute of Social Studies, The Netherlands, 1999.

Documents and Reports

"Aid for Trade: Putting Donors to Work", *Palestine Economic Pulse*, vol. 1, no. 5 (September–October 1996).
Annual Reports of The Palestinian Independent Commission for Citizens Rights, 1997, 1998, 1999, 2000.
Cernea Michael M., *Non-governmental Organizations and Local Development*, World Bank, Discussion Papers, no. 40 (1988).
100 Days Plan of the Palestinian Authority. <www.aljazeera.net>.
Decision Making Positions for Women in Six Palestinian Ministries". Women's Studies Center – The Research Unit. Jerusalem, 1999.
Israeli–Palestinian Interim Agreement on the West Bank and Gaza Strip (Jerusalem: Israeli Foreign Ministry, 1995).
Jerusalem Media and Communication Center (JMCC), public opinion poll no. 12, January 1996.
Jerusalem Media and Communication Center (JMCC) public opinion polls no. 29 & 33 August 1998 and October 1999 respectively.
Jerusalem Media and Communication Center (JMCC). Jerusalem . March 1999.
Journal of Palestine Studies, vol. 24, no. 1 (Autumn 1994): 133.
Journal of Palestine Studies, vol. 28 (Autumn 1996): 209 (Arabic).
Journal of Palestine Studies, vol. 28, no. 1 (Autumn 1998): 145.
Journal of Palestine Studies, vol. 30, no. 1 (Autumn 2000): 144–146.
MERIP Report, no. 205. October–December, 1997.
Middle East International, April 10, 1998, 19.
Monitor, vol. 3, no. 1 (January 1999): 22.
Palestine Policy, vol. 2, no. 5 (Winter 1995): 83–186 (Arabic).
Palestine Policy, Vol. 5, no. 20 (Fall 1998): 121 (Arabic).
Palestine Policy, vol. 5, no. 20 (Fall 1998): 116–130 (Arabic).
Palestine Report, published by Jerusalem Media and Communication Center, 20 December, 1996.
Palestine Report, published Jerusalem Media and Communication Center, vol. 2, no. January 10, 1997.
Palestine Report, published Jerusalem Media and Communication Center, vol. 6, no. 50, June 14, 2000.

Palestine the Revolution, no. 987, June 5, 1994 (Arabic).
Palestinian Central Bureau of Statistics, *Women and Men in Palestine: Directions and Statistics*, 1998
Palestinian Independent Commission for Citizens Rights, *Annual Report*, 2000.
Palestinian Independent Commission for Citizens Rights, *Political Imprisonment By the PA in the Year 2000*, November 2000.
Palestinian Independent Commission for Citizens Rights, *No to the Justice of the Street*, August 2001 (Arabic).
Palestinian Women's Network, vol. 2, no. 5 (Summer/Autumn 1997).
Parliamentary Horizons, vol. 3, no. 8 (November 1999): 2.
Peoples' Rights, no. 5 (July 1997), p. 18.
People's Rights, vol. 1, no. 9 (November 1997): 24.
People's Rights, vol. 1, no. 12 (February 1998): 10.
PLC Report, PLC: Information Department, vol. 3, no. 1 (2000): 1.
PNGO *Working Plan*. October 1997.
PNGO *Annual Report*, 1997.
PNGO *Annual Report*, 1998.
PNGO *Annual Report*, 1999.
PNGO *Annual report*, 2000, p. 16. (Arabic Version).
Polls 29–45, September 1997–December 1999, CPRS, Nablus, The West Bank.
Political Imprisonment, Report Series (3), PICCR, November 2000.
Public opinion poll no. 24, September–October 1996, Center for Palestine Research and Studies, Nablus, The West Bank.
Public opinion polls no. 42–46, July 1999–January 2000, Center for Palestine Research and Studies, Nablus, The West Bank.
Public opinion poll no. 46, January 2000, Center for Palestine Research and Studies, Nablus, The West Bank.
Public Opinion Polls, no. 25–48, December 1996–April 2000, Center for Palestine Research and Studies, Nablus, Palestine.
Report of the Budgetary and Financial Affairs Committee, PLC.
Report of the Council on Foreign Relations: *Strengthening Palestinian Public Institutions.* <www.cfr.org/public/pubs/palinstfull.html>, pp. 32–34.
Report of the Palestinian Human Rights Monitoring Group, *Media in Palestine: Between the PNAs Hammer and the Anvil of Self-Censorship*, November 1999.
Report of PLC Special Committee based on the Report of the Public Oversight Committee (Ramallah: PLC, 1997).
Reporters Sans Frontiers. December 1995.
The Model Parliament: Women and Legislation (Jerusalem: Women's Center for Legal Aid and Counseling. 1998).
The Periodical: A Periodical on the Human Rights of Palestinians (Ramallah: PICCR, 2000).
"West Bank and Gaza Economic Policy Framework Progress Report" *Journal of Palestine Studies*, vol. 30, no. 1 (Autumn 2000), pp. 144–147.

Interviews

Interview with Mahmud Zahhar, "Hamas: Waiting for Secular Nationalism to Self-Destruct", *Journal of Palestine Studies*, vol. 24, no. 3 (Spring 1995): 81–88.

Interview with Mutawakil Taha, the director of the Palestinian Ministry of Information. *Al-Sahafi* (1997) (Arabic).
Interview with the fired Chief Judge in *Al-Risalah*, January 15, 1998.

Interview with the ousted Chief Justice in *People's Rights*, vol. 1, no. 12 (February 1998): 11–13.
Interview with Yasser Abed Rabbo in *Palestine–Israel Journal*, vol. 5, no. 3/4 (1998): 13–20.
Interview with Abu Dhair in *Al-Risalah*, March 9, 2000, p. 12.
Interview with Azmi Shu'aybi, "A Window on the Working of the PA: An Inside View", *Journal of Palestine Studies*, vol. 30, no. 1 (Autumn 2000): 88–97.
Interview with the General Director of the paper and the son of the owner, Marwan Abu Zuluf. Jerusalem, April 6, 2000.
Personal interviews with rank and file people in the districts.
Personal interviews with women's rights activists in the West Bank and Gaza Strip.
Personal interview with Radwan Abu Ayyash in Ramallah, February 8, 2000.
Personal interview with editors and managers in PBC. Ramallah, February 8, 2000.
Personal interview with Khalida Ratrut, Septemper 19, 2001.
Personal interviews with civil activists, Ramallah, July 2001.
Personal interview with Maaruf Zaharan, Qaliqilia's governor, Qaliqilia, April 13, 2004.

Newspapers and Media

Al-Amal Al-Ahli
Al-Ayyam
Al-Hadaf
Al-Hayat Al-Jadida
Al-Esteqlal
Al-Jazeera
Al-Quds
Al-Risalah
Al-Sahafi (1997).
BBC News
Ha'aretz

Web Sites

www.aljazeera.com
www.cprs-palestine.org/polls/index.html
www.haaretz.co.il
www.khalas.org/define
www.jmcc.org
www.lawsociety.org
www.minfo.gov.ps/statements/est_2109.htm
www.newsday.com.
www.pal-watc.org

www.palecon.org/pulsedir/september/pulssep2.html.
www.palestine-pmc.com/details.asp?cat=1&id=1377.5
www.palestinechronicle.com/story
www.pcbs.org/english/culture/media_00/media00
www.pcpsr.org/survey/polls/2001/p2a.html.
www.pna.net/events/decree.htm
www.pna.org/mininfo/general/
www.pngo.net/position.htm

Index